Dog Training For Dummies®

The Do's and Don'ts of Dog Training

Do's	Don'ts
Do be nice to your dog every time he comes to you.	Don't do anything your dog perceives as unpleasant when he comes to you.
Do get into the habit of using only one command. If your dog doesn't respond, reinforce the command.	Don't nag your dog by repeating commands — it teaches him to ignore you.
Do use your dog's name to get his attention and then tell him what you want him to do.	Don't use your dog's name and then expect him to read your mind as to what you want.
Do eliminate the word "no" from your training vocabulary.	Don't expect your dog to know what the exercise "no" means.
Do use a normal tone of voice when you give a command. His hearing is quite acute.	Don't yell at your dog. He's not deaf.
Do be consistent in your actions and expectations.	Don't confuse your dog with unrealistic expectations.
Do provide an outlet for your dog's energies.	Don't try to suppress behaviors that need an outlet.
Do keep your dog mentally stimulated by training him.	Don't let your dog stagnate.
Do understand that your dog is a social animal. Train him so that he can be a part of the family.	Don't lock your dog up or put him out because you haven't trained him to behave.
Do socialize your dog with people and other dogs.	Don't isolate your dog.
Do become your dog's pack leader.	Don't expect your dog to obey if you are not his leader.
Do make learning fun for your dog.	Don't get too serious in your training.
Do reward the behaviors you want.	Don't reward undesirable behaviors.
Do spend plenty of time with your dog and give him lots of exercise.	Don't make him neurotic by neglecting him.
Do keep trying and your dog will reward you by getting the message.	Don't give up when the going gets tough.
Do get outside help when you get stuck.	Don't blame the dog.

Copyright © 2001 IDG Books Worldwide, Inc. All rights reserved.
Cheat Sheet $2.95 value. Item 5286-4.
For more information about IDG Books, call 1-800-762-2974.

For Dummies™: Bestselling Book Series for Beginners

™FOR Dummies
BESTSELLING
BOOK SERIES

Dog Training For Dummies®

Basic Dog Training Tips

Leadership	Practice the 30-minute down and the 10-minute sit, on alternate days, for four weeks.
Sit on command: Use only one command, then reinforce	1. Teach your dog to sit with a treat. Hold treat slightly in front of dog's head, say "sit," and bring hand slightly above his eyes. Give treat when he sits.
	2. Use a treat in one hand, and apply some upward pressure on the collar with the other as you say "sit."
	3. Say "sit," and apply a little upward pressure on the collar. Give lots of praise when dog sits.
	4. Without touching your dog, or showing him a treat, say "Sit." When he responds correctly, reward him with a treat. If not, review Step 3.
Down on command: Use only one command, then reinforce	1. Teach your dog to lie down with a treat. With your dog sitting at your left side, put your left hand on top of his withers. Show him a treat, held in the right hand. Say "down," and lower the treat to the ground between his feet and slide it forward so he has to lie down to get it.
	2. With the treat in your right hand, and your left hand through his collar, say "down," lower the treat and apply downward pressure on the collar.
	3. Say "down," and apply a little downward pressure on the collar. Give lots of praise when he lies down.
	4. Without touching your dog, or showing him a treat, say "down." When he responds correctly, reward him with a treat. If not, review Step 3.
Recall — coming when called	Play the Recall Game as often as necessary. Be sure you can touch your dog's collar every time he comes to you, and before you give him a treat.
	1. On leash, inside
	2. Off leash, inside
	3. Off leash, outside in a confined area
	4. On leash with distractions
	5. Off leash with distractions
Safety — yours and his	Practice having your dog stay before he can
	1. go in or out of a door,
	2. go up or down stairs, or
	3. get in and out of the car.
Sit Stay — not jumping on people	Use the Sit-Stay exercise to teach your dog not to jump on people.
	1. Teach him to stay on leash with you directly in front of him.
	2. Increase the distance to 3 feet in front, while introducing distractions.
	3. Practice until your dog will stay on and off leash around distractions.
	4. Reinforce the sit stay every time your dog greets you.

The IDG Books Worldwide logo is a registered trademark under exclusive license to IDG Books Worldwide, Inc., from International Data Group, Inc.
The ....For Dummies logo and For Dummies are trademarks of IDG Books Worldwide, Inc. All other trademarks are the property of their respective owners.

For Dummies™: Bestselling Book Series for Beginners

Praise for Dog Training For Dummies

"*Dog Training For Dummies* is state of the art. It is an excellent resource for a better understanding of the 'whole' dog. It addresses not only training but also behavior and nutrition. This book is easy to read and is full of tips for the new owner, as well as the experienced one. Congratulations, Jack and Wendy, on another outstanding text."

> — Valerie Rutledge
> Owner, Training Ventures, Motivational Dog
> Obedience Training

"Five years ago, my first dog came into my life. Thanks to Jack and Wendy, I have a great companion. Their influence does not end with mere training. The Volhard's holistic approach to dogs, and their caring for dogs, has led me to find ways to feed my dog, care for his medical needs, and find the right veterinarian. This holistic approach comes through in *Dog Training For Dummies,* which covers everything the novice owner needs to know. Experienced trainers, too, would do well to study this book. I love it and it is my reference tool for any questions I have."

> — Aimee Schilling (and UAGI Murphy's Irish Mischief)
> CD, NA, CGC, Board Member, LaSalle Brittany Club

"*Dog Training For Dummies* carries on Jack and Wendy Volhard's tradition of clear and concise presentation of up-to-date material in an easy-to-read book. The book's organization is such that it can be read cover to cover (as I did) or used as a well-organized reference guide. It packs an amazing amount of knowledge into a remarkably portable volume. Whether the reader is a first time dog owner or an experienced fancier, this book belongs in their library."

> — Bob Payne
> Certified Kennel Operator
> Member, National Association of Dog Obedience
>   Instructors
> Member, American Boarding Kennel Association
> Member, Association of Pet Dog Trainers and Therapy
>   Dogs International

"What an all-around GREAT BOOK. It introduces the pet owner to all the necessary training, from basic commands to nutrition. It also gives him or her so many options on other great things to do with his or her dog. I make it available in all my classes and my students love it."

— Mary Ann Zeigenfuse
Licensed Veterinary Technician
Author of *Dog Tricks - Step-By-Step* (Howell Book
House, 1997)
Owner/operator, Best Friends Obedience School
Member, National Association of Dog Obedience
Instructors

"An exceptionally informative volume on behavior and training. You'll learn as much about yourself as you will about your dog."

— Joel Gavriele-Gold, Ph.D.
Author of *When Pets Come Between Partners*

TM

References for the Rest of Us!™

BESTSELLING BOOK SERIES

Do you find that traditional reference books are overloaded with technical details and advice you'll never use? Do you postpone important life decisions because you just don't want to deal with them? Then our *...For Dummies*® business and general reference book series is for you.

...For Dummies business and general reference books are written for those frustrated and hard-working souls who know they aren't dumb, but find that the myriad of personal and business issues and the accompanying horror stories make them feel helpless. *...For Dummies* books use a lighthearted approach, a down-to-earth style, and even cartoons and humorous icons to dispel fears and build confidence. Lighthearted but not lightweight, these books are perfect survival guides to solve your everyday personal and business problems.

> *"More than a publishing phenomenon, 'Dummies' is a sign of the times."*
>
> — The New York Times

> *"A world of detailed and authoritative information is packed into them..."*
>
> — U.S. News and World Report

> *"...you won't go wrong buying them."*
>
> — Walter Mossberg, Wall Street Journal, on IDG Books' ...For Dummies books

Already, millions of satisfied readers agree. They have made *...For Dummies* the #1 introductory level computer book series and a best-selling business book series. They have written asking for more. So, if you're looking for the best and easiest way to learn about business and other general reference topics, look to *...For Dummies* to give you a helping hand.

IDG BOOKS WORLDWIDE

Dog Training

FOR

DUMMIES®

by Jack and Wendy Volhard

IDG Books Worldwide, Inc.
An International Data Group Company

Foster City, CA ◆ Chicago, IL ◆ Indianapolis, IN ◆ New York, NY

Dog Training For Dummies®

Published by
IDG Books Worldwide, Inc.
An International Data Group Company
909 Third Avenue
New York, NY 10022
www.idgbooks.com (IDG Books Worldwide Web site)
www.dummies.com (Dummies Press Web site)

Copyright © 2001 IDG Books Worldwide, Inc. All rights reserved. No part of this book, including interior design, cover design, and icons, may be reproduced or transmitted in any form, by any means (electronic, photocopying, recording, or otherwise) without the prior written permission of the publisher.

Library of Congress Control Number: 00-107686

ISBN: 0-7645-5286-4

Printed in the United States of America

10 9 8 7 6 5 4 3 2

1B/RW/QR/QR/IN

Distributed in the United States by IDG Books Worldwide, Inc.

Distributed by CDG Books Canada Inc. for Canada; by Transworld Publishers Limited in the United Kingdom; by IDG Norge Books for Norway; by IDG Sweden Books for Sweden; by IDG Books Australia Publishing Corporation Pty. Ltd. for Australia and New Zealand; by TransQuest Publishers Pte Ltd. for Singapore, Malaysia, Thailand, Indonesia, and Hong Kong; by Gotop Information Inc. for Taiwan; by ICG Muse, Inc. for Japan; by Intersoft for South Africa; by Eyrolles for France; by International Thomson Publishing for Germany, Austria and Switzerland; by Distribuidora Cuspide for Argentina; by LR International for Brazil; by Galileo Libros for Chile; by Ediciones ZETA S.C.R. Ltda. for Peru; by WS Computer Publishing Corporation, Inc., for the Philippines; by Contemporanea de Ediciones for Venezuela; by Express Computer Distributors for the Caribbean and West Indies; by Micronesia Media Distributor, Inc. for Micronesia; by Chips Computadoras S.A. de C.V. for Mexico; by Editorial Norma de Panama S.A. for Panama; by American Bookshops for Finland.

For general information on IDG Books Worldwide's books in the U.S., please call our Consumer Customer Service department at 800-762-2974. For reseller information, including discounts and premium sales, please call our Reseller Customer Service department at 800-434-3422.

For information on where to purchase IDG Books Worldwide's books outside the U.S., please contact our International Sales department at 317-572-3993 or fax 317-572-4002.

For consumer information on foreign language translations, please contact our Customer Service department at 1-800-434-3422, fax 317-572-4002, or e-mail rights@idgbooks.com.

For information on licensing foreign or domestic rights, please phone +1-650-653-7098.

For sales inquiries and special prices for bulk quantities, please contact our Order Services department at 800-434-4322 or write to the address above.

For information on using IDG Books Worldwide's books in the classroom or for ordering examination copies, please contact our Educational Sales department at 800-434-2086 or fax 317-572-4005.

For press review copies, author interviews, or other publicity information, please contact our Public Relations department at 650-653-7000 or fax 650-653-7500.

For authorization to photocopy items for corporate, personal, or educational use, please contact Copyright Clearance Center, 222 Rosewood Drive, Danvers, MA 01923, or fax 978-750-4470.

LIMIT OF LIABILITY/DISCLAIMER OF WARRANTY: THE PUBLISHER AND AUTHOR HAVE USED THEIR BEST EFFORTS IN PREPARING THIS BOOK. THE PUBLISHER AND AUTHOR MAKE NO REPRESENTATIONS OR WARRANTIES WITH RESPECT TO THE ACCURACY OR COMPLETENESS OF THE CONTENTS OF THIS BOOK AND SPECIFICALLY DISCLAIM ANY IMPLIED WARRANTIES OF MERCHANTABILITY OR FITNESS FOR A PARTICULAR PURPOSE. THERE ARE NO WARRANTIES WHICH EXTEND BEYOND THE DESCRIPTIONS CONTAINED IN THIS PARAGRAPH. NO WARRANTY MAY BE CREATED OR EXTENDED BY SALES REPRESENTATIVES OR WRITTEN SALES MATERIALS. THE ACCURACY AND COMPLETENESS OF THE INFORMATION PROVIDED HEREIN AND THE OPINIONS STATED HEREIN ARE NOT GUARANTEED OR WARRANTED TO PRODUCE ANY PARTICULAR RESULTS, AND THE ADVICE AND STRATEGIES CONTAINED HEREIN MAY NOT BE SUITABLE FOR EVERY INDIVIDUAL. NEITHER THE PUBLISHER NOR AUTHOR SHALL BE LIABLE FOR ANY LOSS OF PROFIT OR ANY OTHER COMMERCIAL DAMAGES, INCLUDING BUT NOT LIMITED TO SPECIAL, INCIDENTAL, CONSEQUENTIAL, OR OTHER DAMAGES. FULFILLMENT OF EACH COUPON OFFER IS THE RESPONSIBILITY OF THE OFFEROR.

Trademarks: For Dummies, Dummies Man, A Reference for the Rest of Us!, The Dummies Way, Dummies Daily, and related trade dress are registered trademarks or trademarks of IDG Books Worldwide, Inc. in the United States and other countries, and may not be used without written permission. All other trademarks are the property of their respective owners. IDG Books Worldwide is not associated with any product or vendor mentioned in this book.

 is a registered trademark under exclusive license to IDG Books Worldwide, Inc., from International Data Group, Inc.

About the Authors

Jack and Wendy Volhard share their home in upstate New York with a Briard, a German Shepherd, a Labrador Retriever, a Landseer Newfoundland, two Standard Wirehaired Dachshunds, and three cats. The dogs are more or less well-trained, depending on who you ask, and the cats do their own thing. All are allowed on the furniture, but do get off when told. The Volhards are true practitioners, having obtained over 50 conformation and performance titles, multiple High in Trials, and Dog World Awards of Canine Distinction.

Through their classes, lectures, seminars, and training camps in the U.S., Canada, and England, the Volhards have taught countless dog owners how to communicate more effectively with their pets. Individuals from almost every state and 15 countries have attended their five-day training camps. They are regularly consulted by veterinarians, breeders, trainers, and dog owners like yourself on questions about behavior, health, nutrition, and training. Internationally recognized as "trainers of trainers," they are also award-winning authors, and this is their seventh book.

In addition to their work together, both Jack and Wendy are well recognized in the training community for their individual accomplishments.

Jack is the recipient of five awards from the Dog Writers' Association of America (DWAA) and an American Kennel Club obedience judge since 1973. Jack is the author of over 100 articles for various dog publications, co-producer of four training videotapes, and senior author of four books, including *Teaching Dog Obedience Classes: The Manual for Instructors,* known as the "bible" for trainers, and *Training Your Dog: The Step-by-Step Manual,* named Best Care and Training Book for 1983 by the DWAA.

Wendy is the recipient of four awards from the Dog Writers' Association of America (DWAA). She is the author of over 100 articles for various dog publications, a regular columnist for the *American Kennel Gazette,* and co-author of three books, including *Canine Good Citizen: Every Dog Can be One,* named Best Care and Training Book for 1995 by the DWAA. Wendy has also appeared on various TV and radio talk shows in connection with her latest book, *The Holistic Guide for a Healthy Dog,* the definitive guide for a healthier dog, and is the co-producer of four videotapes.

Wendy, whose expertise extends to helping owners gain a better understanding of why their pets do what they do, developed the Canine Personality Profile, and her two-part series, "Drives – A New Look at an Old Concept," was named Best Article for 1991 in a Specialty Magazine by the DWAA. She also developed the most widely used system for evaluating and selecting puppies, and her film, *Puppy Aptitude Testing,* was named Best Film on Dogs for 1980 by the DWAA. Wendy specializes in behavior, nutrition, and alternative sources of health care for dogs, such as acupuncture and homeopathy, and has formulated a balanced homemade diet for dogs.

ABOUT IDG BOOKS WORLDWIDE

Welcome to the world of IDG Books Worldwide.

IDG Books Worldwide, Inc., is a subsidiary of International Data Group, the world's largest publisher of computer-related information and the leading global provider of information services on information technology. IDG was founded more than 30 years ago by Patrick J. McGovern and now employs more than 9,000 people worldwide. IDG publishes more than 290 computer publications in over 75 countries. More than 90 million people read one or more IDG publications each month.

Launched in 1990, IDG Books Worldwide is today the #1 publisher of best-selling computer books in the United States. We are proud to have received eight awards from the Computer Press Association in recognition of editorial excellence and three from Computer Currents' First Annual Readers' Choice Awards. Our best-selling ...*For Dummies*® series has more than 50 million copies in print with translations in 31 languages. IDG Books Worldwide, through a joint venture with IDG's Hi-Tech Beijing, became the first U.S. publisher to publish a computer book in the People's Republic of China. In record time, IDG Books Worldwide has become the first choice for millions of readers around the world who want to learn how to better manage their businesses.

Our mission is simple: Every one of our books is designed to bring extra value and skill-building instructions to the reader. Our books are written by experts who understand and care about our readers. The knowledge base of our editorial staff comes from years of experience in publishing, education, and journalism — experience we use to produce books to carry us into the new millennium. In short, we care about books, so we attract the best people. We devote special attention to details such as audience, interior design, use of icons, and illustrations. And because we use an efficient process of authoring, editing, and desktop publishing our books electronically, we can spend more time ensuring superior content and less time on the technicalities of making books.

You can count on our commitment to deliver high-quality books at competitive prices on topics you want to read about. At IDG Books Worldwide, we continue in the IDG tradition of delivering quality for more than 30 years. You'll find no better book on a subject than one from IDG Books Worldwide.

John J. Kilcullen
John Kilcullen
Chairman and CEO
IDG Books Worldwide, Inc.

Eighth Annual Computer Press Awards ➤1992

Ninth Annual Computer Press Awards ➤1993

Tenth Annual Computer Press Awards ➤1994

Eleventh Annual Computer Press Awards ➤1995

IDG is the world's leading IT media, research and exposition company. Founded in 1964, IDG had 1997 revenues of $2.05 billion and has more than 9,000 employees worldwide. IDG offers the widest range of media options that reach IT buyers in 75 countries representing 95% of worldwide IT spending. IDG's diverse product and services portfolio spans six key areas including print publishing, online publishing, expositions and conferences, market research, education and training, and global marketing services. More than 90 million people read one or more of IDG's 290 magazines and newspapers, including IDG's leading global brands — Computerworld, PC World, Network World, Macworld and the Channel World family of publications. IDG Books Worldwide is one of the fastest-growing computer book publishers in the world, with more than 700 titles in 36 languages. The "...For Dummies®" series alone has more than 50 million copies in print. IDG offers online users the largest network of technology-specific Web sites around the world through IDG.net (http://www.idg.net), which comprises more than 225 targeted Web sites in 55 countries worldwide. International Data Corporation (IDC) is the world's largest provider of information technology data, analysis and consulting, with research centers in over 41 countries and more than 400 research analysts worldwide. IDG World Expo is a leading producer of more than 168 globally branded conferences and expositions in 35 countries including E3 (Electronic Entertainment Expo), Macworld Expo, ComNet, Windows World Expo, ICE (Internet Commerce Expo), Agenda, DEMO, and Spotlight. IDG's training subsidiary, ExecuTrain, is the world's largest computer training company, with more than 230 locations worldwide and 785 training courses. IDG Marketing Services helps industry-leading IT companies build international brand recognition by developing global integrated marketing programs via IDG's print, online and exposition products worldwide. Further information about the company can be found at www.idg.com. 1/26/00

Dedication

This book is for those who like their dogs and who have them first and foremost as pets and companions.

Author Acknowledgments

"We are each the sport of all that goes before us."

Clarence Darrow

All of us are the product of our own life experiences. Ours started in the 1960s, when we were exposed to many of the famous behaviorists of the day. Being avid readers, we absorbed as much information as we could from individuals such as Konrad Most, Konrad Lorenz, and Eberhard Trummler. We learned why dogs do what they do and how to apply a behavioral approach to training, one that copies how dogs interact with each other. John Fuller's work at Bar Harbor, Maine, and Clarence Pfaffenberger's work with Guide Dogs for the Blind, as well as the experiments done in Switzerland by Humphrey and Warner to indicate the working abilities of German Shepherds, all went into the mix that eventually became our *motivational method.* Other individuals who influenced the way we train are Milo Pearsall, Olive Point, and Karen Pryor.

Since the 1960s, we have had nine generations of dogs, all of whom have been our teachers. We ran an obedience school for nearly 25 years, and all the students and their dogs have been our teachers as well. We continue today with our five-day instructor/training camps and weekend seminars, and we are fortunate enough to be presented with enough doggy challenges to continue our quest for knowledge. So to all of you who have passed through our doors in these last years, we thank you and your dogs for providing us with the interest that still drives us today.

Publisher's Acknowledgments

We're proud of this book; please register your comments through our IDG Books Worldwide Online Registration Form located at `http://my2cents.dummies.com`.

Some of the people who helped bring this book to market include the following:

Acquisitions, Editorial, and Media Development

Project Editor: Michael Kelly

Senior Editor: Scott Prentzas

General Reviewer: Mary Ann Zeigenfuse

Editorial Manager: Pam Mourouzis

Editorial Coordinator: Michelle Hacker

Cover Photos: © Kent and Donna Dannen

Illustrator: Barbara Frakes

Production

Project Coordinator: Emily Wichlinski

Layout and Graphics: Joseph Bucki, Kristin Pickett, Jacque Schneider, Jeremey Unger, Brian Torwelle, Erin Zeltner

Special Art:

Proofreaders: Andrew Hollandbeck, Carl Pierce, Nancy Price, Sossity R. Smith

Indexer: Sherry Massey

Special Help

Sandra Blackthorn, Keith Peterson

General and Administrative

IDG Books Worldwide, Inc.: John Kilcullen, CEO; Bill Barry, President and COO; John Ball, Executive VP, Operations & Administration; John Harris, CFO

IDG Books Consumer Reference Group

Business: Kathleen A. Welton, Vice President and Publisher; Kevin Thornton, Acquisitions Manager

Cooking/Gardening: Jennifer Feldman, Associate Vice President and Publisher

Education/Reference: Diane Graves Steele, Vice President and Publisher; Greg Tubach, Publishing Director

Lifestyles: Kathleen Nebenhaus, Vice President and Publisher; Tracy Boggier, Managing Editor

Pets: Dominique De Vito, Associate Vice President and Publisher; Tracy Boggier, Managing Editor

Travel: Michael Spring, Vice President and Publisher; Suzanne Jannetta, Editorial Director; Brice Gosnell, Managing Editor

IDG Books Consumer Editorial Services: Kathleen Nebenhaus, Vice President and Publisher; Kristin A. Cocks, Editorial Director; Cindy Kitchel, Editorial Director

IDG Books Consumer Production: Debbie Stailey, Production Director

IDG Books Packaging: Marc J. Mikulich, Vice President, Brand Strategy and Research

◆

The publisher would like to give special thanks to Patrick J. McGovern, without whom this book would not have been possible.

◆

Contents at a Glance

Cartoons at a Glance

By Rich Tennant

page 5

page 73

page 169

page 345

page 219

page 297

Cartoon Information:
Fax: 978-546-7747
E-Mail: richtennant@the5thwave.com
World Wide Web: www.the5thwave.com

Table of Contents

Introduction

●●●

*B*oth of us have had dogs of one kind or another since we were children. Although neither one of us was the primary caregiver, we did have the responsibility of walking the dog.

Children have entirely different expectations of their dogs than adults do. For one thing, they don't believe in leashes. And because both of us were brought up in a city, we had to train our respective dogs to stay close by during our walks. Neither one of us remembers exactly how we did that. No doubt our dogs were smarter than we were and viewed their daily outings as having to keep an eye on us rather than the other way around.

It wasn't until 1968 that we got involved in training in a more structured way. We had obtained a Landseer Newfoundland and were encouraged to join the local obedience-training club. As these things go, one thing led to another, and before we knew it, a pleasant pastime turned into a hobby and then an avocation. Before long, we were conducting seminars and five-day training camps, which have taken us to almost every state in the United States, Canada, and England.

So here we are, more than 30 years later, sharing with you what we have learned along the way. Every dog we have ever had has been more of a teacher than a pupil, and we have learned much more from our dogs than we could ever have hoped to teach them. This book is our attempt to pass on to you what our dogs have taught us.

Not many people can become proficient, much less expert, in a given field without help. We certainly have had lots of that. A well-trained dog is the result of education, actually more yours than your dog's. You need to know what makes a dog a dog, how he thinks, how he reacts, how he grows, how he expresses himself, what his needs are, and most important, why he does what he does. When you understand your dog, you will achieve a mutually rewarding relationship. Dogs are not a homogenous commodity. Each one is a unique individual, and in their differences lies the challenge.

About This Book

We want this book to be a useful tool for you. And we don't want dog training to feel like a chore that you have to slog through step by step. So we've structured this book in such a way that you can jump in and out of the text as it interests you and applies to your situation. Is your dog partially trained, but needs to learn a few things? Then go directly to the chapters you need. Are you planning to pick up a new puppy and want to prepare yourself for a complete training regimen? Then start at the beginning and work your way through the book at a pace that you and your new pooch are comfortable with.

We don't expect you to internalize every bit of information in the book, either. Throughout the text, we include reminders of key points and cross-references to more information about the topic at hand. Remember, dog training is fun! It isn't a series of tests that you have to pass (unless you and your dog enter the advanced world of competition).

Foolish Assumptions

In writing this book, we assumed a few things about you:

- ✔ You have a dog or plan to get one.
- ✔ You want your dog to be well-behaved — for his sake as well as yours.
- ✔ You have little or no knowledge of proper dog training techniques — or if you have done some reading on the subject, you've had limited success in training your dog up to now.

Even if you do have experience with dog training, you'll find this book helpful. Through our many years of experience with a wide variety of dog breeds and personalities, we have picked up many tricks that are sure to prove useful even to experienced dog trainers.

How This Book Is Organized

In structuring this book, we went from basic to intermediate and finally advanced training. Each part contains the respective training progressions you need, plus some supplementary information to ensure success. You can apply all of it to your dog.

Part 1: Training the Trainer — You

This part helps you prepare yourself for the task of training your dog. Here you can find chapters on setting the stage for training, understanding your dog's mind, purchasing training equipment such as collars and leashes, and training your dog in the basics — sitting, staying, and so on.

Part II: Giving Your Dog's Training Its Best Shot

In this part, you find out about some things you can do to ensure training success, from surviving the puppy period to providing for your dog's nutritional needs to dealing with the not-so-pleasant behaviors that your dog may exhibit from time to time.

Part III: Getting Down to Training Your Dog

Here's where you really get down to the business of training your dog in specific areas. For information about housetraining, training your dog to walk on a leash, teaching your dog how to retrieve, and more, turn to this part of the book.

Part IV: Training for Competition

If you have ambitions beyond getting your dog to be polite, this is the part for you. Here you can find information about various forms of competition (namely Companion Dog, Companion Dog Excellent, and Utility) and how to train your dog for the exercises they require.

Part V: Beyond Training

Your dog's health contributes a great deal to his behavior, so this part talks about the importance of quality health care. You also can find a chapter about dealing with doggie aggression — behavior that can be frightening but usually is fairly easy to overcome.

Part VI: The Part of Tens

Every *For Dummies* book has a Part of Tens. In this part, you find quick lists of ten items each — bits of handy information about dog training and other related topics that you can read through in a flash.

Icons Used in This Book

To help you navigate your way through the text, we have included some high-lights of important material, some hints, some cautions, and some true stories of success. This key information is marked with icons in the margins. Here's what the icons tell you:

This icon draws your attention to ways to save time, money, energy, and your sanity.

This icon raises a red flag; your safety or your dog's may be at risk. It also tells you about the don'ts of dog training. Proceed at your own risk!

This icon directs you to information that's important to remember — key points that you'll want to focus on.

This icon highlights more in-depth information that isn't critical for you to know, but will enhance your knowledge of dog trainer and may make you a better teacher.

This icon points out dog training techniques and strategies that we and our clients have found to be successful.

Where to Go from Here

The important thing about dog training is to get started *today*. The sooner you train your dog to behave the way you want him to, the sooner the two of you can live in peace together, and the more problems you can prevent down the road. So turn the page (or use the Table of Contents or Index to get to the information you need the most) and get going! Your dog will thank you for it.

Part I
Training the Trainer — You

The 5th Wave   By Rich Tennant

"WE'VE HAD SOME BEHAVIOR PROBLEMS SINCE GETTING 'SNOWBALL', BUT WITH PATIENCE, REPETITION AND GENTLE DISCIPLINE, I'VE BEEN ABLE TO BREAK ROGER OF MOST OF THEM."

In this part . . .

You can't expect a dog to do what you want him to do (or *don't* want him to do) unless you show him what your expectations are. And your dog won't learn properly or be willing to heed your commands unless you use effective training methods. In this part, we explain how to prepare yourself, the human part of the equation, for training: how to choose the right approach, how to adapt your methods to your particular dog's nature, and how to establish yourself as the leader of the pack. We also help you select the best leashes and collars for training and explain why bribery in the form of treats really works. Finally, we walk you through basic training maneuvers such as sitting, staying, and coming when called — the things that every well-behaved dog needs to know.

Chapter 1

Setting the Stage for Training

. . . .

In This Chapter

▶ What a well-trained dog means for you and your home

▶ What the mother dog teaches you about training

▶ When training is more than just saying no

▶ Who the trainer is — you or your dog

▶ What training method is most effective

. . . .

A well-trained dog is a joy to have around. He is welcome almost any-where because he behaves around people and around other dogs. He knows how to stay, and he comes when called. He is a pleasure to take for a walk, and he can be let loose for a romp in the park. He can be taken on trips and family outings. He is a member of the family in every sense of the word.

The most important benefit for your dog, we'll call him Buddy, is his own safety. A dog that listens and does what he is told rarely gets into trouble. Instead of being a slave to a leash or a line, a trained dog is truly a free dog — he can be trusted to come when called, not to chase a cat across the road, or not to try to retrieve a car.

As a gift to yourself and your dog, as well as your family and your friends and neighbors, train your dog. It will mean sanity for you, safety for your dog, and compliments from those you meet. Make him an ambassador of good will for all dogs.

Your dog has a life expectancy of 8 to 16 years. Now is the time to ensure that these years are mutually rewarding for you and your dog. Teach him to be the well-trained dog you want him to be. Believe us, it's well worth the investment.

Identifying a Well-Trained Dog

For more than 30 years, we have taught dog training classes, two-day seminars, and five-day training camps. We listen carefully when our students tell us what a well-trained dog should be. First and foremost, they say, he has to be housetrained, of course. After that, in order of importance, a well-trained dog is one who

- ✔ Doesn't jump on people.
- ✔ Doesn't beg at the table.
- ✔ Doesn't bother guests.
- ✔ Comes when called.
- ✔ Doesn't pull on the leash.

Note that these requirements, with one exception, are expressed in the negative — that is, *dog, don't do that.* For purposes of training, you need to express these requirements in the positive so that you can teach your dog exactly what you expect of him. Here is what the new list of requirements for a well-trained dog looks like:

- ✔ Sit when I tell you.
- ✔ Go somewhere and chill out.
- ✔ Lie down when I tell you and stay there.
- ✔ Come when called.
- ✔ Walk on a loose leash.

As you can see, the sit and down-stay commands are the building blocks for a well-trained dog; if Buddy knew nothing else, you could live with him. Of course, your Buddy might have some additional wrinkles that may need ironing out, some of which are more matters of management than training. He may enjoy *landscaping*, as do our Dachshunds, who delight in digging holes in the backyard and can do so with amazing speed and vigor. Unless you are willing to put up with what can become major excavation projects, the best defense is to expend this digging energy with plenty of exercise, training, and supervision.

Another favorite pastime of some dogs is raiding the garbage. Prevention is the cure here: Put the garbage where your dog can't get to it.

One of our Dachshunds learned to open the refrigerator by yanking on the towel we kept draped through the door handle and to help himself to anything he could reach. Prevention was the answer. We removed the towel.

What is an untrained dog?

The untrained dog has few privileges. When guests come, he is locked away because he is too unruly. When the family sits down to eat, he is locked up or put outside because he begs at the table. He is never allowed off leash because he runs away and stays out for hours at a time. Nobody wants to take him for a walk because he pulls, and he never gets to go on family outings because he is such a nuisance.

Dogs are social animals, and one of the cruellest forms of punishment is to deprive them of the opportunity to interact with members of the family on a regular basis. Isolating a dog from contact with humans is inhumane. Spending quality time with your dog by training him will make him the beloved pet he deserves to be.

Defining Training

We use the term *training* to describe two different concepts:

- To teach Buddy to do something that you want him to do, but that he would not do on his own. For example, Buddy knows how to sit and sits on his own, but you want him to sit on command, something he will not do on his own without training.

- To teach Buddy to stop doing something he would do on his own, but that you don't want him to do. For example, Buddy chases bicyclists, something he does on his own that you want him to stop.

We call this *action training* and *abstention training:*

- **Action training:** To teach your dog to do something that you want him to do, which he would not do on his own. For action training, you mainly use positive reinforcement, such as a treat or lots of praise. A simple definition of *positive reinforcement* is any response together with a given action that makes the response likely to occur again. For example, you call your dog, and when he comes to you, you reward him with a treat. Giving your dog a treat after he has responded to the come command increases the likelihood that he'll respond again.

- **Abstention training:** To teach your dog to stop doing something he would do on his own, which you don't want him to do. For abstention training, you may have to use negative reinforcement, such as a check on the leash. A simple definition of *negative reinforcement* is an action the dog perceives as unpleasant that is performed immediately before or during a behavior and that the dog can avoid by stopping the behavior. For example, your dog is pulling on the leash, and you check him.

A *check* is a tug on the leash, followed by an immediate release of tension on the leash, that is an unpleasant experience for the dog but one he can avoid by not pulling (see Figure 1-1). The mother dog uses a similar approach when teaching her puppies to stop doing something they'd do on their own but that she doesn't want them to do. For example, when the puppies are 6 to 7 weeks old, she begins to wean them. At this age the puppies now have their baby teeth, which can be quite painful to the mother when they feed. When the mother dog wants them to stop what they're doing, she snarls or growls or snaps at them. The puppies perceive her action as an unpleasant experience and stop whatever they're doing. The check is based on the same principle.

The commands sit, down, stand, and come all involve action training and are the fundamentals for not only the well-trained pet but also any further training. Teaching your dog to *heel* — that is, walk on your left side and pay strict attention to you, as in competitive events or when you need absolute control — is also action training. The stay command is an example of abstention training; you are teaching Buddy not to leave.

Figure 1-1:
A check reinforces something that you don't want your dog to do.

The object of any training is to have your dog respond reliably to your command. Ideally, he responds on the first command. There is nothing more frustrating than telling your dog to do something only to be ignored. It is especially annoying when somebody is watching or you are trying to show off. Male dogs in particular have that favorite trick of absolutely having to lift a leg just one more time, and sometimes several times, before they deign to acknowledge our presence.

Think of it in terms of choices. Do you want Buddy to think he has a choice of responding to you? We don't think so. We think you want a dog that understands, after you have trained him, that he has to do what you tell him, no ifs or buts.

Selecting a Training Model

Basically, three training models exist, each with varying degrees of effectiveness. Table 1-1 offers a quick look at these models.

Table 1-1	Training Methods and How Effective They Are		
Training Model	*Method*	*Effectiveness*	*Stress Involved*
No-No	The dog is always wrong — he is punished unless he can figure out on his own by trial and error what you want.	Takes a long time and sometimes the dog doesn't get it, depending on what the dog is expected to learn.	Extremely high, to the point where the dog may give up trying altogether.
Yes-Yes	The dog is always right — he is rewarded for every correct response but still has to learn on his own what is expected.	Takes a considerable amount of patience and time.	Can be high, depending on the dog.
Yes-No	The dog knows immediately whether he is right or wrong.	Very fast.	Very little.

The No-No model is the least desirable of the three. Imagine trying to learn a new skill, and the only instruction you receive is a reprimand when you do something wrong. The stress level would be incredible, and it wouldn't take long before you gave up in disgust.

On the face of it, the Yes-Yes model looks quite appealing. After all, how much can go wrong when every correct response is rewarded? Actually, quite a bit — when you consider that there are still no instructions of any kind and that the subject, be it a person or a dog, has to figure out how to get the reward. For a sensitive person or dog, such uncertainty can be very stressful, and the higher the level of stress, the slower the rate of learning. Moreover, with this model, it's difficult to set the parameters of what is acceptable behavior and what is unacceptable behavior.

The drawback of both the No-No and Yes-Yes models is that they tend to be excessively slow in getting the point across to the subject in comparison to the Yes-No model.

Because you are a busy, results-oriented person, this book shows you how to use the Yes-No method to train Buddy. The main advantage of the Yes-No method is that there's no guesswork involved for the dog. He knows immediately what it is you want. For example, when introducing your dog to the sit command, you can use a treat to coax him into a sit. As soon as he responds, he gets the treat; if he doesn't respond, he doesn't get the treat. It'll take only a few repetitions before your dog has figured out how to get the treat. You can also show him what you want him to do by physically placing him into a sit and then giving him a treat and telling him what a clever boy he is (see Chapter 4 for more info on basic training).

The following sections cover a few ground rules for applying the Yes-No model.

Establish trust with your dog

Picture Buddy chasing a cat across the road. Your heart is in your mouth because you are afraid he might get run over. When he finally returns, you are angry and soundly scold him for chasing the cat and giving you such a scare.

Here is how Buddy looks at this situation: First, he chased the cat, which was lots of fun. Then he came back to you and was reprimanded, which was no fun at all.

What you wanted to teach him was not to chase the cat. What you actually taught him was that coming to you can be unpleasant.

One of the commands you want your dog to learn is to come when called. To be successful, remember this principle: Whenever your dog comes to you, be nice to him. Put another way, don't do anything he perceives as unpleasant. If you want to give him a bath or a pill, don't just call him to you. Instead, go get him or call him; then first give him a cookie before the bath or pill.

No matter what he may have done, be pleasant and greet him with a kind word, a pat on the head, and a smile. Teach your dog to trust you by being a safe place for him. When he is with you, follows you, or comes to you, make him feel wanted.

If you call him to you and then punish him, you undermine his trust in you. When your dog comes to you on his own and you punish him, he thinks he is being punished for coming to you.

You may ask, "How can I be nice to my dog when he brings me the remains of one of my brand-new shoes or when he wants to jump on me with muddy paws or when I just discovered an unwanted present on the carpet?"

We can certainly empathize with these questions, having experienced the same and similar scenarios on a number of occasions ourselves. We know how utterly frustrating a dog's behavior can be. What we have learned and what we have had to accept is that at that moment in time, the dog does not understand that he did anything wrong. He only understands our anger — but not the why of it. Hard as it may be, you have to grin and bear it, lest you undermine the very relationship of mutual trust you are trying to achieve through training. (Take a look at Chapter 2 for info on how to understand your dog's mind and check out Chapter 10 for info on housetraining.)

Punishment after the fact is cruel and inhumane. Even if the dog's behavior changes as a result of being punished, it changes in spite of it and not because of it. The answer lies in prevention and training. *Prevention* means providing the dog with plenty of outlets for his energies in the form of exercise, play, and training. It also means not putting the dog in a position where he can get at your brand-new pair of shoes. *Training* means teaching your dog to sit on command so that he does not jump on you (see Chapter 4 for training basics).

Be consistent with commands and tone

If there is any magic to training, it is consistency. Your dog cannot understand *sometimes, maybe, perhaps,* or *only on Sundays.* He can and does understand *yes* and *no.* Here's an example: You confuse your dog when you encourage him to jump up on you while you're wearing old clothes but then get angry with him when he joyfully plants muddy paws on your best suit.

Here's another example: Bill loved to wrestle with Brandy, his Golden Retriever. Then one day, when Grandma came to visit, Brandy flattened her. Bill was angry, and Brandy was confused — she thought roughhousing was a wonderful way to show affection. After all, that's what Bill had taught her.

Consistency in training means handling your dog in a predictable and uniform manner. If more than one person is in the household, everyone needs to handle the dog in the same way. Otherwise, the dog becomes confused and unreliable in his responses.

So does this mean that you can never permit your puppy to jump up on you? Not at all. But you have to teach him that he may only do so when you tell him it's okay. But beware: Training a dog to make this distinction is more difficult than training him not to jump up at all. The more black and white, or yes and no, that you can make it, the easier it will be for Buddy to understand what you want.

Outlast your dog — be persistent

Training your dog is a question of who is more persistent — you or your dog. Some things he will learn quickly; others will take more time. If several tries don't bring success, be patient, remain calm, and try again.

How quickly your dog will learn a particular command depends on the extent to which the behavior you're trying to teach him is in harmony with the function for which he was bred. For example, a Labrador Retriever, bred to retrieve game birds on land and in the water, will readily learn how to fetch a stick or a ball on command. On the other hand, an Afghan Hound, bred as a coursing hound who pursues its quarry by sight, may take many repetitions before he understands the command to fetch and then responds to it each and every time. A Shetland Sheepdog, bred to herd and guard livestock, will learn to walk on a loose lead more quickly than a Beagle, bred to hunt hares. A Newfoundland, with its relaxed temperament, will learn the down-stay more quickly than the lively Wirehaired Fox Terrier. You get the idea. (Check out Chapter 8 for info about breed-specific behaviors.)

Know to avoid no

As of right now, eliminate the word *no* from your training vocabulary. All too often, *no* is the only command a dog hears, and he is expected to figure out what it means. There is no exercise or command in training called "no." Avoid negative communications with your dog; they undermine the relationship you are trying to build. Don't use your dog's name as a reprimand. Don't nag your dog by repeatedly using his name without telling what you want him to do.

At one of our recent training camps, one of the participants wore a T-shirt depicting a dog greeting another dog with "Hi. My name is 'No, No. Bad Dog.' What's yours?" Begin to focus on the way in which you communicate with Buddy. Does he perceive the interaction as positive or negative, pleasant or unpleasant, friendly or unfriendly? How many times do you use the word *no,* and how many times do you say "Good dog" when interacting with your dog? Our experience during more than 30 years of teaching has been that by the time we see the dogs, most have been no'ed to death. Everything the dog does brings forth a stern "Don't do this," "Don't do that," or "No, bad dog."

The dogs are sick of it and have no interest or desire in learning what the owners want them to do.

In dealing with your dog, ask yourself, "What exactly do I want Buddy to do or not to do?" Use a *do* command whenever possible so that you can praise your dog instead of reprimanding him. You'll notice a direct relationship between your dog's willingness to cooperate and your attitude. Get out of the blaming habit of assuming that Buddy's failure to respond is his fault. Your dog only does what comes naturally. More importantly, your dog's conduct is a direct reflection of your training. Train Buddy — in a positive way — what you expect from him, and more than likely he'll enthusiastically go along with the program.

Does this mean you can never use the *n* word? In an emergency, you do what you have to do. But, remember, only in dire need.

Take charge

Dogs are pack animals, and a pack consists of followers and one leader. The leader is in charge and dictates what happens when.

From Buddy's perspective, a pack leader's Bill of Rights looks something like this:

- To eat first and to eat as much as he wants to.
- To stand, sit, or lie down wherever he wants to.
- To have access to the prime spots in the household, including the furniture and the beds.
- To control entry to or from any room in the house.
- To proceed through all narrow openings first.
- To demand attention from subordinate pack members any time he wants to.
- To ignore or actively discourage unwanted attention.
- To restrict the movements of lesser ranking members of the pack.

In a multidog household, we often see the leader of the dog pack exercise these rights on a daily basis. Does Buddy exercise any of these rights with you?

You and your family are now Buddy's pack, and someone has to be in charge — become the leader. The principles of democracy do not apply to pack animals. Your dog needs someone he can respect and look up to for direction and guidance.

You may just want to be friends, partners, or peers with your dog. You can be all of those, but for the well being of your dog, you must be the one in charge. In today's complicated world, you cannot rely on him to make the decisions.

Debbie did not think much about the "being in charge" theory. She wanted to be pals with Thor, her Labrador Retriever. After all, he had always listened to her before and had never given her any trouble.

She changed her mind when one day Thor made the decision, "Now I will chase the cat across the road," just as a car was coming. She realized that if she wanted Thor to be around for a while, he had to learn that she was in charge and that she made the decisions.

Few dogs actively seek leadership and most are perfectly content for you to assume the role, so long as you do. But you must do so, or even the meekest of dogs will take over. Remember, it's not a matter of choice. For his safety and your peace of mind, you have to be the one in charge.

How do you know which of you is in charge? Here are a few signs to watch for:

- Does Buddy get on the furniture and then growl at you when you tell him to get off?
- Does Buddy demand attention from you, which you then give?
- Does Buddy ignore you when you want him to move out of the way, when he is in front of a door or cupboard?
- Does Buddy dash through doorways ahead of you?

If the answer to two or more of these questions is "yes," you need to become pack leader, and we show how to do that in a positive and nonconfrontational way in Chapter 2.

Just Who Is Training Whom?

Training is a two-way street: Buddy is just as involved in training you as you are in trying to train him. The trouble is that Buddy is already a genius at training you, a skill with which he was born. Put another way, a dog comes into the world knowing what is to his advantage and what is not, and he will do whatever he can to get what he wants. You, on the other hand, have to learn the skills of training him, just as we had to learn them. A good part of the skills you have to learn is to recognize when you are inadvertently reinforcing behaviors you may not want to reinforce. Begging at the dinner table is a good example: When Buddy begs at the table and you slip him some food, he is training you to feed him from the table. You need to ask yourself, "Is this a behavior I want to reinforce?" If the answer is no, then stop doing it, no matter what. (And check out Chapter 4.)

Now look at the converse situation: Buddy has taken himself for an unauthorized walk through the neighborhood. You are late for an appointment but don't want to leave with Buddy out on the streets. You frantically call and call. Finally, Buddy makes an appearance, happily sauntering up to you. You, on the other hand, are fit to be tied, and you let him know your displeasure in no uncertain terms by giving him a thorough scolding. You now need to ask yourself, "Is this the kind of greeting that will make Buddy want to come to me?" If the answer is no, then stop doing it, no matter what. (And check out Chapter 4.)

To succeed, you must become aware of how your dog is training you so that he doesn't by accident become the one in charge. Take the following quiz:

What do you do when Buddy

- Drops his ball in your lap while you are watching television?
- Nudges or paws your elbow when you are sitting on the couch?
- Rattles his dish?
- Sits at the door?

Do your answers closely reflect the following:

- Throw it for him.
- Pet him.
- Give him something to eat.
- Open the door to let him out.

If so, he has you well trained. Nothing is wrong with this (all six of our dogs have us perfectly trained to perform these tricks). Or is there? The answer depends on whether or not your dog has accepted you as pack leader. Review the earlier section called "Take charge," which should give you the answer.

Chapter 2

Understanding Your Dog's Mind

. . . .

In This Chapter

▶ Distinguishing your dog's instinctive behaviors

▶ Knowing what drives your dog to certain behaviors — and how to respond to them

▶ Profiling your dog

▶ Applying your dog's profile to your training plans

▶ Understanding how your dog thinks

▶ Understanding how *your* thinking affects training

▶ Becoming pack leader

. . . .

*T*o train Buddy, you need some insight into what's happening at any given moment in that little brain of his. Here, your powers of observation will help you. In many instances, Buddy's behavior is quite predictable based on what he has done in similar situations before. You'll be surprised at what you already know. You can almost see the wheels turning when he's about to set chase in pursuit of a car, bicycle, or jogger, giving you just enough time to stop him.

You don't, however, have to rely on observation alone. To help you understand how Buddy's mind works, we have devised a simple Personality Profile that is an amazingly accurate predictor of his behavior, such as his propensity to chase moving objects.

To be successful in your efforts to train Buddy, you must also convince him that you are the one in charge, the pack leader. You can accomplish this task with the long down and long sit exercises while you're watching TV.

Such is the stuff of this chapter. Read on.

Recognizing Your Dog's Instinctive Behaviors

To give you a better understanding of your dog, we have grouped instinctive behaviors into three *drives:*

- ✔ Prey
- ✔ Pack
- ✔ Defense

These drives reflect instinctive behaviors that your dog has inherited from his ancestors and that are useful to you in teaching him what you want him to learn. Each one of these drives is governed by a basic trait.

Your dog and every other dog is an individual who comes into the world with a specific grouping of genetically inherited, predetermined behaviors. How those behaviors are arranged, their intensity, and how many component parts of each drive the dog has determine temperament, personality, and suitability for the task required. Those behaviors also determine how the dog perceives the world.

Prey drive

Prey drive includes those inherited behaviors associated with hunting, killing prey, and eating. The prey drive is activated by motion, sound, and smell (see Figure 2-1). Behaviors associated with prey drive include the following:

- ✔ Seeing and hearing
- ✔ Scenting and tracking
- ✔ Stalking and chasing
- ✔ Pouncing
- ✔ High-pitched barking
- ✔ Jumping up and pulling down
- ✔ Shaking
- ✔ Tearing and ripping apart
- ✔ Biting and killing
- ✔ Carrying
- ✔ Eating
- ✔ Digging and burying

Figure 2-1:
The prey
drive is an
active drive.

You see some of these behaviors when Buddy is chasing the cat or gets excited and barks in a high-pitched tone of voice as the cat runs up a tree. Buddy may also shake and rip soft toys or bury dog biscuits in the couch.

Pack drive

Pack drive consists of behaviors associated with reproduction, being part of a group or pack, and being able to live by the rules. Dogs are social animals that evolved from the wolf. To hunt prey that is mostly larger than themselves, wolves have to live in a pack. To assure order, they have to adhere to a social hierarchy governed by strict rules of behavior. An ability to be part of a group and to fit in is important, and, in the dog, is translated into a willingness to work with us as part of a team.

Pack drive is stimulated by rank order in the social hierarchy. Behaviors associated with this drive include the following:

- Physical contact with people and/or other dogs
- Playing with people and/or other dogs

✔ Behaviors associated with social interaction with another dog, such as reading body language

✔ Reproductive behaviors, such as licking, mounting, washing ears, and all courting gestures

✔ The ability to breed and to be a good parent

A dog with many of these behaviors is the one that follows you around the house, is happiest when with you, loves to be petted and groomed, and likes to work with you (see Figure 2-2). A dog with these behaviors may be unhappy when left alone too long, which can express itself in separation anxiety.

Defense drive

Defense drive is governed by survival and self-preservation and consists of both fight and flight behaviors. The defense drive is complex because the same stimulus that can make a dog aggressive (fight) can elicit avoidance (flight) behaviors, especially in a young dog.

Figure 2-2:
Many of your dog's behaviors around you are associated with the pack drive.

Fight behaviors are not fully developed until the dog is about two years of age, and sometimes later, although you can see tendencies toward these behaviors at an earlier age. Behaviors associated with fight include the following:

- Hackles up from the shoulder forward
- Standing tall and staring at other dogs
- Standing ground or going to unfamiliar objects
- Guarding food, toys, or territory against other people and dogs
- Dislike of being petted or groomed
- Lying in front of doorways or cupboards and refusing to move
- Growling at people or dogs
- Putting the head over the shoulder of another dog
- Biting people or other dogs

Flight behaviors demonstrate that the dog is unsure, and young dogs tend to exhibit more flight behaviors than older dogs. The following behaviors are associated with flight:

- Hackles that go up the full length of the body, not just at the neck
- Hiding or running away from a new situation
- A dislike of being touched by strangers
- General lack of confidence
- Urinating when being greeted by a stranger or the owner
- Flattening of the body when greeted by people or other dogs

Whoa! Buddy's got his hackles up

Hackles refers to the fur along the dog's spine from the neck to the tip of his tail. When a dog is frightened or unsure, the fur literally stands up and away from his spine. In a young dog, it may happen frequently because the dog's life experiences are minimal. When he meets a new dog, for example, he may be unsure whether or not that dog is friendly, and so his hackles go up. His whiskers are also a good indication of his insecurity; they're pulled back, flat along his face. His ears are pulled back, and his tail is tucked.

And he cringes, lowering his body posture and averting his eyes. All in all, he'd rather be somewhere else.

On the flip side, when the hackles go up only from the neck to the shoulders, the dog is sure of himself. He's the boss, and he's ready to take on all comers. His ears are erect, his whiskers are forward, all his weight is on his front legs, and he stands tall and makes direct eye contact. He's ready to rumble.

Freezing — not going forward or backward — is interpreted as inhibited flight behavior.

How the drives affect training

Since dogs were originally bred for a particular function and not solely for appearance, you can, as a general rule, predict the strength or weakness of the individual drives. For example, the northern breeds, such as Alaskan Malamutes and Siberian Huskies, were bred to pull sleds. They tend to be low in pack drive, and training them to heel or not to pull on the leash can be a bit of a chore. Herding dogs, on the other hand, tend to be high in pack drive and should be relatively easy to train not to pull on the leash. The guarding breeds, such as the German Shepherd, the Doberman, and the Rottweiler, tend to be high in fight drive with a desire to protect family and property, a trait that can get them into trouble. The Retrievers tend to be high in prey drive and should easily learn to retrieve on command. (Check out the following section's sample profiles for an idea of what you can expect in terms of ease or difficulty in training your own dog. Also check out Chapter 8.)

Determining Your Dog's Personality Profile

To help you understand how to approach your dog's training, we created *Volhards' Canine Personality Profile*. The profile catalogs ten behaviors in each drive that influence a dog's responses and that are useful in training. The ten behaviors chosen are those that most closely represent the strengths of the dog in each of the drives. The profile does not pretend to include all behaviors seen in a dog, nor the complexity of their interaction. Although it is an admittedly crude index of Buddy's behavior, you will find it surprisingly accurate.

The results of the profile will give you a better understanding of why Buddy is the way he is and the most successful way to train him. You can then make use of his strengths, avoid needless confusion, and greatly reduce training time.

When completing the profile, keep in mind that we devised it for a house dog or pet with an enriched environment, perhaps even a little training, and not a dog tied out in the yard or kept solely in a kennel — such dogs have fewer opportunities to express as many behaviors as a house dog. Answers should indicate those behaviors Buddy would exhibit if he had not already been trained to do otherwise. For example, did he jump on people to greet them, or jump on the counter to steal food, before he was trained not to do so?

The questionnaire for the profile suggests three possible answers to each question with a corresponding point value. The possible answers and their corresponding values are as follows:

- ✔ Almost always — 10
- ✔ Sometimes — 5
- ✔ Hardly ever — 0

For example, if Buddy is a Beagle, the answer to the question "When presented with the opportunity, does your dog sniff the ground or air?" is probably "almost always," giving him a score of 10.

Many of the behaviors for which dogs were bred, such as herding and hunting, are the very ones that get them into trouble today. These behaviors involve the prey drive and result in chasing anything that moves.

You are now ready to find out who Buddy really is.

You may not have had the chance to observe all of these behaviors, in which case you leave the answer blank.

When presented with the opportunity, does your dog

1. Sniff the ground or air? _____
2. Get along with other dogs? _____
3. Stand his ground or investigate strange objects or sounds? _____
4. Run away from new situations? _____
5. Get excited by moving objects, such as bikes or squirrels? _____
6. Get along with people? _____
7. Like to play tug-of-war games to win? _____
8. Hide behind you when he feels he can't cope? _____
9. Stalk cats, other dogs, or things in the grass? _____
10. Bark when left alone? _____
11. Bark or growl in a deep tone of voice? _____
12. Act fearfully in unfamiliar situations? _____
13. When excited, bark in a high-pitched voice? _____
14. Solicit petting, or like to snuggle with you? _____
15. Guard his territory? _____
16. Tremble or whine when unsure? _____

17. Pounce on his toys? _____

18. Like to be groomed? _____

19. Guard his food or toys? _____

20. Cower or turn upside down when reprimanded? _____

21. Shake and "kill" his toys? _____

22. Seek eye contact with you? _____

23. Dislike being petted? _____

24. Act reluctant to come close to you when called? _____

25. Steal food or garbage? _____

26. Follow you around like a shadow? _____

27. Guard his owner(s)? _____

28. Have difficulty standing still when groomed? _____

29. Like to carry things? _____

30. Play a lot with other dogs? _____

31. Dislike being groomed or petted? _____

32. Cower or cringe when a stranger bends over him? _____

33. Wolf down his food? _____

34. Jump up to greet people? _____

35. Like to fight other dogs? _____

36. Urinate during greeting behavior? _____

37. Like to dig and/or bury things? _____

38. Show reproductive behaviors, such as mounting other dogs? _____

39. Get picked on by older dogs when young? _____

40. Tend to bite when cornered? _____

Score your answers by using Table 2-1.

Table 2-1		Scoring the Profile	
Prey	*Pack*	*Fight*	*Flight*
1.	2.	3.	4.
5.	6.	7.	8.
9.	10.	11.	12.
13.	14.	15.	16.

Prey	Pack	Fight	Flight
17.	18.	19.	20.
21.	22.	23.	24.
25.	26.	27.	28.
29.	30.	31.	32.
33.	34.	35.	36.
37.	38.	39.	40.
Total Prey	**Total Pack**	**Total Fight**	**Total Flight**

After you have obtained the totals, enter them into the appropriate column of the profile at a glance that's shown in Figure 2-3.

To make best use of the concept of drives in your training, you need to know what you want Buddy to do or stop doing. Usually, you want him to be in pack drive and he wants to be in prey. Once you have mastered how to get him out of prey and into pack, you have a well-trained dog.

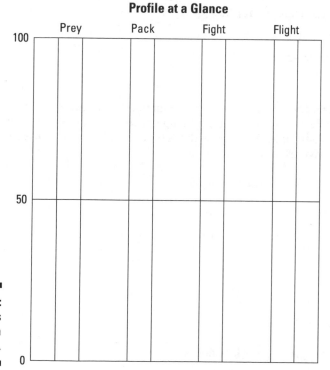

Profile at a Glance

Figure 2-3:
Your dog's profile at a glance.

Deciding How You Want Buddy to Act

Before you can use the results of the profile, you need to look at what you want Buddy to do or — and this is often more important — stop doing. For example, when you walk Buddy on leash and want him to pay attention to you, he has to be in pack drive. Buddy, on the other hand, wants to sniff, maybe follow a trail, or chase the neighbor's cat; he is in prey drive.

For most of what you want Buddy to do, such as the following, he needs to be in pack drive.

- ✔ Come
- ✔ Walk on a loose leash
- ✔ Sit
- ✔ Down
- ✔ Stay

For most of what Buddy wants to do, such as the following, he is going to be in prey drive.

- ✔ Chase a cat
- ✔ Follow the trail of a rabbit
- ✔ Retrieve a ball or stick
- ✔ Sniff the grass
- ✔ Dig

You can readily see that those times when you want him to behave, you have to convince Buddy to forget about being in prey drive. Most often prey drive gets dogs into trouble. The dog with high pack and low prey drive rarely needs extensive training, if any at all.

Such a dog doesn't do the following:

- ✔ Chase bicycles, cars, children, or joggers
- ✔ Chase cats or other animals
- ✔ Roam from home
- ✔ Steal food
- ✔ Chew your possessions
- ✔ Pull on the leash

In other words, he is a perfect pet.

Theoretically, Buddy does not need defense drive (fight) behaviors for what you want him to learn, but the absence of these behaviors has important ramifications. A very low defense drive determines how Buddy has to be trained. For example, our first Labrador, Bean, was low in defense drive. If we, or anyone else, would lean over him, he would collapse on the floor and act as though he had been beaten. Katharina, our German Shepherd, on the other hand, who was high in fight drive, would just look at you if you leaned over her, as though to say, "Okay, what do you want?"

Training each dog required a different approach. Checking Bean caused him to literally collapse — he didn't have enough fight behaviors to cope with the check. A slight tug on the leash or a quietly uttered command was sufficient to get him to ignore chasing our proverbial rabbit. Katharina required a firm check to get the same result because she had sufficient fight behavior to cope with a firm check. (Refer to the following sections for the different profiles and how to deal with them.)

The beauty of the drives theory is that, if used correctly, it gives you a tool to overcome areas where your dog may be weak.

Bringing out drives

When you grill hamburgers on the barbecue, the aroma stimulates your appetite, as well as everyone else's in the neighborhood. In effect, it brings out your prey drive. The smell becomes a cue. Incidentally, the smell also brings out Buddy's prey drive.

Following is a short list of cues that bring out each of the dog's major drives:

- **Prey drive** is elicited by the use of motion — hand signals (except stay) — a high-pitched tone of voice, an object of attraction (stick, ball, or food), chasing or being chased, and leaning backward with your body as the dog comes to you.

- **Pack drive** is elicited by touching, praising and smiling at the dog, grooming, and playing and training with your body erect.

- **Defense drive** is elicited by a threatening body posture, such as leaning or hovering over the dog either from the front or the side (this is how people get bitten), checking the dog, using a harsh tone of voice, and exaggerated use of the stay hand signal (see Chapter 4).

Switching drives

Buddy can instantaneously switch himself from one drive to another. Picture this scene — Buddy is lying in front of the fireplace:

- ✔ Playing with his favorite toy
- ✔ When the doorbell rings he drops the toy, starts to bark, and goes to the door
- ✔ You open the door; it is a neighbor and Buddy goes to greet him and then
- ✔ Returns to play with his toy

Buddy has switched himself from prey into defense into pack and back into prey.

During training, your task is to keep Buddy in the right drive, and if necessary, switch him from one drive into another. For example, you are teaching Buddy to walk on a loose leash in the yard when a rabbit pops out of the hedge. He immediately spots it, runs to the end of the leash, straining and barking excitedly in a high-pitched voice. He is clearly in full-blown prey drive.

Now you have to get him back into pack where he needs to be to walk at your side. The only way you can do that is by going through defense. You cannot, for example, show him a cookie in an effort to divert his attention from the rabbit. The rabbit is going to win out.

The precise manner in which you get Buddy back into pack drive — you must go through defense — depends on the strength of his defense drive. If he has a large number of defense (fight) behaviors, you can give him a firm tug on the leash (check), which switches him out of prey into defense. To get him into pack, touch him gently on the top of his head, smile at him and tell him how clever he is. Then continue to work on your walking on a loose leash.

If he is low in defense (fight) behaviors, a check may overpower him, and a voice communication, such as "Ah, ah" will be sufficient to get him out of prey into defense, after which you put him back into pack drive.

For the dog that has few fight behaviors and a large number of flight behaviors, a check on the leash is often counter-productive. Body postures, such as bending over the dog, or even using a deep tone of voice, are usually enough to elicit defense drive. Your dog, by his response to your training — cowering, rolling upside down, not wanting to come to you for the training session — will show you when you overpower him, thereby making learning difficult, if not impossible.

Here are the basic rules for switching from one drive to another:

- ✔ **From prey into pack:** You must go through defense.

    How you put your dog into defense depends on the number of defense (fight) behaviors he has. As a general rule, the more defense (fight) behaviors the dog has, the firmer the check needs to be. As the dog learns, a barely audible voice communication or a slight change in body posture will suffice to encourage your dog to go from prey through defense into pack drive.

✔ **From defense into pack:** By touching or smiling at your dog.

✔ **From pack into prey:** Use an object (such as food) or motion.

Your dog can switch himself from one drive into another. To switch your dog from prey into pack, you must go through defense.

Applying the concept of drives, learning which drive Buddy has to be in and how to get him there speeds up your training process enormously. As you become aware of the impact your body stance and motions have on the drive he is in, your messages will be perfectly clear to your dog. Your body language is congruent with what you are trying to teach. Because Buddy is an astute observer of body motions, which is how dogs communicate with each other, he will understand exactly what you want.

Applying drives to your training

By looking at your dog's profile (see the questionnaire earlier in this chapter), you know the training techniques that work best and are in harmony with your dog's drives. You now have the tools to tailor your training program to your dog.

✔ **Defense (fight) — more than 60:** Your dog will not be bothered too much by a firm hand. Correct body posture is not critical, although incongruent postures on your part will slow down the training. Tone of voice should be firm, but pleasant and non-threatening.

✔ **Defense (flight) — more than 60:** Your dog will not respond to force training, and you will have to rely mainly on the other drives. Correct body posture and a quiet, pleasant tone of voice are critical. Avoid using a harsh tone of voice and any hovering, either leaning over or toward your dog. There is a premium on congruent body postures and gentle handling.

✔ **Prey — more than 60.** Your dog will respond well to a treat or a toy during the teaching phase. A firm hand may be necessary, depending on strength of defense drive (fight), to suppress prey drive when in high gear, such as when chasing a cat or spotting a squirrel. This dog is easily motivated, but also easily distracted by motion or moving objects. Signals will mean more to this dog than commands. There is a premium on using body, hands, and leash correctly so as not to confuse the dog.

✔ **Prey — less than 60.** Your dog is probably not easily motivated by food or other objects, but is also not easily distracted by or interested in chasing moving objects.

✔ **Pack — more than 60.** This dog responds readily to praise and touch. The dog likes to be with you and will respond with little guidance.

✔ **Pack — less than 60.** Start praying. Buddy probably does not care whether he is with you or not. He likes to do his own thing and is not easily motivated. Your only hope is to rely on prey drive in training. Limited pack drive is usually breed-specific for dogs bred to work independently of man.

Dogs with defense drive of less than 60 rarely get into trouble — in fact, they avoid it. Many young dogs without life experience fall into this category, and while their numbers may be quite low as pups, they may vary slightly with age.

With such a dog, a straight body posture is more important, and to greet him, you need to bend down to the dog's level to build his confidence. Use of voice commands is more effective than a check on the leash with this kind of dog.

If your dog is high in both prey and defense (fight), you may need professional help. He is by no means a bad dog, but you may become exasperated with your lack of success. The dog may simply be too much for you to train on your own.

Dogs that exhibit an overabundance in prey or pack are also easily trained, but you will have to pay more attention to the strengths of their drives and exploit those behaviors most useful to you in training. You now have the tools to do it!

Here are some other important hints to keep in mind when planning your training strategy:

✔ If your dog is high in defense (fight), you need to work especially diligently on your leadership exercises and review them frequently (see the section "Assuming Your Role as Pack Leader," later in this chapter).

✔ If your dog is high in prey, you also need to work on these leadership exercises, not necessarily because your dog wants to become pack leader, but to control him around doorways and moving objects.

✔ If your dog is high in both defense (fight) and prey, you may need professional help with your training.

Here are the nicknames for some of the profiles. See if you can recognize your dog.

✔ **The Couch Potato — low prey, low pack, low defense:** Difficult to motivate and probably does not need extensive training. Needs extra patience if training is attempted because he has few behaviors with which to work. On the plus side, this dog is unlikely to get into trouble, will not disturb anyone, will make a good family pet, and does not mind being left alone for considerable periods of time.

✔ **The Hunter — high prey, low pack, low defense:** This dog will give the appearance of having an extremely short attention span, but is perfectly able to concentrate on what he finds interesting. Training will require the channeling of his energy to get him to do what you want. Patience will be required because the dog will have to be taught through prey drive.

The dog that is high in prey and defense (fight) and low in pack is independent and is not easy to live with as a pet or companion. He is highly excitable by movement and may attack anything that comes within range.

✔ **The Gas Station Dog — high prey, low pack, high defense (fight):** This dog is independent and not easy to live with as a pet. Highly excitable by movement, he may attack anything that comes within range. He doesn't care much about people or dogs and will do well as a guard dog. Pack exercises such as walking on a leash without pulling need to be built up through his prey drive. This dog is a real challenge.

✔ **The Runner — high prey, low pack, high defense (flight):** Easily startled and/or frightened. Needs quiet and reassuring handling. A dog with this profile is not a good choice for children.

✔ **The Shadow — low prey, high pack, and low defense:** This dog will follow you around all day and is unlikely to get into trouble. He likes to be with you and is not interested in chasing much of anything.

✔ **Teacher's Pet — medium (50-75) prey, pack, and defense (fight):** Easy to train and motivate, and mistakes on your part are not critical. Teacher's Pet has a nice balance of drives. He is easily motivated and therefore quite easy to train — even when your training skills are not particularly keen. At our training camps and seminars, we have the owners put the profile of their dogs in graph form for easy "reading." Figure 2-4 shows the graph for Teacher's Pet.

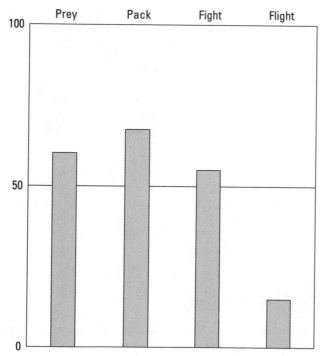

Figure 2-4: A typical Teacher's Pet profile.

By now, you have gathered that the easiest dogs are those that are balanced among all drives. No matter what you do, the dog seems to be able to figure out what you want. If you are lucky enough to have a dog like that, take good care of him. By applying the principles of drives, he will be easy to turn into a well-trained dog.

For your dog's profile at a glance, use the graph in Figure 2-3, shown earlier in this chapter.

How Your Dog Thinks

Does your dog think? Certainly. He just thinks like a dog, and to anyone who has been around dogs sometimes it's uncanny! It's almost as though he can read your mind. But is it your mind he is reading, or has he simply memorized patterns of your behavior?

Here is an example: Before leaving for work, Wendy always put Heidi in her crate. It wasn't long before Heidi went into her crate on her own when Wendy was about to leave. "What a clever puppy," thought Wendy, "She knows that I'm going to work."

Dogs often give the appearance of being able to read your mind. What happens in actuality is that by observing you and studying your habits, they learn to anticipate your actions. Because they communicate with each other through body language, they quickly become experts at reading yours.

What Heidi observed was that immediately before leaving for work, Wendy invariably put on her make-up and then crated her. Heidi's cue to go into her crate was seeing Wendy putting on her make-up.

Then one evening, before dinner guests were to arrive, Wendy started "putting her face on." When Heidi immediately went into her crate, Wendy realized the dog had not been reading her mind, but had learned the routine through observation.

Using your powers of observation, you too can learn what goes through Buddy's mind. The direction of his eyes, his body posture, his tail position, the position of his ears, up or down, and the direction of his whiskers, pointed forward or pulled close to his muzzle, are all indicators of what he is thinking at the moment. The more the two of you interact, the better you'll become at knowing what Buddy thinks.

"Reading" your dog

Just as your dog takes his cues from watching you, so can you learn to interpret what's on his mind by watching him.

You know Buddy has the propensity to jump on the counter to see whether he can find any food to steal. Because he has done this a number of times before, you begin to recognize his intentions by the look on his face — for example, head and ears are up, whiskers pointed forward, intent stare — and the way he moves in the direction of the counter — with deliberate tail wagging.

What should you do? You interrupt Buddy's thought process by derailing the train. Say "just a minute, young man, not so fast," in a stern tone of voice. You can also whistle or clap your hands, anything to distract him.

After that, tell him to go lie down and forget about stealing food.

What if he has already started the objectionable behavior? He has his paws firmly planted on the counter and is just about to snatch the steak. Use the same words to stop the thought process, physically remove him from the counter by his collar, and take him to his corner and tell him to lie down.

When you don't read your dog in time

What if your dog has already managed to achieve the objectionable behavior? Punishment after the fact is useless and inhumane. Your dog cannot make the connection. "Go to bed without supper" doesn't work any better with dogs than it does with children. The ideal time to intervene is when your dog is thinking about what you don't want him to do.

Do not attempt any discipline after the offending deed has been accomplished. Your dog cannot make the connection between the discipline and his actions. Your dog may look guilty, but not because he understands what he has done; he looks guilty because he understands you are upset.

Visualize yourself preparing a piece of meat for dinner. You leave the counter to answer the phone and after you return, the meat is gone. You know Buddy ate it. Your first reaction is anger. Immediately, Buddy looks guilty, and you assume it is because he knows he has done wrong.

Buddy knows no such thing. He is reacting to your anger and wonders why you are mad and, perhaps based on prior experience, expects to be the target of your wrath.

Look at it from Buddy's point of view. He thoroughly enjoyed the meat. Unfortunately, it's gone, and you can't bring it back. Nor can you make him un-enjoy it. What's worse, if you punish Buddy now, he will not even understand why because he can't make the connection between the punishment and the meat he just ate. He can only make the connection between your anger and being punished.

He knows you are angry, but does not know it has anything to do with the meat. Punch a pillow, if you have to, but not your dog.

If you don't believe us, try this experiment. Without Buddy's seeing you, drop a crumpled up piece of paper on the floor. Call Buddy to you and point accusingly at the paper and say in your most blaming voice, "What have you done, bad dog!" He will reward you with his most guilty look without having a clue what it's all about (see Figure 2-5).

Moral of the story: Don't leave your valued belongings such as shoes, socks, or anything else near and dear to your heart lying about, where your dog can destroy them. Look at it this way — if you weren't a neat freak before you got your dog, you will be now.

If you attribute human qualities and reasoning abilities to your dog, your dealings with him are doomed to failure. He certainly does not experience guilt. Blaming the dog because "he ought to know better," or "he shouldn't have done it," or "how could he do this to me" will not improve his behavior. He also does not "understand every word you say," and is only able to interpret your tone of voice and body language.

Dogs begin to learn at three weeks of age. At seven weeks, their brains are neurologically complete, and all the circuits are wired. Their mind is a blank page, and all you have to do is fill it with the right information. What they learn in the next few weeks will never be forgotten. If you wait until your dog is older, he will probably have picked up a lot of bad habits. That means erasing the page and starting all over, a much more tedious job than starting when he is a puppy.

Figure 2-5:
Scolding
your dog
often does
not achieve
your desired
result.

Can dogs "reason"?

The answer is no, not in the sense that we can. Dogs can, however, solve simple problems. By observing your dog, you learn his problem-solving techniques. Just watch him try to open the cupboard where the dog biscuits are kept to help himself for a between-meal snack. Or see how he works at trying to retrieve his favorite toy from under the couch.

During your training, you'll also have the opportunity to see Buddy trying to work out what you're teaching him (see Chapter 6).

Our favorite story involves a very smart English Springer Spaniel who had been left on our doorstep. The poor fellow had been so neglected that we did not know he was a pure-bred Spaniel until after he paid a visit to the groomer. He became a delightful member of the family for many years. One day, his ball had rolled under the couch. He tried everything — looking under the couch, jumping on the back rest to look behind it, and going around to both sides. Nothing seemed to work. In disgust, he lifted his leg on the couch and walked away. So much for problem solving.

Your dog is already an expert at reading you. With a little time and practice, you, too, will be able to tell what's on his mind and read him like a book. His behavior is just as predictable as yours.

Understanding the YOU Factor

Several factors influence how successful you will be in turning your pet into a well-trained dog. Some of these are under your direct control, and some of them come with your dog.

The factors that are under your direct control are

- ✔ Your expectations
- ✔ Your attitude
- ✔ Your dog's environment
- ✔ Your dog's social needs
- ✔ Your dog's emotional needs
- ✔ Your dog's physical needs
- ✔ Your dog's nutritional needs

There is a direct relationship between your awareness and understanding of these factors and your success as a trainer. This section focuses on the first two factors: your expectations and your attitudes. We deal with the other factors in Chapter 5.

Your expectations

All of us have varying ideas of what we expect from our companions. Some of these expectations are realistic, others are not. You have heard people say, "My dog understands every word I say," and perhaps you think that your dog does. If it were as easy as that, there would be no need for books like this one.

Sometimes your dog may seem to really understand what you say. However, if a dog understands every word his owner says, how come the dog doesn't do what he is told?

Still, there is enough truth here to perpetuate the myth. Although dogs don't understand the words you use, they do understand tone of voice, and sometimes even your intent.

Are your expectations realistic?

Do you believe your dog obeys commands because he

- ✔ Loves you?
- ✔ Wants to please you?
- ✔ Is grateful?
- ✔ Has a sense of duty?
- ✔ Feels a moral obligation?

We suspect that you answered "yes" to the first and second questions, became unsure at the third question, and then realized that we were leading you down a primrose path.

If your approach to training is based on moral ideas regarding punishment, reward, obedience, duty, and the like, you're bound to handle the dog in the wrong way.

No doubt your dog loves you, but he will not obey commands for that reason. Does he want to please you? Not exactly, but it sometimes seems like he does. What he is really doing is pleasing himself. Unfortunately, Buddy also does not have the least bit of gratitude for anything you do for him and will not obey commands for that reason either. He is interested in only one thing: What are you doing for me right now?

Buddy certainly has no sense of duty or feelings of moral obligation. The sooner you discard beliefs like that, the quicker you will come to terms with how to approach his training.

Are your expectations too low?

Do you believe your dog does not obey commands because he

- Is stubborn?
- Is hardheaded?
- Is stupid?
- Is ungrateful?
- Lies awake at night thinking of ways to aggravate you?

If you answered yes to any of the questions, you are guilty of *anthropomorphizing,* that is, attributing human characteristics and attributes to an animal. It's an easy habit to fall into, but will not help in your training.

Dogs are not stubborn or hardheaded. To the contrary, they are quite smart when it comes to figuring out how to get their way. And they do not lie awake at night thinking of ways to aggravate you — they sleep, just like everybody else.

What should your expectations be?

So why does your dog obey your command? Usually for one of three reasons:

- He wants something.
- He thinks it's fun, like retrieving a ball.
- He has been trained to obey.

When he obeys for either the first or the second reason, he does it for himself; when he obeys for the third reason, he does it for you. This is an important distinction because it deals with reliability and safety.

Ask yourself this question: If Buddy obeys only because he wants something or because it's fun, will he obey when he does not want something or when it is no longer fun? The answer is obvious.

The well-trained dog obeys because he has been trained. This does not mean you and he can't have fun in the process, so long as the end result is clearly understood. When you say "come," there are no options, even though he may want to play a little longer, and even though you don't have a cookie.

Your attitude

One of the most important aspects of training is your attitude toward your dog. During training, you want to maintain a friendly and positive attitude.

For many of us, maintaining this attitude can be enormously difficult because frequently we don't start to think about training until Buddy has become an uncontrollable nuisance. He is no longer cute, he has become incredibly rambunctious, everything he does is wrong, and he certainly doesn't listen.

Don't train your dog when you are irritable or tired. You want training to be a positive experience for your dog. Should you get frustrated during training, stop and come back to it at another time.

Your communications by the time you've lost your positive attitude consist of "no," "bad dog," "how could you do this," and "get out and stay out." You are unhappy and Buddy is unhappy.

A better approach is to train him with firm kindness, so both of you can be happy. An unfriendly or hostile approach will not gain you your dog's cooperation and will needlessly prolong the training process. When you become frustrated or angry, the dog becomes anxious and nervous, and is unable to learn.

When you feel that you are becoming a little irritable, it is best to stop training and come back to it in a better frame of mind. You want training to be a positive experience for Buddy.

Your dog's age and training

From birth until maturity, your dog goes through physical and mental developmental periods. What happens during these stages can, and often does, have a lasting effect on your dog. Its outlook on life will be shaped during these periods, as will its behavior.

The age at which a puppy is separated from its mother and littermates will have a profound influence on its behavior as an adult. Taking a pup away from the mother too soon may have a negative effect on its ability to handle training. For example, housetraining may be more difficult under these circumstances. A pup's ability to learn is important to becoming a well-trained dog. It will also affect its dealings with people and other dogs.

So what is the ideal time for your puppy to make the transition to its new home? All the behavioral studies that have been done recommend the 49th day, give or take a day or two.

Assuming Your Role as Pack Leader

Remaining in place, in either the sit or down position, is one of the most important exercises you can teach your dog. Aside from its practical value, this exercise has important psychological implications.

Teaching your dog to stay still at your command is at the top of the list of critical exercises. Not only can you keep Buddy out from underfoot, but you also reinforce in his mind that you are the one in charge — you are the pack leader.

One way a dog exerts his leadership over a subordinate dog is by restricting the movement of the subordinate, or keeping him in his place. We remember an amusing incident involving our Yorkshire Terrier, Angus. Friends had come to visit and brought their six-month-old Doberman, Blue. Things went fine with the two dogs until we noticed that Blue was sitting in a corner with Angus lying in front of him a few feet away. Every time Blue tried to move, Angus would lift his lip, and Blue shrank back into the corner. It seems Angus had exploited the "home-field advantage" and convinced Blue that he was in charge.

Using the same principle, we have successfully taught countless dog owners to become pack leader in a nonviolent and nonconfrontational way. To accomplish this, you need to learn to place your dog into a sit and a down.

Placing your dog in a sit and down

For the sit, with Buddy on your left, kneel next to him, both of you facing in the same direction. If Buddy is a small dog, you can put him on a table for these exercises. Place your right hand against his chest and your left hand on his withers. (The withers are located directly behind the neck where the shoulder blades meet.) Say "Sit," run your left hand over his back, all the way down to his knees, and with equal pressure of both hands, collapse him into a sit. Keep your hands in place to the count of five and verbally praise Buddy, saying "good dog." Then release him with "Okay."

For the down, with Buddy sitting on your left, kneel next to him, both of you facing in the same direction. Reaching over his back, place your left hand behind his left foreleg; place the right hand behind the right foreleg. Keep your thumbs up so as not to squeeze Buddy's legs, something he may not like and may cause him to resist (see Figure 2-6). Say "down" and lift Buddy into the begging position and then lower him to the ground. Keep your hands in place to the count of five and verbally praise him. Then release him with "Okay."

Figure 2-6:
Preparing
your dog for
the down.

The long sit and down exercise: A recipe for leadership

The purpose of the long sit and down exercise is to teach Buddy in a non-violent way that you are his pack leader. For this reason, it is the foundation of all further training. Training your dog is next to impossible unless he accepts you as the one in charge.

Week 1: Five times during the course of a week, practice the long down exercise for 30 minutes at a time as follows:

1. **Sit on the floor beside your dog.**

2. **Place him in the down position.**

3. **If he gets up, put him back.**

4. **Keep your hands off when he is down.**

5. **Stay still.**

6. **After 30 minutes, release him.**

As a general rule, the greater a dog's leadership aspirations, the more frequently he will try to get up and the more important this exercise becomes. Just remain calm and each time he tries to get up, replace him in the down position.

If your dog is particularly bouncy, put him on leash and sit on a chair and the leash so your hands are free to put him back.

Some dogs immediately concede that you are the pack leader, while others need some convincing. If your dog is in the latter group, your, as well as his, first experience with the long down will be the hardest. As he catches on to the idea and gradually (if not grudgingly) accepts you as pack leader, each successive repetition will be that much easier.

Practice the long down under the following conditions:

- ✔ When your dog is tired
- ✔ After he has been exercised
- ✔ When interruptions are unlikely
- ✔ When you are not tired

If the situation allows it, you can watch television or read, so long as you don't move.

Week 2: On alternate days, practice three 30-minute downs and 10-minute sits while you sit in a chair next to your dog.

Week 3: On alternate days, practice three 30-minute downs and 10-minute sits while you sit across the room from your dog.

Week 4: On alternate days, practice three 30-minute downs and 10-minute sits while you move about the room but in sight of your dog.

After week 4, practice a long down and a long sit at least once a month.

We guarantee you that if you follow this regimen, your dog will unconditionally accept you as pack leader.

Chapter 3

Equipping for Training Success

. . . .

In This Chapter

▶ Implementing yourself (and your dog) for training

▶ Distinguishing between collars

▶ Balancing fit and safety concerns

▶ Taking advantage of treats

. . . .

Dog training is no different from any other activity — you need the right equipment for the job. Many choices are available to you, and in this chapter we address the factors that determine what training equipment to use under what circumstances.

Just because it's a collar or a leash doesn't mean you can use it to *train* your dog. In Chapter 1, we discuss how the mother dog teaches her puppies to stop doing something she doesn't want them to do. She uses negative reinforcement, something the puppies perceive as unpleasant, to get them to stop. This unpleasant experience, in turn, teaches the puppies the responsibility for their own behavior. A puppy says to himself, "If I use my teeth on Mommy, I'll get nailed. If I don't, mommy will lick my face." So puppy chooses not to use his teeth on Mommy. That, at any rate, is the gist of the puppy's thought process.

The key to making negative reinforcement work is that the dog has to perceive it as unpleasant so he can avoid it. If he doesn't perceive it as unpleasant, there's nothing to avoid and the undesired action continues. Hence, the importance of the right training equipment.

Choosing the Right Training Equipment

The type of training collar and leash you need depends on a number of factors, including those in the following list:

✔ The strength or weakness of your dog's drives

✔ Your dog's touch sensitivity

✔ Your dog's size and weight in relation to your size and weight

✔ The equipment's effectiveness

✔ Your dog's safety

✔ Your aptitude for training your dog

Keep in mind that training is not a matter of strength but finesse. For you, the trainer of Buddy, it should not have to be a heavy aerobic workout.

Before we talk about each of the preceding points, we want you to take a look at some commonly available leashes and collars.

Pulling on leashes

Leashes come in an assortment of styles, materials, widths, and lengths. The following are the most common materials:

✔ Chain

✔ Leather

✔ Canvas

✔ Nylon

We have never quite understood the purpose of chain leashes or why anyone would want to use them, but they exist. Chain leashes are often used with large dogs, but they are heavy and unwieldy. For example, if you wanted to fold the leash neatly into one hand or the other, as required by the training techniques we teach in this book, you'd not be able to do so without considerable discomfort. It is definitely not a leash you can use for training Buddy.

For a training leash, our materials of choice are canvas or nylon. Both can be readily manipulated, an important factor for the method we use, and they are economical. Canvas, especially with larger dogs, is easier on your hands than nylon.

Leather leashes are also quite popular, although more expensive than canvas leashes. But leather leashes, too, don't readily lend themselves to our approach to training.

The best training leash is a 6-foot canvas leash — it is easy on the hands, easily manipulated, and just the right length. It is also the most economical. For the average-size or larger dog, such as a Labrador, we use a canvas leash that is ½-inch wide. For toy dogs, such as a Yorkshire Terrier, we use a leash that is ¼-inch wide.

Canvas leashes are readily available in pet stores and come in a variety of colors, although olive green seems to be the most common.

Choosing among collars

Collars also come in a dazzling assortment of styles, colors, and materials. We distinguish between two types of collars:

- ✔ Training collars
- ✔ Collars for the trained dog, which can be ornamental

The purpose of a *training* collar is for you to be able to guide your dog and, if necessary, to check your dog. (A *check* is a tug on the leash, followed by an immediate release of tension on the leash.) A check is used mainly for abstention training, when you want your dog to stop doing something that he wants to do but that you don't want him to do. The check is a form of negative reinforcement — it is an unpleasant experience the dog can avoid by stopping the unwanted behavior, similar to a mother dog snapping at a puppy (see Chapter 1 for more on the check).

Collars for the trained dog are the buckle type — also called *buckle collars* — and they're either leather, nylon, or canvas. For the untrained dog, buckle collars are virtually useless. Picture yourself trying to hang on as a fully-grown Rottweiler decides to take off after a cat. Trying to control that dog with a buckle collar would definitely be a heavy aerobic workout.

Some owners prefer a harness, which is perfectly fine for dogs that do not pull or for small dogs, where pulling is not terribly objectionable. But for a medium-sized or large dog that pulls, harnesses are not a good idea because you give up the control you're trying to achieve. The dog literally leans into the harness and happily drags you wherever he wants to go. The only exception we can think of for using a harness on an untrained dog is if the dog has a neck injury.

Use the two types of collars — training collars and buckle collars — correctly. Remove the training collar when you are not training your dog or when you cannot supervise him. When not training, your dog should wear his buckle collar with ID tags attached.

You can find any number of training collars. The advantages and disadvantages of each are described in the following sections.

Chain or nylon slip-on collars

A slip-on collar, usually made of chain or nylon, is one that slips over the dog's head. As a result, it is generally much too big to be an effective training tool. Table 3-1 lists the pros and cons of this type of collar.

Table 3-1	Pros and Cons of Slip-On Collars
Advantages	*Disadvantages*
Readily available in pet stores and through catalogs	Not very effective
Inexpensive	Great potential for damaging the dog's trachea and neck
Easy to put on	Therefore, easy to come off — not very helpful when trying to make Buddy walk alongside you

Studies have shown a high incident of significant tracheal and spinal injuries among dogs that are trained with this type of collar. Animal chiropractors have made similar observations of spinal misalignment caused by this collar.

Not only are slip-on collars ineffective for purposes of training, but they also pose a danger to the trachea and spine of your dog. Avoid them! Because slip-on collars aren't very effective to begin with and have a poor safety record, we recommend that you save your money and get something that works, such as the nylon snap-around collar.

Nylon snap-around collars

The principal difference between a slip-on and a snap-around collar is that the latter has a clasp that enables you to fasten the collar around the dog's neck instead of having to slip it over his head. That way, you can fit the collar high on your dog's neck where you have the most control. The slip-on collar, on the other hand, slides down all the way to the point where the dog's neck joins the shoulders — the strongest area of the dog's body and where you have the least control.

The snap-around collar is our collar of first choice because of its effectiveness and versatility. The ones we use are actually made of a material other than nylon and don't stretch or fray.

The principal advantage of the snap-around collar is that it does not have to slip over your dog's head; it can be snapped directly around Buddy's neck, ensuring a snug fit. It should fit high on his neck, just below his ears, as snug as a turtleneck sweater, for a maximum of control. Table 3-2 presents some other advantages (and disadvantages) to a snap-around collar.

Table 3-2	Pros and Cons of Nylon Snap-Around Collars	
Advantages	*Disadvantages*	
Nylon collars are readily available through pet shops and catalogs	Nylon will stretch and fray	
Fairly inexpensive	If you choose another material besides nylon, you have to order one made from the right material	
Can be fitted exactly to your dog's neck	Not as easy to put on as a slip-on collar	
Very effective	A puppy will grow out of it quickly, and you may have to purchase others	
Quite safe		
Can be used as a training collar or a buckle collar		

The snap-around collar is guaranteed to fit your dog properly. The collar should sit just below your dog's ears. Measure the circumference of your dog's neck directly behind his ears with a piece of string. Place the string next to a ruler to get the exact length and then get a collar that size. These collars come in half-inch increments.

The snap-around collar consists of

- A clasp on one side
- A ring on the other side
- A loose or floating ring

Start with you and your dog facing each other. Then follow these steps to place a snap-around collar on your dog:

1. **Take the clasp in your left hand and the two rings in your right hand.**

2. **Place the collar under your dog's neck and bring the ends up to the top of his neck, directly behind the ears.**

   When you begin to put on the collar, the dog flexes his neck muscles, expanding the circumference of the neck by as much as ½ inch, creating the impression that the collar is much tighter than it actually is (similar to the effect produced by a horse taking in air as it is being saddled).

3. **Attach the clasp to the floating ring.**

   The smooth side of the clasp should be next to the dog's skin.

You may get the impression that the collar is much too tight and that you can barely get it around Buddy's neck. We suggest that after the first time you put the collar on you wait for five minutes. After the dog has relaxed, you then can test for correct snugness. You should be able to slip two fingers between the collar and your dog's neck (one finger if you have a toy dog). If you can't, the collar is too tight; if you can get three or more fingers through, the collar is too loose. One way to make the collar smaller is to tie a knot in it.

Once you have the collar on, you can use it as a training collar by attaching the leash to the *live ring* of the collar or as a buckle collar by attaching it to the *dead ring* of the collar.

The *live ring* of the training collar is the stationary ring; the *dead ring* of the collar is the floating ring (see Figure 3-1).

Some dogs don't respond to a check on a snap-around collar — that is, the check doesn't create an unpleasant experience for the dog so he doesn't learn to accept the responsibility for his behavior. The dog may be touch-insensitive and have a high discomfort threshold (see Chapter 8 for breed-specific behaviors). Or the dog's size and weight in relation to your size and weight may be such that he doesn't feel your check.

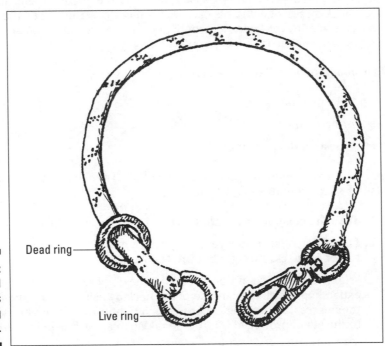

Figure 3-1:
The live and dead rings on a training collar.

Dead ring

Live ring

When one of us (okay, Wendy) was training one of our Newfoundlands (Cassandra), she outweighed Wendy by 20 pounds. Although she had begun her training as a puppy and was very responsive (Wendy and Cassandra had a wonderful relationship), when she spotted a rabbit, she'd drag Wendy helter-skelter after her quarry in hot pursuit. When Wendy tried to check her, it made absolutely no impression on her. It felt as though Wendy was trying to control a Mack truck with a shoestring. It was extremely frustrating, and Wendy's negative emotions were affecting their relationship because Cassandra didn't know the reason for Wendy's frustration.

So, as a last resort, Wendy went to the pinch collar — it was the only way she could get through to Cassandra not to go after the rabbit. Afterward, when Wendy gave a check, it did make an impression on her, and she responded immediately. Wendy was relieved that she could control Cassandra, and Cassandra was relieved that Wendy was no longer frustrated.

The moral of the story is this: A dog's *touch sensitivity*, or threshold of discomfort, increases proportionally with the interest the dog has in what he is pursuing (see Chapter 2 for more info about understanding your dog's mind).

Note that many people are put off by the pinch collar (which is covered in the next section) because it looks like a medieval instrument of torture. Your perception of a given piece of equipment, however, is immaterial. What counts is your dog's perception. It is your dog's response to your check that will tell you how he perceives the collar.

Take the training collar off your dog when he is not being trained and whenever he is not under your direct supervision. Do not attach any tags to the training collar. When you are not training your dog, use a buckle collar to which you have attached his tags.

Pinch collars

For old-time trainers, the pinch collar was the only collar to use.

Also called a German collar or prong collar, a pinch collar certainly is effective and efficient, and the dog understands immediately where his advantage lies. We've heard those who use one for the first time refer to it as power steering. We call it the *religious collar* because it makes an instant believer out of the dog.

According to our veterinarian, who is also a certified animal chiropractor, the pinch collar is generally the safest training collar. From our perspective, it is also the most effective training collar. Table 3-3 offers some of the highlights and lowlights of using the pinch collar.

Table 3-3	Pros and Cons of Pinch Collar
Advantages	*Disadvantages*
Readily available in pet stores and through catalogs	Looks like a medieval instrument of torture
Very effective	Twice as expensive as a snap-around collar
Can be fit to the exact size of the dog's neck	Not as easy to put on as a slip-on collar
Very safe — it is self-limiting in that it constricts very little and not to the point where the dog's air can be cut off	

Pinch collars come in four sizes: large, medium, small, and micro. We have never used or recommended the large size because it appears to have been made for elephants. For a large, strong, and rambunctious dog, the medium size is more than adequate. For Golden Retriever-sized or smaller dogs, the small size is sufficient. For toy dogs, use the micro version, which must be ordered.

For many dogs, the pinch collar is the most humane training collar. If you have to use one, put it on the same way you put on the snap-around collar. Simply expand or contract it by adding or removing links, respectively.

Electronic collars

We do not recommend that you try using an electronic collar to train your dog. To use such a collar requires a great deal of skill and experience. Moreover, they are quite expensive.

We do, however, recommend an electronic bark collar for uncontrollable barking — it's a lot cheaper than being evicted.

Hedging toward head halters

The head halter is a hybrid piece of equipment. It works on the premise that where the dog's head goes, sooner or later the rest of the body has to follow. It is an adaptation from head halters used for horses.

Whereas the pinch collar looks downright menacing, the head halter looks quite inviting and almost user friendly. Interestingly, your dog's reaction, and he *is* the one that counts, is likely to be quite the opposite. He will readily accept a pinch collar but vigorously and vociferously object to the halter, at least initially.

The following list describes the principal advantages of the halter, once your dog has learned to accept the effect it has on him:

- ✔ **Calming and tranquilizing:** Helpful with nervous, timid, shy, or hyperactive dogs
- ✔ **Equalizing:** Helps smaller handlers with larger dogs, senior citizens, and handicapped handlers control their dogs
- ✔ **Muzzling:** Helps with inappropriate sniffing behavior, whining or barking, some forms of aggression, and play biting or nibbling

Table 3-4 provides some additional advantages to the head halter, as well as some disadvantages.

Table 3-4	Pros and Cons of the Head Halter
Advantages	*Disadvantages*
Readily available in pet stores and through catalogs	Greatest potential for serious damage to your dog's neck
Not very expensive	Transition tool only
Minimum strength required to use it	The dog does not learn to accept responsibility for his behavior

The great potential for damage is due to the nature of the halter. Because it controls the head, a strong pull by the dog or the handler can do serious damage to the dog's neck. In this regard, it is not quite the same principle as the head halter for horses. Because most people are smaller than horses, the halter is used to control the horse's head from below.

In contrast, most people are taller than dogs, and any pull or tug is going to be upward and, at times, simultaneously to the side. Tugging the dog's neck in this way creates great potential for injury. We also feel that the halter can and often does have a depressing effect on the dog. We find it ironic that this highly marketable tool has such a great potential for damage, while the torturous-looking pinch collar is the safest.

Finally, the halter is a transition tool, at best, because it does not teach the dog to assume the responsibility for his behavior. He is being guided by the muzzle instead of being trained by the Yes-No model. And the dog is not learning through positive/negative reinforcement what is expected from him (see Chapter 1 for details about the Yes-No model and positive/negative reinforcement).

Treats Are Your Training Buddies

Other than your ingenuity and intellect, treats are the most powerful positive training tool you can use. Treats are used in one of two ways:

✔ **As a reward for a desired response:** For example, you say "down," and Buddy lies down. When used as a reward, the treat is hidden from the dog, who does not know whether or not he is going to get it.

To be effective, the treat has to *immediately* follow the desired response so the dog understands that he is being rewarded for that particular response. Don't diddle around fumbling for a treat and give it to him just as he is getting up again. That would be rewarding Buddy for getting up, not what you wanted at all.

✔ **As a lure or inducement to obtain a desired response:** Now the treat is in the open and is used to entice the dog to lie down, and when he does, he gets the treat. When used as an inducement, it is within the dog's control whether or not he gets the treat.

Because you are going to use treats both as a reward and an inducement, you need to decide where to carry them. Some people use fanny packs, which may be okay, depending on your dog. Some dogs begin to focus in on the fanny pack because they know that's where the treats are kept. If that happens, you need to find another way to carry your treats.

We use our pockets and wear trousers that are loose enough so that we can quickly get a treat. If your dog has to wait who knows how long while you struggle to get a treat out of your pocket, the treat may no longer mean anything. Worse yet, he may have done something else during the wait, something you don't want to reward.

Making the ideal treat

We like to use dry treats rather than something soggy, and there are many dry and semi-dry treats available. You do, however, need to be careful of both salt and sugar content so that treats don't ruin your dog's diet. Experiment to find out what your dog likes and to what he responds. It's of no use trying to train a dog with treats he doesn't like. Treats are also not going to be very effective after Buddy has just been fed.

Our dogs' favorites are homemade liver treats. They are simple to make using the following steps and contain no salt or sugar:

1. **Partially boil some beef liver.**

2. **Cut liver into ¼-inch cubes.**

3. **Place on a baking sheet and liberally sprinkle with garlic powder.**

4. **Bake in a 350-degree oven until dry, about one hour.**

5. **Store in the refrigerator.**

Our dogs also like raisins and carrots, but obviously not as much as they like liver.

When treats don't work

Some dogs do not respond as well to treats as they do to other objects, such as a ball, Frisbee, stone, or stick. In that case, use whatever turns your dog on, so long as it does not become a hindrance in your training.

Our German Shepherd, Katharina, would not take treats in training — must be that German work ethic. She would, however, respond to a stick or a toy, so that is what we used.

Whatever you use for treats, be sure to keep them handy and accessible. If you can't get at the treat quickly, there's a good chance that Buddy will do something that you don't want to reward — and you'll have lost the moment to reinforce the right behavior.

Chapter 4

Basic Training

*O*ne question almost every dog owner asks is, "How do I keep my dog from jumping up on people?"

Dogs jump on people usually as a form of greeting, like saying, "Hello, nice to meet you!" Even the briefest of separations from the owner, as little as five minutes, can set off this behavior.

Different styles of greetings have been perfected by dogs. Bean, the Labrador, would literally launch himself at his owner from a distance of about six feet. The owner did not appreciate having to catch this missile.

Dogs perceive jumping up as a friendly gesture. Jumping is a dog's way of letting the object of his affection know that he's happy to see him or her. You can train your dog to greet people in a less rambunctious fashion, but you don't want to punish your happy pet simply because he is glad to see you.

As annoying as it may be at times, remember that jumping up is a gesture of affection and good will. We certainly do not recommend any form of punishment to deal with it.

Even more annoying is the dog's habit of sniffing an area of our anatomy we would prefer he didn't. And downright embarrassing is his apparent special fondness for engaging in this behavior with guests. While this behavior may be normal for the dog — he uses his nose to identify the rank, sex, and age of other dogs he meets — you should insist that he get this information in a less intrusive way.

So how do you get him to stop these behaviors without dampening his enthusiasm? By teaching him to sit and stay on command. Your dog can't jump on you when he is sitting — the two behaviors are mutually exclusive.

You also need to teach Buddy a release word to let him know he can move again after you have told him to stay. If you do not release from the command after a reasonable period of time, he will release himself, and the length of time he stays will become shorter and shorter. Our release word is *OK*, meaning "You can move now."

The other commands you need to teach Buddy are the down and the come. Both of these commands are important for your peace of mind and for his safety. The down command lets you eat dinner without having to put up with a begging dog, and the come command ensures that your dog doesn't try to retrieve cars, which can have disastrous consequences.

Teaching the Basics

The sit and stay is one of the simplest and yet most useful exercises you can teach your dog. It gives you a wonderfully easy way to control him when you need to most. It is also one of the most basic of commands that you and your dog can quickly achieve.

Of all the commands your dog could learn, he must know the following commands:

- Sit
- Stay
- OK (the release command)
- Down
- Come

Since you will not be checking Buddy for these exercises, he needs to be on a leather or material buckle collar, sufficiently snug so that he can't slip out of it. (For more on checking, see Chapter 1.)

Sitting

The importance of teaching a dog to sit and stay cannot be overemphasized. Not only does Buddy stop jumping up on Grandma when she walks into the room, he can't run into the street after the neighbor's cat if he knows that he must sit.

Use the sit and stay command when you want your dog to remain quietly in one spot for a short time. For example, Kaiser, a German Shepherd, would become so excited when Jane was about to feed him that he sent the dish flying out of her hands. Once taught the sit and stay, he sat like a perfect gentleman as she put his dish down.

Getting your dog to sit — the easy part

Teaching your dog to sit on command is actually quite simple. Try the following time-tested technique.

If your dog already knows how to sit, he has to learn what *you* expect from him when you say "sit." He must learn to obey you every time you give him the command, and to obey on the first command.

Begin by showing your dog a small, bite-sized treat, holding it just a little in front of his eyes, slightly over his head. Say "sit" as you bring your hand above his eyes. When your dog looks up at the treat, he should sit.

When he sits, give him the treat and tell him what a good puppy he is. Tell him without petting him. If you pet him at the same time as you praise him, he will probably get up, but what you really want him to do is sit. Praising is verbal, so use a phrase such as "good dog" in a pleasant tone of voice. Rewarding is giving the dog a treat for a correct response.

When using this method of teaching your dog to sit, it is important to properly position your hand in relation to the dog's head. If your hand is held too high, your dog will jump up; if it is too low, he will not sit. Hold your hand about two inches above his head.

If your dog does not respond on his own, say "sit" again and put your dog into a sit by placing your left hand under his tail and behind his knees, and your right hand on his chest, and then tuck him into a sit. Keep your hands still and count up to five, before giving him the treat.

Practice making your dog sit five times in a row for five days. Some dogs catch on to this idea so quickly that whenever they want a treat they sit in front of their owner.

Getting your dog to sit on command — the hard part

Working with your dog to sit using treats is just the opening chapter of the real task at hand — teaching your dog to sit on command. Saying "sit" when getting your dog to sit using treats is essential, as he starts to associate the command with the action.

When he understands what the word "sit" means, you can start to teach him to obey your command. Put the hand that has the treat at your side and slide your other hand through his collar at the top of his neck, palm facing up, and tell him to sit. If he does, give him a treat and tell him how good he is; if he does not, pull up on his collar and wait until he sits; then praise and reward him with a treat.

Practice until he sits on command, that is, without having to pull up on, or touch the collar. Give him a treat and praise him with "good puppy" for every correct response.

As your dog demonstrates that he has mastered sitting on command, start to reward the desired response every other time. Finally, reward him on a *random* basis — every now and then give him a treat after he has sat on command. A random reward is the most powerful reinforcement of what your dog has learned. It is based on the simple premise that hope springs eternal. To make the random reward work, all you have to do is use it and keep using it!

Now when Buddy wants to greet you by jumping up, tell him to sit. Bend down and briefly pet him and tell him what a good puppy he is; then release him.

Following this simple method consistently, you can change your dog's greeting behavior from trying to jump on you to sitting to be petted.

Staying

An easy way to teach your dog to understand the stay command is to make him sit and stay for his supper. As you are getting ready to feed him, bowl in hand, tell him "sit," then "stay," and finally lower the bowl to the ground. As he starts for it, pick up the bowl before he gets even a mouthful. Put him back where he was supposed to sit and stay and start all over. Repeat until you can put the bowl down and count to five before telling him "OK." Then let him eat in peace.

Successful training depends on who is more determined and persistent — you or your dog.

After several days of following this regimen, your dog should sit all on his own as soon as he sees you approaching with his supper and wait until you release him with "OK." Thus, you've created a much more pleasant way to feed your dog than having him jump up and down trying to knock his dish out of your hands.

When Buddy has proven that he can sit and stay on command using his meal as incentive, you want to begin working on him staying when the doorbell rings or someone knocks on the door. If your dog is anything like ours, the doorbell causes an immediate charge amidst paroxysms of barking. While you likely want your dogs to be alert, you also likely then want them to stop, sit, and stay, so you can answer the door.

To accomplish this goal, you need to enlist the aid of a friend or neighbor to ring the doorbell. When the bell rings and your dog goes through his paces, take him by the collar and make him sit. Tell him "stay" and then go to open the door. When he gets up, which he surely will, put him back.

If Buddy is an excitable soul, be prepared for many repetitions of putting him back before he takes you seriously. Other dogs catch on after two or three attempts.

When he stays as you go to the door, open it to admit your accomplice. At this point, Buddy will more than likely want to say hello. Again, put him back and have your helper approach him holding out the palm of his or her hand, let Buddy sniff the palm, and then have your helper ignore him. You may have to be right next to Buddy to reinforce the sit and stay.

To help make your helper's arrival as traditional as possible, have him or her ring the doorbell only once. Ask him or her to wait for you to open the door.

You need to repeat this procedure several times until Buddy is reliable and holds the sit and stay while you open the door.

Doing the sit-stay

As a part of his grade school education, your dog has to learn the sit-stay in a more formal manner — not just at home, but anywhere. Because he already has some idea what the concept means, reinforcing the sit-stay should go relatively quickly. Using these steps, you and your dog should achieve success in just a few minutes in one training session:

1. **With your dog sitting at heel position, put the rings of his training collar between his ears and attach the leash to the dead ring of the collar.**

   Heel position is defined as the area from the dog's head to his shoulder in line with your left hip with both of you facing in the same direction.

   Fold the leash accordion-style into your left hand with the part of the leash going toward the dog coming out at the bottom of your hand.

2. **Apply a little upward tension on the collar — just enough to let him know the tension is there but not enough to make him uncomfortable.**

3. **Say "stay" and give the stay signal — a pendulum motion with the right hand, palm facing the dog, stopping in front of the dog's nose, and then returning to your right side (see Figure 4-1).**

   Before you step away from your dog, make sure your right hand is at your side again.

4. **Take a step to the right, count to ten, return to your dog's side, release tension, tell him how good he is, and release with "OK."**

5. **Repeat, only this time step directly in front of your dog, count to ten, step back, release tension, tell him what a good boy he is, and release with "OK."**

6. **With your dog sitting at your left side, put the rings of the training collar under your dog's chin and attach the leash to the live ring of the collar.**

   Neatly fold your leash accordion-style into your left hand, and place it against your belt buckle, allowing one foot of slack.

Figure 4-1:
Giving the
stay signal.

7. **Say and signal "stay" and then place yourself one foot in front of your dog.**

8. **Without applying tension to the leash, turn and face your dog, keeping your left hand at your belt buckle and your right hand at your side, palm open, facing your dog.**

When you see that your dog's attention is drifting, there's a good chance that he is about to move. When you see this happening, reinforce the stay command.

If your dog is thinking about moving, or should actually try to move, take a step toward your dog with your right foot and, with your right hand, firmly slap the leash straight up to a point directly above his head. Bring back your right foot and right hand to their original position without repeating the stay command. Count to 30 and pivot back to your dog's right side. Verbally praise him and release him with "OK."

Repeat over the course of several training sessions until your dog is steady on this exercise.

You can tell your dog is thinking about moving when he starts to look around and begins to focus on something other than you. Any time you see that, reinforce the stay command by slapping the leash straight up.

Reinforcing the extended stay

The *review progression* is one of the sequences you can use to teach your dog a particular exercise. Every exercise has a review progression, which is one of the sequences used to teach the dog that particular exercise. Refreshing the dog's recollection of what you expect from him, this sequence is most helpful when your dog is still learning and when you think he needs to be reminded of his responsibilities. The following steps, using the leash on the dead ring of the collar, involve testing your dog's understanding of "stay," while extending the time and distance of the result of the stay command:

1. **Starting in heel position, with your left hand holding the leash and placed against your belt buckle, say and signal "stay" and then step three feet in front of your dog, leaving no tension on the leash.**

2. **Slightly rotate your left hand to apply tension on the leash.**

   This is called the sit-stay test. If your dog moves to come to you, reinforce the stay. Test three times, increasing the tension until you get physical resistance on the part of your dog. Your tension should be commensurate to the size and weight of your dog. In other words, Terrier-strength tension applied to your Golden Retriever isn't going to produce the desired results.

   For the sit-stay test, use a downward rotation of the left wrist. Maintain tension for a few seconds and then release tension. You are looking for physical resistance on the part of your dog. From now on, practice this quick test before you do a sit-stay with your dog. (And don't forget to release from the earlier stay before starting.)

3. **Starting at heel position, with the leash now on the live ring, go three feet in front of your dog.**

   The goal is to have him stay for one minute. If he moves, reinforce the stay.

4. **Move six feet in front, to the end of the leash.**

You need to practice the sit-stay on a fairly regular basis, but you don't want to bore yourself or the dog. After Buddy understands what you want, once or twice a week is perfectly adequate.

Releasing

OK is the release command. When you say "OK," your dog should know that he can move now and is on his own time. Make it a strict rule to give him the release command, which allows him to move again, after every time you tell him to stay. If you get lax about releasing and forget, Buddy will get into the habit of releasing himself. That teaches him that he can decide when to move — not a good idea and the opposite of what you want him to learn.

TIP

Attention to inflection

You should give commands in a normal tone of voice. For example, when giving the sit command, remember that it is "sit!" — the command — and not "sit?" — the question.

When releasing, you should give the release word "OK" in a more excited tone of voice, as in "That's it, you're all done!"

Unless impaired, a dog's sense of hearing is extremely acute and when giving a command there is absolutely no need to shout. In fact, the opposite is true — the quieter you give your commands, the quicker your dog learns to pay attention to you.

When teaching a new command, you may have to repeat it several times during the initial introduction before your dog catches on. After the first session, teach him to respond to the first command. Give the command and if nothing happens, show your dog exactly what it is you want by physically helping him. Consistency is the key to success.

TIP

As quickly as you can, get into the habit of using only one release command. If you do not get the desired response on the first command, reinforce the command by showing the dog what you want without repeating it. You can do this by simply walking forward. Make sure that Buddy knows the difference between being praised for doing his exercise correctly and being released from work. You say "good boy" when you are teaching Buddy to do something, and when the exercise is finished, you release with "OK." By being consistent early on, your dog learns he has to respond to the first command.

Teaching down and go lie down

You say the command "Go lie down" when you want Buddy to go to his place and remain there for an extended period until you release him. You'll use this command most frequently when you are eating or when friends visit and you don't want your dog making a pest of himself. When you give him the command, he is expected to go to his favorite spot and make himself comfortable. When he can get up again, release him.

"Down" is the command you use when you want your dog to lie down in place, right now, and stay there until you release him.

Your dog already knows how to lie down. The following steps will help you teach him to do it when you tell him.

1. **With your dog sitting at your left side and a treat in your right hand, put two fingers of your left hand, palm facing you, through his collar at the side of his neck.**

2. **Show him the treat and lower it straight down and in front of your dog as you apply gentle downward pressure on the collar, at the same time saying "Down."**

   When he lies down, give him the treat and praise him by telling him what a good puppy he is. Keep your left hand in the collar and your right hand off your dog while telling him how clever he is so that he learns he is being praised for lying down. With a small dog, you may want to do this on a table.

3. **Reverse the process by showing him a treat and bringing it up slightly above his head with upward pressure on the collar as you tell him to sit.**

   Practice having your dog lie down at your side five times in a row for five days, or until he does it on command with minimal pressure on the collar. Praise and reward with a treat every time.

4. **Sit your dog at your left side and put two fingers of your left hand, palm facing you, through his collar at the side of his neck.**

   Keep your right hand with the treat at your right side.

5. **Say "Down" and apply downward pressure on the collar.**

   When he lies down, praise and give him a treat every other time. Practice over the course of several days until he will lie down on command without any pressure on the collar.

Make a game out of teaching your dog to lie down on command. Get him eager about a treat and then in an excited tone of voice say, "Down." Then give him his treat. After that, when he lies down on command you can randomly reward him.

You can now start to teach your dog to lie down in one place for several minutes. Tell him to "go lie down" and take him to his favorite spot; if necessary, place him down with a little pressure on his collar and the command "down." Keep an eye on him and when he tries to get up, place him down again. Teach him to stay at that spot in the down position for five minutes, then praise him and release him with "OK."

As he learns where you want him to stay, gradually and over the course of several sessions, increase his time in that spot until he stays up to 30 minutes before you release him. The long down exercise described in Chapter 2 will help this exercise go quickly.

You must release him from the spot when he can move again. If you forget, he will get into the habit of releasing himself, thereby undermining the purpose of the exercise.

From then on, when you want him out from under foot, tell him to "go lie down." At this stage, you may still have to take Buddy to the spot, but after several repetitions he will go by himself.

As always, the key to your success lies in how consistent you are in your dealings with Buddy.

While the sit-stay is used for relatively short periods, the down-stay is used for correspondingly longer periods. Traditionally, the down-stay is also taught as a safety exercise — to get Buddy to stop wherever he is and stay there. For example, Buddy finds himself on the other side of the road. He sees you and is just about to cross the road when a car comes. You need a way to get him to stay on the other side until the car has passed by.

The object of the down-stay command is to have your dog respond to your command whether he is up close or at a distance. Pointing to the ground will not work from a distance, so you need to train your dog to respond to an oral command.

This is where the down-stay command comes in — the theory being that the dog is least likely to move in the down position. Be that as it may, you will find this command not that hard to teach, and you do want to be able to stop your dog in his tracks.

Winning the game of coming when called

One of the greatest joys of owning a dog is going for a walk in a park or the woods and letting him run, knowing he will come when he is called. A dog that does not come when called is a prisoner of his leash and, if he gets loose, is a danger to himself and others.

This section offers some proven rules for helping you and your dog realize the benefits of coming when called.

Rule #1: Exercise, exercise, exercise

Many dogs do not come when called because they do not get enough exercise. At every chance, they run off and make the most of this unexpected freedom to move around by staying out for hours at a time.

Consider what your dog was bred to do and that will tell you how much exercise he needs. Just putting him out in the backyard will not do. You have to participate. Think of it this way: Exercise is as good for you as it is for your dog.

Rule #2: Whenever your dog comes to you, be nice to him

One of the quickest ways to teach your dog not to come to you is to call him to punish him or do something the dog perceives as unpleasant. Most dogs consider being given a bath or a pill unpleasant. When Buddy needs either, go and get him instead of calling him to you.

Another example of teaching your dog not to come is to take him for a run in the park and call him to you when it's time to go home. Repeating this sequence several times, teaches the dog that the party is over. Soon, though, he may become reluctant to return to you when called because he is not ready to end the fun.

You can prevent this kind of unintentional training by calling him to you several times during his outing, sometimes giving him a treat, sometimes just a pat on the head. Then let him romp again.

Rule #3: Teach him to come when called as soon as you get him

Ideally, you acquired your dog as a puppy, which is the best time to teach him to come when called. Start right away. But remember, sometime between four and eight months of age your puppy begins to realize there is a big, wide world out there.

While he is going through this stage, it is best to keep him on leash so that he does not learn he can ignore you when you call him.

Rule #4: When in doubt, keep him on leash

Learn to anticipate when your dog is likely not to come. You may be tempting fate trying to call him once he has spotted a cat, another dog, or a jogger. Of course, there will be times when you goof and let him go just as another dog appears out of nowhere.

Don't set your dog up for failure at coming when called. Be confident that if you let Buddy off leash, you are not doing so in a place where he is bound to spot a rabbit hopping by.

Resist the urge to make a complete fool of yourself by bellowing "come" a million times. The more often you holler "come," the quicker he learns he can ignore you when he is off leash. Instead, patiently go to him and put him on leash. Do not get angry with him once you have caught him or you will make him afraid of you and he will run away from you when you try to catch him the next time.

Rule #5: Make sure your dog always comes to you and lets you touch his collar before you reward

Touching his collar prevents the dog from developing the annoying habit of playing "catch" — coming towards you and then dancing around you, just out of reach. So teach him to let you touch his collar before you offer him a treat or praise.

The game of coming when called

You need two people, one hungry dog, one six-foot leash, plenty of small treats, and two whistles (optional). Some people prefer to train their dog to come to a whistle instead of the verbal command "come." Some people train their dog to do both.

What works best depends on the dog, and you may want to experiment. Consider trying the verbal command first, because there may be times when you need to call your dog but don't have your whistle. You can then do it over with a whistle, which will go very quickly because Buddy already has some understanding of what he is supposed to do.

For this exercise, you should be inside the house, with your dog on a six-foot leash. You and your partner are sitting on the floor, six feet apart, facing each other, and your partner gently restrains the dog while you hold the end of the leash.

1. **Call your dog by saying "Buddy, come" and use the leash to guide him to you.**

2. **When Buddy comes to you, put your hand through his collar, give him a treat, pet him, and praise him enthusiastically.**

   Now you can and should pet Buddy so that he understands how happy you are that he came to you. This situation is different from the sit or the down, where you want him to remain in place and petting him would cause him to get up.

   Some dogs find it entertaining to come when you call, only to prance around you when they arrive. Prevent this habit by training your dog to allow you to touch his collar prior to a treat or praise.

3. **Now you hold Buddy and pass the leash to your partner, who says "Buddy, come," guides the dog in, puts his hand through the collar, gives him a treat, and praises the dog.**

   Keep working on this exercise until your dog responds on his own to being called and no longer needs to be guided in with the leash.

4. **Repeat the exercise with Buddy off leash, gradually increasing the distance between you and your partner to 12 feet.**

5. **Have your partner hold Buddy by the collar while you hide from him in another room and then call him.**

6. **When he finds you, put your hand through the collar, give him a treat, and praise him.**

   If he can't find you, go to him, take him by the collar, and bring him to the spot where you called. Reward and praise.

7. **Now have your partner hide and then call your dog.**

   Repeat the exercise until Buddy doesn't hesitate in finding you or your partner in any room of the house.

Now you're ready to go outside. Take Buddy outside to a confined area, such as a fenced yard, tennis court, park, or school yard, and repeat Steps 1, 2, and 3 from the preceding exercise.

Now you are ready to practice by yourself. Let Buddy loose in a confined area and ignore him. When he is not paying any attention to you, call him. When he gets to you, give him a treat and make a big fuss over him. If he does not come, go to him, take him by his collar, and bring him to the spot where you called him; then reward and praise him. Repeat until he comes to you every time you call him.

Once Buddy is trained, you don't have to reward him with a treat every time, but do so frequently.

Dashing Your Dog's Dashing Habits

Almost as annoying as unrestrained greeting behavior, but far more dangerous, is the dog's habit of dashing through doors just because they are open, racing up and down stairs — with, ahead, or behind you — and jumping in and out of the car without permission.

These behaviors are dangerous to your dog because he may find himself in the middle of the road and get run over. These behaviors are dangerous to you because you might get knocked over or down the stairs.

These potential accidents can be prevented by teaching Buddy to sit and stay while you open the door and to wait until you tell him it's okay to go out.

Sit and stay also apply to going up and down stairs — we don't like the thought of having both arms full while going down a staircase with a dog dashing by, or having a dog scramble around us as we get in or out of a car.

Start by sitting Buddy in front of a door that is closed to the outside. You know that if you open that door he will want to go through. Tell him to stay and start opening the door. When he starts to get up, close the door, put him back in the exact spot where you told him to stay, and start all over.

You will find that after you have put him back three or four times, he begins to get the message and will stay. Practice until you can open the door all the way before closing it again with Buddy on a stay. From now on, each time you let him out, make him sit first, open the door, and then release him with "OK."

Also, get into the habit of having him sit and stay before you open any door. Some of us prefer to go through the doorway first, while others want the dog to go through first. It makes no difference, so long as your dog stays until you release him. Practice through doors your dog uses regularly, including the car door. Every time you make him sit and stay it reinforces your position as pack leader and the one in charge.

If you have stairs, start teaching Buddy to stay at the bottom while you go up. First sit him and tell him to stay. When he tries to follow, put him back and start again. Practice until you can go all the way up the stairs with him waiting at the bottom before you release him to follow.

Repeat the same procedure for going down the stairs.

Once Buddy has been trained to wait at one end of the stairs, you will discover that he will anticipate the release. He will "jump the gun" and get up just as you are thinking about releasing him. Before long, he will only stay briefly and release himself when he chooses. It may happen almost as soon as he has grasped the idea, or it may take a few weeks or even months, but it will happen.

When it does, stop whatever you are doing and put him back, count to ten, and release him. Do not let him get into the habit of releasing himself. Consistency is just as important here as it is teaching any other exercise.

Setting the Tone for Proper Table Manners

Teaching Buddy table manners is your responsibility, and you only have to remember one rule: Don't feed the dog from the table. This sounds a lot simpler than it is, especially in a multiperson household. Moreover, don't ever underestimate your dog's ability to train you.

Every time you reward your dog's efforts with a treat from the table, you are systematically teaching him not to take "no" for an answer.

When Buddy was a puppy, nobody thought much about occasionally slipping him something from the table. But now he is six months old, almost fully grown, and has started to beg at the table. Because it is no longer cute, and embarrassing when there are guests, the family resolves to put a stop to it.

At first, Buddy does not believe you are serious; after all, you were the one who started it in the first place. He digs a little deeper into his repertoire of begging routines. He may sit up, nudge you, paw you, or whine in the most pathetic tone as though he is near death's door from starvation. Sure enough, little Sally takes pity on him and slips him something.

As this scenario repeats itself, often with longer intervals before someone gives in, Buddy is systematically being trained to persevere at all cost and never to give up. Looking at it from his point of view, you are rewarding, even encouraging, the very behavior you want to stop.

When you stop rewarding the undesired behavior (begging), your dog will stop begging at the table.

As soon as you stop giving in to Buddy, his efforts will decrease, until over time, and provided you don't have a relapse, he will stop begging altogether. In technical jargon, you have extinguished the undesired behavior by refusing to reward it.

You can also save yourself all this aggravation by teaching Buddy to lie quietly in his favorite spot while you enjoy your meals in peace.

Part II
Giving Your Dog's Training Its Best Shot

The 5th Wave   By Rich Tennant

WHY TIMID FAMILIES SHOULDN'T PICK BORDER COLLIES AS HOUSEHOLD PETS.

I have to go to the bathroom, Dad.

In this part . . .

Of course you want your dog to succeed at training, because a well-trained dog is a happy dog, and happy dogs make happy owners. You can do several things to ensure training success, and those things are the focus of this part. For example, selecting a dog whose innate personality meshes with yours — or really under-standing your existing dog's nature — sets the stage for good communication between dog and owner. Knowing what a puppy goes through can help you understand what he needs both physically and emotionally and help you excuse those bad behaviors that come from instinct or simple ignorance. (Patience and understanding come in handy with older dogs, too!) And feeding your dog foods that keep him physically healthy contributes a great deal to his overall well-being — which ensures that training will be fun and rewarding for both of you.

Chapter 5

Developing Training Savvy

*T*he ability of your dog — just like your ability — to learn and retain information is directly related to what goes on around him and to how he feels. A noisy and distraction-filled environment will make it difficult for Buddy to concentrate on learning new commands. Strife in the household may cause Buddy to become irritable, even aggressive — feelings that impede the learning process. Even what you feed your dog can have an effect on his ability to learn.

Similarly, how Buddy feels, both mentally and physically, influences his ability to learn. If he feels anxious, depressed, or stressed, learning and retention decrease in direct proportion to the degree of the dog's distress. If he is physically ill or in pain, he can't learn what you're trying to teach him.

These observations are stating the obvious — just think how you would react under similar circumstances — and yet we need to point these things out in this chapter because dog owners seem to be oblivious of their effect on the dog's ability to learn.

Managing Your Dog's Environment

Your dog has a keen perception of his environment. Continuous or frequent strife or friction in your household can have a negative impact on your dog's ability to learn. Many dogs are also adversely affected by excessive noise and activity and may develop behavior problems.

Look for the following signs that your dog has a negative perception of his environment:

✔ Lethargy

✔ Hyperactivity

✔ Irritability

✔ Aloofness

✔ Aggression

Under these circumstances, learning is retarded — if it takes place at all — or the lesson will not be retained.

However, if you also have a keen perception of how your dog responds to his environment, your training goals will be more easily attained. This section provides some tips on creating for your dog the best possible environment for learning.

Starting on the right foot

You have heard the saying "You don't get a second chance to make a first impression." You also know that the first impression leaves the most lasting impact. The stronger that impression, the longer it lasts.

Introductions to new experiences should be as pleasant as possible. A dog can have a hard time "unlearning" that something or someone is best avoided. For example, Buddy's first visit to the veterinarian should be a pleasant experience, or he will have an unpleasant association with going to the veterinarian. Have the doctor give him a dog biscuit first and then do the examination, before giving another treat at the end.

The importance of making a good first impression applies to your dog's training as well. A particularly traumatic or unpleasant first experience can literally ruin a dog for life. The object is to make your dog's first impression of training as pleasant as you can. Any introduction to a new activity should be a pleasant experience.

Recognizing your dog's social needs

Dogs are social animals that do not do well being isolated (see Figure 5-1). For example, if you work, you likely have to leave your dog alone at home. Then when you get home, your dog is terribly excited and wants to play and be with you. But you might also go out in the evening, leaving your dog alone again.

Photo courtesy of Ed Camelli

Figure 5-1:
Your dog
responds to
quality time
with you.

Sometimes, your dog retaliates. In our younger (and more socially active) days, we had a lovely, well-trained Collie named Duke. Both of us worked, and we frequently went out in the evening. If this happened three days in a row, Duke would urinate on our bed. It took us a while to figure out this pattern; we solved the problem by not going out three days in a row, or by taking Duke with us.

Day-care centers for dogs are being established in many communities. You can leave your dog for the day without having to feel guilty about not giving him time to socialize. If you simply do not have the time to give your dog the attention he craves, consider finding a day-care center for dogs. Their popularity is proof of the need for these services. You can leave your dog for the day without having to feel guilty. He will spend much of his time socializing with other dogs and having a good time.

In addition to keeping Buddy entertained and amused, many dog day-care facilities provide other services such as bathing, grooming, and training. Perhaps the best feature, depending on your perspective, is that when you pick up Buddy on your way home, he will be too tired to make many demands on you.

Just like with any behavior, when it comes to exercise, your dog has a limited amount of energy. Once that energy has been expended, Buddy is happy and tired. If that energy is not expended, it may redirect itself into barking, chewing, digging, house soiling, self-mutilation, and similar behaviors. Clearly not what you have in mind for the well-trained pet.

Identifying your dog's emotional needs

Whether dogs have emotional needs depends on whether you accept that dogs have emotions. We certainly do, and here are some of them:

- Joy
- Happiness
- Sadness
- Depression
- Anger
- Apprehension
- Fear

You can see your dog exhibit some of these emotions, such as joy and happiness, on a daily basis, but what about sadness and depression? Dogs react with the same emotions that we have with the loss of a loved one, be it a member of the family or another dog.

For the last 30 years, we have always had more than one dog, at times as many as ten. When one of them passed on, there is no question that those closest to him or her experienced grief. We had a brother and sister pair of Landseers named Cato and Cassandra. When Cassandra died, Cato showed all the signs of clinical depression.

Cassandra died when Cato was seven years old and had been retired from a very successful dog-show career. Because Cato really enjoyed pre-show training and going to dog shows, we started showing him all over in Canada to get him out of his depression. And it worked. He competed for another three years and finally retired for good at the age of ten.

How can you tell whether your dog is experiencing any of these negative emotions? Pretty much the way you can tell with a person. If your dog mopes around the house, doesn't seem to enjoy activities he previously enjoyed, is lethargic, is not particularly interested in food, and sleeps a lot, chances are he's depressed. Under those circumstances, he won't feel much like training.

We sometimes see dogs with anxiety, apprehension, and fear — behaviors that can be hereditary, situational, or caused by some physical ailment. Whatever the cause, to train such a dog requires a great deal of patience and an understanding of how difficult it is for him to learn. On the other hand, the rewards are significant because through the structure of training, the dog's confidence is increased, sometimes to the point where these behaviors disappear altogether.

Keeping up with your dog's physical needs

Every dog, whether shorthaired or longhaired, needs to be groomed on a regular basis. Dogs also need to be bathed regularly. Dogs love to be clean and groomed, evidenced by how playful they become after their grooming sessions. They enjoy being told how beautiful they look, and a clean dog is a lot more fun to train than a dirty dog.

Bathing your dog

The general guideline in bathing is this: When your dog smells like a dog, bathe him. Some dogs' coats repel dirt and pollution more effectively than others. Dogs live in a variety of environments, and his environment, as well as how much your dog is exposed to dirt or how dirty your dog becomes just eating his food, will dictate how often to bathe.

The easiest way to bathe your dog is in the bathtub because you need hot and cold water to get the shampoo out of his coat (see Figure 5-2). You need to get a spray attachment for the faucet and a rubber mat so he doesn't slip. Start bathing your dog when he is still a puppy and you can easily get him in and out of the tub. As he grows up, size permitting, he'll get into the tub by himself. Make it a pleasant experience by giving him a treat after you've placed him into the tub and after his bath. Having taught your dog to stand on command helps considerably.

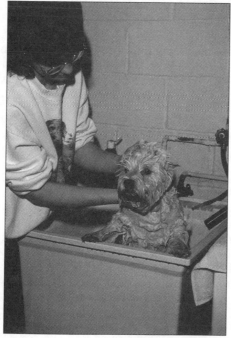

Figure 5-2:
A clean dog
is a happy
dog.

Photo courtesy of Jeannie Harrison

Use a gentle shampoo diluted with water 10 to 1. If you use the shampoo full strength, it'll take forever to rinse him and get all the shampoo out of his coat. Dry him with a towel, and you're done.

If Buddy is a small dog, bathing him in the kitchen sink will be easier on your back. Another alternative is to bathe him in a washtub outside, although you may not have access to warm water, and in some parts of the country, bathing him outside wouldn't work too well in the winter.

Contrary to popular belief, few dogs mind getting a bath. And most actually enjoy it. They love the attention, and the warm water makes them droopy and relaxed.

We have a Briard, a French sheep-herding dog. We look at him as a giant Yorkshire Terrier. He has a huge mustache and a long coat. He must be brushed at least three times a week and bathed once a week; otherwise, he begins to smell and his hair mats. He is a high-maintenance dog.

Our Standard Wirehaired Dachshunds, however, require little grooming. Their hair, which does not shed, is taken out — literally pulled out with a special grooming tool — three times a year. Apart from a comb through whiskers, eyebrows, and legs, these dogs require practically no maintenance at all. Still, our little female Dachshund, Diggy, loves to roll in anything she can find in the woods, so she frequently finds herself in the bath tub. The difference between the two dogs is that Diggy takes only five minutes to shampoo and towel-dry, whereas the Briard takes half an hour in the tub and several hours to dry.

For bathing Buddy, choose a mild herbal shampoo, something you would use for yourself. Rinsing your dog in a solution of apple cider vinegar and water — half vinegar and half water — helps to repel fleas and other skin parasites. This solution also balances out the pH levels of the skin and is excellent for minor skin irritations. Your dog will have a wonderfully shiny coat after this treatment.

How often your dog should be bathed is relatively simple to assess. Let your nose be your guide.

Trimming your dog's toenails

A dog's toenails need to be trimmed once a week. If the nails are not cut, your dog is unable to use the pads of his feet (see Figure 5-3). Ultimately, the nails will grow and turn backward into the feet, causing a great deal of pain and discomfort to the dog. In breeds that have long backs, such as Corgis, Dachshunds, and Bassets, keeping toenails short is critical. Left unattended, the nails force these dogs to walk on the back pad on their feet, which in turns pushes the shoulders back and ultimately causes horrible back problems.

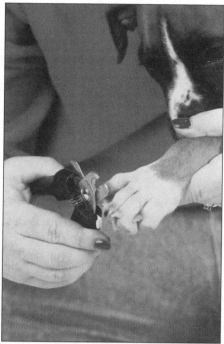

Figure 5-3:
Trimmed
nails are not
just for good
looks.

Photo courtesy of winter/churchill aka dogphoto.com

Basically, two kinds of clippers are available. One is like a guillotine blade that is very sharp. It is a small tool that's best for dogs under 20 pounds. Dogs over 20 pounds, who have larger nails, need a clipper that looks like a pair of pruning shears.

A grinder makes nail trimming very easy. The grinder is an electric hobby tool made by Dremel, and it grinds the nail like a nail file. The grinder is our tool of choice because it leaves the nails with smooth edges, whereas the clipper leaves sharp edges. Your dog may object to the sound of the grinder at first, but many dogs adjust comfortably. (The instructions that follow apply for both the clipper and the grinder.)

How can you tell when Buddy's nails need to be trimmed? If you can hear his toenails when he walks across an uncarpeted floor, they are too long.

Here's how you can train your dog to accept nail cutting. Of course, you can also take him to a groomer or the veterinarian.

1. **Sitting with your dog on the floor or the couch, take his paws, one at a time, and gently get him used to having them touched and looked at.**

   Give him a treat when he allows you to hold his paw without jerking it away.

2. **Once Buddy is comfortable, hold his paw in your hand and, with your index finger, gently apply pressure to a nail.**

   Pat the nail a couple of times, praise your dog, and give him a treat. Do this until your dog is comfortable with having his nails touched.

3. **Show your dog the nail clipper/grinder and let him smell it.**

   If you are using the grinder, turn it on so he gets accustomed to the noise.

4. **Take your dog's foot and hold it firmly, but not hard, and clip/grind off the end of one nail.**

   You need to usually remove about 1/16 inch. Praise your dog and reward with a treat. Go slowly and aim to finish up one foot per session.

5. **Trim the nails at the rate of one foot per day until all four feet are done.**

   After that, you can move to trimming once a week and do all four feet at the same session. Always remember to reward your dog.

If you have let your dog's nails go, take him to your veterinarian or a groomer. Nail cutting can be painful to your dog if you don't do it on a regular basis. Dogs that have had bad experiences are fretful when it comes to nail-cutting time. With these dogs, training them to accept a grinder is often the best route to take. We also use the grinder to round off the rough edges left after cutting the nails with a clipper.

Cleaning ears

Ears need to be cleaned out once a week as part of your grooming sessions. Take a piece of cotton and wet it with a solution of apple cider vinegar and warm water (50 percent of each). The solution is a good maintenance cleaner, because the acidity of the vinegar prevents the growth of all sorts of bacteria and fungi. Wipe out ears, paying attention to the little folds that collect earwax. Do not go down too deep inside the ear.

Expressing anal glands

Anal glands are small sacs inside the rectum. In earlier times, dogs used to express these glands to mark their territory. Little use is found for these holdover glands today.

All dogs have anal glands, and they can become a nuisance. If you see your dog scooting along the ground, chances are he is trying to express them himself. If this behavior continues, take him to your veterinarian and have him show you how to express these glands; it is childishly simple. Left unattended, the glands can block the end of the rectum and become infected and painful, and your dog will not be able to eliminate. In severe cases, surgery is required.

Feeding your dog's nutritional needs

The most important influence on your dog's ability to learn, and the one under your most immediate control, is what you feed him. Because feeding is so important, we have devoted a separate chapter to this topic (see Chapter 7).

For the well-trained dog, you need to become familiar with what foods are available and what is best for your dog. So many dog foods are on the market today that making the correct choice for Buddy can be a bewildering task. Just as you do when buying food for yourself or your family, you need to look at the ingredients. Dogs are carnivores and need animal protein. Select a food that lists an animal protein, such as chicken, beef, or lamb, in the first three ingredients.

Managing the Dog Within

Besides the principal influences on your dog's ability to learn that are *under your control,* there are influences that come *with* your dog:

- ✔ Breed-specific behaviors
- ✔ Temperament
- ✔ Mental sensitivity
- ✔ Responses to visual stimuli
- ✔ Sound sensitivity
- ✔ Touch sensitivity

All these things affect how the dog learns, what he finds difficult, and what comes almost naturally.

Breed-specific behaviors

Whether you have a designer dog — a dog of mixed origin — or a purebred, he comes with breed-specific behaviors, such as hunting or herding, among others. These behaviors, in turn, have been further refined. Some dogs hunt large game, others small, and yet others hunt birds. Some hunt close by, and others hunt far away. Some herd and guard, and others just herd; some were developed to herd cows, and others, sheep. You get the picture.

There are many different breeds of dogs. The American Kennel Club (AKC), the main governing body of dogdom, recognizes 148 different breeds, but there are many others that are not recognized.

These breeds are divided into seven groups, largely based on behavioral similarities. Some of these breeds are fairly close cousins, whereas others are as different as night and day. (There is also a Miscellaneous Class for newly accepted breeds.)

For example, Group VII, the Herding Group, includes the Belgian Malinois, the Belgian Sheepdog, and the Belgian Tervuren, which are closely related. It also includes the two Welsh Corgis, the Cardigan, and the Pembroke, which have no resemblance to any of the other dogs in that group but in turn are related to one another. The most obvious difference between the two is that the Cardigan has a tail and the Pembroke's tail is docked. Appearance aside, what all the dogs in that group share in common is the instinct to herd. In addition, many of them share the instinct to guard. The German Shepherd, for example, is a member of that group.

Table 5-1 shows the various groups.

Table 5-1	American Kennel Club Dog Groups
Group	*Type of Dog*
Group I	Sporting dogs — Pointers, Retrievers, Setters, and Spaniels
Group II	Hounds
Group III	Working dogs — includes sled and draft dogs, water dogs, and guard dogs
Group IV	Terriers
Group V	Toys — from Affenpinscher to Yorkshire Terrier
Group VI	Non-sporting dogs — sort of a catch-all category for those that don't fit into any of the other groups
Group VII	Herding dogs — those that herd, some of which also guard

Because the dogs in a given group, with the exception of Group VI, are there because of behavioral traits, you can get a pretty good idea of what is going to be easy for your dog and what is going to be hard.

Terriers, for example, like to dig because they were bred to go after little furry things that live in holes in the ground. Shetland Sheepdogs like to round up kids, because they were bred to herd. Pointers are bred to finger the game, Retrievers to bring it back, Spaniels to flush it, and so on, each one with its own special talents.

The very traits for which dogs were bred in the first place are the ones that sometimes interfere with being a good pet, such as the instinct to hunt or herd.

Because dogs were bred to work with or under the direction of man, these talents help with our training efforts. But sometimes the dog's instinct to do what he was bred for is what gets him into trouble today. Put another way, we may not want him hunting or herding or whatever. So some of our training efforts are spent in redirecting these energies. Whenever you run into a road-block in your training, ask yourself, "Is that what this dog was bred to do?" If not, it will take him more time to learn that particular exercise, and you have to be patient.

Temperament

Most people readily agree that good temperament is the most important quality for pets. Unfortunately, the explanation of exactly what that means is often vague and elusive, and sometimes contradictory. The official breed standard of most breeds makes a statement to the effect that the dog you are considering is loyal, loving, intelligent, good with children, and easy to train.

If only it were true!

Simply defined, *temperament* is having the personality traits suitable for the job you want the dog to do. If you want your dog to be good with children, and your dog has that personality trait, then he has good temperament. He may not do so well on other things, such as guarding or herding, but that may not have been what you were looking for.

Similarly vague and elusive have been attempts to define the dog's intelligence. Again, it goes back to function. We define a dog's *intelligence* as the ease with which he or she can be trained for the function the dog was bred for. For example, as a general rule, it is childishly simple to teach a Labrador Retriever to retrieve. After all, that's what he was bred to do.

On the other hand, you'd be dead wrong to refer to an Afghan Hound as stupid just because he may have difficulty in learning to retrieve. That's not what he was bred to do; it's not his job. And that's the whole point.

You need to recognize and be aware of your dog's strengths and limitations. They have a profound influence on the ease or difficulty of teaching your dog a particular task. Circus trainers have an old saying: "Get the dog for the trick and not the trick for the dog." Exploit your dog's strengths.

Mental sensitivity

Dogs, like people, vary in their ability to deal with negative emotions. Most dogs, however, are keenly aware of our emotions. Moreover, the more you work with Buddy, the greater the bond that develops. It seems as though he can read your mind.

He may not be able to read your mind, but he certainly senses your emotions. If you are feeling frustration, disappointment, or anger, Buddy will sense it.

Because dogs are ill-equipped to deal with these emotions, they tend to become anxious and confused. That slows down or even prevents the learning process. Your job in training Buddy is to maintain an upbeat attitude.

It is your job, as your dog's trainer, to teach him what you want him to do and what you don't want him to do. Without your guidance, your dog will simply do what comes naturally to him — he's a dog!

Blaming Buddy for what you perceive to be a shortcoming on his part doesn't help and undermines the very relationship you're trying to build. Remember, Buddy only does what comes naturally, and it's your responsibility to teach him what is acceptable and what is not.

You are the trainer, and Buddy is the student. He responds only to the commands you have taught him.

Responses to visual stimuli

Responses to visual stimuli is a fancy way of saying how a dog responds to moving objects. For purposes of training, it relates to the dog's distractibility when faced with something that moves.

This, too, varies from breed to breed, as well as the nature of the moving object. Terriers are notoriously distractible. Our Yorkshire Terrier, although technically a member of the Toy Group, was convinced that every moving leaf or blade of grass had to be investigated. Although this made perfect sense to him, it made training him to pay attention a real challenge.

In the Hound Group, some breeds, such as Afghan Hounds, Borzois, or Salukis, called *sight hounds,* are not much interested in objects close by and, instead, focus on those far away. Others, such as the Basset Hound, Beagle, or Bloodhound, are more stimulated by scents on the ground or in the air than by moving objects. Training a Beagle to *heel* — that is, walk on a loose leash while paying attention to you and without sniffing the ground — becomes a Herculean task.

The guarding breeds, such as the German Shepherd, Doberman Pinscher, and Rottweiler, were bred to survey their surroundings — to keep everything in sight, as it were. They, too, find it difficult to focus exclusively on you in the presence of distractions. Remember, it's their job to be alert to what's going on around them.

The Bernese Mountain Dog was used as a draft dog by the weavers of the Canton of Berne, drawing small wagons loaded with baskets to the marketplace. As a breed, these dogs are usually not excited by moving objects. After all, it would hardly do for the little fellow to chase a cat with the little wagon bouncing behind him.

The Newfoundland, an ordinarily sedate companion, becomes a raving maniac near water with his instinctive desire to rescue any and all swimmers, totally disregarding that they may not want to be rescued.

Sound sensitivity

Some dogs have a keener sense of hearing than others, to the point where loud noises literally hurt their ears. One of our Landseers would leave the room anytime the TV was turned on. Fear of thunder can be the result of sound sensitivity.

Under ordinary circumstances, sound sensitivity is not a problem, but it can affect the dog's ability to concentrate in the presence of moderate to loud noises. A car backfiring will cause this dog to jump out of his hide, whereas it'll only elicit a curious expression from another dog.

Touch sensitivity

A dog's threshold of discomfort depends on two things:

- His touch sensitivity
- What he is doing at the particular time

For purposes of training, and for knowing what equipment to use, you need to have some idea of Buddy's touch sensitivity. For example, when a dog doesn't readily respond to the training collar, he is all too quickly labeled as stubborn or stupid. But nothing could be further from the truth. It's the trainer's responsibility to select the right training equipment so that the dog does respond.

Discomfort thresholds tend to be breed-specific. For example, we'd expect that a Labrador Retriever, which is supposed to be able to cover all manner of terrain, as well as retrieve in ice-cold water, would have a high discomfort threshold. Shetland Sheepdogs tend to be quite touch sensitive and respond promptly to the training collar. What one dog hardly notices makes another one sit up and take notice. And therein lies the secret of which piece of training equipment to use.

Touch sensitivity is not size-related. Our Yorkshire Terrier had a very high discomfort threshold. That, plus his sight sensitivity, made training him a real challenge.

Neither is it age-related. A puppy does not start out as touch sensitive and, as he grows older, become insensitive. There may be some increase in insensitivity, but it is insignificant.

Finally, a dog's touch sensitivity is affected by what he is doing. In hot pursuit of a rabbit, his discomfort threshold goes up, as it would during a fight.

Once you have an idea of Buddy's discomfort threshold, you will know how you have to handle him and the type of training equipment you need.

Stressing the Stressful Effects of Stress

Stress is the buzzword of the new millenium. If it isn't one thing, it's another — health, family, job, state of the economy, state of the country, state of the world. Even pleasurable experiences, such as taking a vacation, are a source of stress.

In order to deal with all these stresses, we get ourselves one or more of the following (check appropriate response):

❑ Boat

❑ Motor home

❑ Cabin in the woods

❑ Dog

❑ _____ (fill in the blank)

Now *it* becomes a source of stress, and so it goes.

Stress is defined as the body's response to any physical or mental demand. It is a physiological, genetically predetermined reaction over which the individual, be it a dog or person, has no control. Stress is a natural part of our daily lives and affects each person in different ways. Dogs are no different. Just like people, they experience stress. As your dog's teacher, you must recognize the circumstances that produce stress, its manifestations, and how to manage it.

Your personal experiences with stress will help you relate to what your dog is experiencing. Learning the signs and symptoms is not difficult once you know what you are looking for.

Understanding stress

Stress is defined as the body's response to any physical or mental demand. The response prepares the body either to fight or flee. Stress increases blood pressure, heart rate, breathing, and metabolism, and it triggers a marked increase in the blood supply to the arms and legs.

When stressed, the body becomes chemically unbalanced. To address the imbalance, the body releases chemicals into the bloodstream in an attempt to re-balance itself. The reserve of these chemicals is limited. You can dip into it only so many times before it runs dry and the body loses its ability to re-balance. Prolonged periods of imbalance result in neurotic behavior and the inability to function.

Stress takes its toll on the body, be it a person's or a dog's. When the body's ability to counteract stress has been maxed out, the stress is expressed behaviorally. This is as true for your dog as it is for you.

Mental or physical stress ranges from tolerable all the way to intolerable — that is, the inability to function. Your interest here lies with the stress experienced during training, whether you are teaching a new exercise or practicing a familiar one, or during a test, as for example, the Canine Good Citizen test (see Chapter 13). You need to be able to recognize the signs of stress and what you can do to manage the stress your dog may experience.

Positive and negative stress — manifestations

Stress is characterized as positive — manifesting itself in increased activity — and negative — manifesting itself in decreased activity.

Picture yourself returning home after a hard day at work. You are welcomed by a mess on the brand-new white living room carpet. What is your response? Do you explode, scream at poor Buddy, your spouse, and the children, and then storm through the house slamming doors? Or do you look at the mess in horror, shake your head in resignation, feel drained of energy, ignore the dog, the spouse, and the children, and retire to your room?

In the first sample response, your body was energized by the chemicals released into the bloodstream. In the second sample response, your body was debilitated. Dogs react in a similar manner, as noted in the following sections.

Help, I'm hyperactive

So-called positive stress manifests itself in hyperactivity, such as running around, not being able to stay still, not being able to slow down, not paying attention, bouncing up and down, jumping on you, whining, barking, mouthing, getting in front of you, anticipating commands, or inability to learn. You may think your dog is just being silly and tiresome, but for the dog those are coping behaviors.

Why am I so depressed?

So-called negative stress manifests itself by lethargy, such as showing no energy, being afraid, freezing, slinking behind you, running away, giving a slow response to a command, showing no interest in exercise or training, or inability to learn. In new situations, Buddy gets behind you, or he seems tired and wants to lie down, or he seems sluggish and disinterested. These are not signs of relaxation but are the coping behaviors for negative stress.

Recognizing the symptoms of stress

In dogs, signs of either form of stress — positive or negative — are muscle tremors; excessive panting and drooling; sweaty feet that leave tracks on dry, hard surfaces; dilated pupils; and, in extreme cases, urination or defecation — usually in the form of diarrhea — or self-mutilation.

Stress is a normal part of our lives, and the little stresses that go on every day add to the wear and tear of the body, the mess on the rug being the last straw. It becomes the threshold beyond which you can no longer concentrate or function normally and thereby become anxious.

Anxiety is a state of apprehension, uneasiness. When it is prolonged, two things happen:

- ✔ The ability to learn and to think clearly is diminished and ultimately stops. It can also cause a panic attack.

- ✔ Anxiety depresses the immune system thereby increasing our chances of becoming physically ill. It affects our dogs in the same way. The weakest link in the chain is attacked first. If the dog has structural flaws, such as weak *pasterns* (the region of foreleg between the wrist and digits), it may begin to limp or show signs of pain. Digestive upsets are another common reaction to stress.

Stress is part of life and it is important to experience some stress for the body to continue functioning properly. A dog responds to stress by getting ill only when he cannot find an acceptable way to respond to it behaviorally.

Stress, in and of itself, is not bad or undesirable. A certain level of stress is vital for the development and healthy functioning of the body and its immune system. It is only when there is no behavioral outlet for stress — when the dog is put in a no-win situation — that the burden of coping is born by the body and the immune system starts to break down.

Origins of stress — intrinsic and extrinsic

Intrinsic sources of stress are all the things that come with the dog, including structure and health. They are inherited and come from within the dog. Dogs vary in coping abilities and stress thresholds. Realistically, there is not much you can do to change your dog, such as training a dog to deal better with stress. You can use stress-management techniques to mitigate its impact (see the section "Managing Stress," later in this chapter).

Extrinsic sources of stress range from the diet you feed to the relationship you have with your dog. They come from outside the dog and are introduced externally. Extrinsic sources include the following:

- Lack of adequate socialization
- Appropriateness of the training method being used
- Training location
- Frustration and indecision on your part
- How the dog perceives his environment

Fortunately, all these sources of stress are under your control (again, see the section "Managing Stress").

Relating stress to learning

All learning is stressful. For many people, ourselves included, one of the most recent stress-inducing learning experiences was brought on by the computer revolution. In our case, there were plenty of times during the learning process when we were tempted to throw the agonizing contraption out the window. At that moment, learning, and the ability to think rationally, had stopped. There was no point in trying to go on until the body had the chance to re-balance itself.

When you train Buddy, you cannot prevent him from experiencing some stress, but you can keep it at a level where he can still learn. Recognize the signs of stress, as discussed earlier in this chapter, and when you should stop. When Buddy reaches the point where he can no longer learn, whatever he does will not be committed to memory.

If you find that your dog is overstressed during a training session, it is time to stop the session. At that point, your dog's ability to learn is critically diminished, and neither of you will benefit from continuing.

There are going to be times when Buddy just doesn't get the message. It can happen at any time, especially when you are working with distractions. Nothing you do works, and you feel that you're not making progress.

"What can I do?" we are often asked. "If I stop, Buddy will think he has won and he will never do it for me." This argument is completely without merit because it presumes that you and Buddy are adversaries, in some kind of a contest, such as, "you will do it no matter what." If you approach training with this attitude, you are doomed to failure; at best, you will have an unrewarding relationship with your dog.

Training Buddy has nothing to do with winning, but with teaching. You can walk away from a training session at any time, whether or not you think you have been successful. When you see that no further learning is taking place, stop! If you don't, and you insist on forcing the issue, you will undermine both your dog's trust in you and the relationship you are trying to build.

Let Buddy rest for four hours and try again. You will find that all of a sudden the light bulb seems to have gone on. By having taken a break at that point, you give latent learning — the process of getting the point through time — a chance to work. Our advice is to quit training when you find yourself becoming irritable or when Buddy starts to show signs of severe stress.

Konrad Most, considered to be the "father" of modern dog training, recognized the importance of maintaining the dog's equilibrium. In his 1910 training manual he wrote, "Good training needs a kind heart as well as a cool and well-informed head . . . ." Anyone can dominate a dog by physical or mental pressure, but only through the building of confidence by positive reinforcement can reliability and enjoyment of performance be achieved. Buddy must perceive you as trustworthy, or he will begin to exhibit neurotic behaviors.

Stress and distraction training

When distractions are introduced in training, your dog may not respond as you expect. As a result, you may become a little frustrated, taking the attitude, "How could you do this to me?" Buddy senses your feelings and becomes apprehensive and anxious. He only understands that you are upset, but does not understand why. Unless you now calm yourself and him, and reassure him that he is a good boy and should keep trying, your training session will deteriorate to the point where all learning stops.

SUCCESS STORY #1

A stressful first impression

A classic example of the impact of the first impression is the following incident: Pinny had entered her one-year old Landseer Newfoundland, Immy, in a Newfoundland Club of America Water Test. These events test the dog's rescue abilities and, when found satisfactory, result in a Water Dog title, attesting the fact the dog is a water rescue dog.

The Newfoundland Club of America conducts Water Tests where the dogs can demonstrate their water rescue abilities. Two levels exist: Water Dog and Water Rescue Dog. The Club also conducts Draft Dog tests.

The first part of this test is on land, where the dogs are expected to demonstrate a passing familiarity with basic obedience commands, such as heel, come, and stay. Immy was very well trained to do all this.

When Pinny and Immy approached the area in which they were to be tested, which had been roped off into a large square with yellow tape, she noticed that Immy was becoming extremely agitated. He outright refused to get close to, much less into, the roped-off enclosure. His eyes rolled back in his head, he wanted to bolt, and he became almost uncontrollable.

Pinny walked away from the area, calmed him down and tried again. No way was Immy going close to the yellow tape that was flapping in the wind. Pinny didn't push the issue, but Immy went on and did the water part of the trial with great success.

Driving home, she was trying to think why Immy should have been so frightened of the yellow tape. And then she remembered. When Immy first came to her, he was already 6 months old. He was a tall and gangly puppy with lots of energy and a propensity for jumping straight up in the air. It wasn't long before he took this great talent and experimented with jumping the fence in the back garden. He took himself for a nice walk around the neighborhood and found visiting other dogs lots of fun.

Living on a rather busy street, Pinny was worried that he would get run over. So she came to the conclusion that an electric fence was the best solution to her problem.

When the salesperson installed the fence, he asked Pinny if she had ever trained a dog to the fence before. She answered that she had not. "Don't worry, I'll show you how to do it," said the salesman. He took Immy on a leash, went up to the fence which had yellow flags on it, and as Immy approached curiously, he yanked him back as hard as he could, and screamed "no." Immy fell to the ground in shock, and Pinny was horrified.

Looking back, Immy clearly associated this most unpleasant experience with the yellow tape, and when he encountered it again at the Water Test, he wanted nothing to do with it.

Prepare to be patient when you first introduce your dog to training with distractions. Naturally, Buddy is going to be distracted (that is the point!), but over time, he will learn to respond in the way that you want. If you feel yourself becoming distraught, it is time to take five.

When you take your Canine Good Citizen test (see Chapter 13), it is especially important for you to remain calm and control any nervousness you may experience. Your dog is acutely aware of your emotions, which are likely to interfere with his performance. Remember, the object of training and the test is to make both a positive experience for you and your dog.

Most of the tests for the Canine Good Citizen involve some form of distraction. You need to monitor your dog's reaction to these distractions so that you can help him cope. One test requires you be out of your dog's sight for three minutes, which can be a source of significant stress to your dog. You need to introduce him to and condition him for this exercise in such a way that any stress he may experience is minimized.

Try to make every new exercise or distraction a positive experience for your dog. A favorable introduction will have a positive long-term impact.

The first impression leaves the most lasting impact. Whenever you introduce your dog to a new exercise or distraction, make it as pleasant and as stress-free as possible so that it leaves a neutral, if not favorable, impression.

Managing Stress

Become aware of how Buddy reacts to stress, positively or negatively, and the circumstances under which he stresses. Something you are doing, or even a location, may cause him stress.

Understand that Buddy has no control over his response to stress — he inherited this behavior — and that it is your job to manage it as best as you can. Through proper management, Buddy will become accustomed, with every successful repetition, to coping with new situations and handling them like an old trooper.

Managing positive stress

For example, say that Buddy stresses in a "positive" way, which means he gets overexcited and bouncy. In the case of a person, you might say that he or she is hysterical. In the old movies, when someone started screaming uncontrollably, this was handled by slapping the person on the cheek. (For Buddy, a check on the collar to settle him down would be the same thing.) However, we advise that you keep your hands still and off your dog and keep your voice quiet, or you will excite him even more. Instead, give him the down command and enforce it.

Every behavior has a time frame, and experience tells you how long it takes Buddy to calm down under different circumstances. During times of severe stress, Buddy is unable to learn or respond to commands, even those he knows well, until his body re-balances itself. Your goal is to restore your dog's breathing pattern and body posture to normal.

With the right management on your part, Buddy will become comfortable with any new situation.

Managing negative stress

If Buddy stresses in a "negative" way, take him for a walk to get the circulation going and redistribute the chemicals that have been released, so his breathing can return to normal. Massage the top of his shoulders to relax him — just because he is quiet does not mean he is calm. Try to get him excited with an object or food. Do not, under any circumstances, use a check to get him "out of it." This will just produce even greater lethargy.

Stress manifests itself in so many ways, and it is up to you, the owner, to know your dog. Remember, it is a response over which the dog has no control. It is also up to you to play detective to find out what triggers the stress behavior.

Other remedies for managing stress

Some dogs get unduly stressed during thunderstorms. Others, perhaps because of lack of socialization, get stressed when they are away from home, left in a kennel, taken to a class for the first time, riding in the car, and the like.

Products now exist on the market that make dealing with stress so much easier. Homeopathic remedies and Bach Flower Remedies are excellent to use for this purpose.

For fear of thunderstorms, we recommend Aconite 30c. This remedy comes in liquid or pellet form. Usually one dose gives the dog a feeling of being able to cope with the storm.

When taking a dog to a place where he experiences fear, such as the animal hospital, we use a product called Calm Stress. It is a liquid homeopathic that you can put it into your dog's mouth just before you enter. It lasts about 20 minutes. Once your dog understands that he need not be afraid and that he has coped well with the environment, further dosing will be unnecessary.

A simple remedy for carsick dogs is a ginger cookie. Ginger has a wonderful way of settling the stomach, and if you give your dog a ginger cookie just as he gets into the car, the car becomes a good place to be in. If the trip is a long one, you can give a ginger cookie periodically. Dogs can get quite stressed in a car, not only by the movement but also by things flashing by the windows. Using a crate for such a dog is a good idea, because you can cover the crate so the dog is not constantly exposed to visual stimuli. Rescue Remedy, together with Calm Stress, also works well to combat carsickness.

We also use the Calm Stress remedy to rehabilitate rescue dogs with great success, as well as another one called Rescue Remedy. A Bach Flower Remedy is used when the dog gets so stressed that he is in danger of shock. This remedy can be dropped directly into the dog's mouth, about 4 drops, or put into his water bowl.

A stressful reaction to a physical problem

Perhaps the strangest case we have had to deal with was that of one of our own dogs. D. J. is an extremely handsome black Briard. When D.J. was a young dog, he got stressed by almost everything. If we put him in the car, he would throw up and turn in circles. When he got out, he would be wet from drooling and would want to pace and pace. Around other dogs, he was anxious and wanted nothing to do with them. If they came too close, he would lunge out at the end of the leash, teeth flashing — a frightening sight for any dog or person that happened to be close.

Knowing that D. J. was on the very best diet he could be on, we ruled out food-related problems. He had every medical test in the book to try to find out the cause of his stressful behavior. Nothing was found, and so we lived with him, always seeking some kind of answer. The answer came when he was nearly three years old.

We were told of a veterinarian who was also a Certified Animal Chiropractor and who was giving a clinic for dogs and horses. Because we had tried everything else, visiting this veterinarian was the last ditch attempt to help D. J. The journey to the clinic was memorable in itself. The car was a mess from D.J.'s vomit, drool, and diarrhea. Every tollbooth collector risked being attacked through the window.

The chiropractor was in a horse barn, working on some dogs when we arrived. Leaving D. J. in the car, we went in and introduced ourselves. The doctor was the model of patience with D. J. She told us to bring in D. J. and just let him sit and watch what was going on for a while, so he could get the feeling of his surroundings. She went on adjusting other dogs.

In the barn were horses, goats, and chickens. D. J. was fascinated by the smells and was fine so long as nothing or no one came close to him. We carefully inched him closer and closer to the doctor who was sitting on a small stool. D.J. stood with his back to her, and all of a sudden, decided to back into her. She talked to him for a while, without touching his body. She asked him if he minded if she petted him. He sat still. She touched him and he jumped, and we all jumped.

We started again. She felt up and down his back while his attention was glued on a chicken. As she felt his back and then his tail, she told us that many vertebrae were out of alignment, and there had been some kind of break in his tail. We surmised that this must have happened during the birthing process, which apparently is not uncommon. She very gently manipulated him back into position. But she really felt the problem was his neck.

Slowly, slowly, she moved up his body and he was motionless. Thank goodness the chicken was obliging and stayed within a nose length of D. J. who was still staring at it. The doctor finally was able to feel his neck and with two rather quick movements, adjusted the vertebrae. He stood up and shook himself, sat down suddenly, and then just lay down.

She told me that his neck was such a mess that the nerves connected to his eyes were severely displaced. She felt that he had never been able to see properly, either his vision was so distorted he couldn't make out shapes, or that he was seeing upside down. My light bulb went on.

This of course explained all his behavior and the severe stress that he felt. If his vision was poor, naturally he always felt threatened when away from home. Because he was never off leash when we took him out, and couldn't run away as he wanted to do, he would then be forced into a defensive posture, hence the teeth and the growling. We felt both relieved and saddened.

The journey home was amazing. After cleaning out the car, we put D. J. into the back of the station wagon on a nice clean blanket. He slept the whole way home, without even acknowledging the tollbooth attendants. We took him out in the car every day after that, to training classes, everywhere we could think of. He was totally at ease and at almost nine years of age, has become a very cuddly and sweet dog. Most visitors to our house pick out D. J. as our most friendly dog.

So the moral of this story is that when your dog is stressing, there is a reason for it. You just have to work at it until you find the answers.

Chapter 6

Dealing with Doggie Don'ts

Does your dog have what you think is a behavior problem? Does Buddy bark too much, but otherwise behave like a model dog? Does he jump on people when he first meets them, but is perfectly well behaved the rest of the time? Does Buddy have occasional accidents in the house, pull your arms out when you walk him on leash, or chew on your favorite possessions when left unattended?

Dogs can exhibit one or two irritating habits that are not necessarily "behavior" problems. Some can be solved with very little training; others require more time and effort on your part. Whatever your situation, any training starts with convincing Buddy that you are the boss. Dogs are pack animals that come into the world with the expectation that someone has to be in charge of the pack. They need a leader, and that leader has to be you.

Without making the effort to become Buddy's leader, your attempts at training are going to be haphazard at best. The method we recommend to best establish your authority is an exercise called the *long down*. The long down is nonviolent and nonthreatening, and one exercise Buddy readily understands because it mimics behaviors used in a pack to maintain rank order. You can find details on this exercise in Chapter 2.

Figuring Out the Cause of Behavior Problems

Many dog behavior problems have a common cause or a combination of causes. In order of importance, they include the following:

- ✔ Boredom and frustration due to insufficient exercise
- ✔ Mental stagnation due to insufficient quality time with you
- ✔ Loneliness caused by too much isolation from human companionship
- ✔ Nutrition and health-related problems

Loneliness is perhaps the most difficult problem to overcome. By necessity, many dogs are left alone at home anywhere from eight to ten hours a day with absolutely nothing to do except get into mischief. Fortunately, there are some things you can do in addition to spending quality time with him when you are together. If Buddy is really unhappy, take him to doggie day care or get another dog as his companion. You can find more on combating loneliness in Chapter 21.

Before addressing behavior problems specifically, we give you our general prescription for good behavior:

- ✔ Sufficient exercise
- ✔ Good company
- ✔ Good health
- ✔ Good nutrition
- ✔ Good training

Exercise

You notice that exercise is at the top of the list. Exercise needs vary, depending on the size and energy level of your dog. Many dogs need a great deal more exercise than their owners realize. Bull Terriers are a good example. If the owner of an English Bull Terrier lives in an apartment in a large city and the dog doesn't get enough free-running exercise, he is bound to develop behavior problems. These problems can range from tail spinning, which is a neurotic behavior, to ripping up furniture. This kind of dog would show none of these behaviors if he were living in a household where adequate exercise, both mental and physical, were provided.

Dog trainers have a maxim that says that "tired dogs are happy dogs." Dogs that have adequate exercise and can expend their energy through running, retrieving, playing, and training rarely show objectionable behaviors. Dogs denied those simple needs frequently redirect their energy into unacceptable behaviors.

When your dog engages in behaviors that you consider objectionable, it can be a vexing problem. Sometimes the behavior is instinctive, such as digging. Sometimes it occurs out of boredom, but never because the dog is ornery. Before you attempt to deal with the behavior, you need to find out the cause.

The easiest way to stop a behavior is by addressing the need that brought it about in the first place, rather than by trying to correct the behavior itself. If there is one single cause for behavior problems, it is the lack of adequate exercise.

Good company

Many years ago, we labeled a set of behaviors we used to see in our obedience classes as *single-dog syndrome*. These behaviors were expressed mostly by dogs living in a single-dog household. These dogs would run away from their owners more frequently than those dogs living in multi-dog households. They would growl around their food bowls, be picky eaters, be possessive about toys, and be much more unruly than dogs living in homes where there were other dogs.

Good company means not only that you act as a companion to your dog but also that your dog shares the company of other dogs as frequently as possible. Some possibilities include taking regular walks in parks where other dogs roam, joining a dog club where dog activities are offered, or putting your puppy into day care several days a week. Dogs are pack animals and thrive in the company of other dogs. Socialization of your pet is a continuing process. For more information on doggie activities, see Chapter 21.

Good health

Keeping Buddy in good health is not nearly as easy as it was 50 years ago. It seems that with the advance of science in so many dog-related fields, dogs should be healthier than ever. This is not the case. Too often through poor breeding practices, poor nutrition, and over-vaccination, a dog's health has been threatened as never before.

It's not fun to have a dog that has constant health problems from minor skin irritations, picking up fleas, smelling, ear infections, and the like, to more serious conditions that affect his internal organs, such as kidneys, heart, liver, and thyroid. Your dog not feeling well can cause many behavior problems, from aggression to timidity, and health-related conditions are often confused with behavior problems. Buddy may have eaten something that upset his stomach, causing a house-soiling accident. He may have a musculoskeletal disorder making changes of position painful and causing irritability and sometimes snapping. These concerns are obviously not amenable to training solutions, and certainly not discipline. For more on your dog's health, see Chapter 19.

Good nutrition

You are what you eat equally applies to our dogs as it does to ourselves. Feeding properly makes the difference between sickness and health and has a profound effect on your dog's behavior. And with the abundance of dog foods on the market, it can be difficult to figure out what is best for your pet.

There are basically three ways to correctly feed your dog. The first is to select a commercial kibble that has two animal proteins in the first three ingredients. To that you can add some fresh, raw foods. The second is to buy a dehydrated version of a natural diet dog food, to which you can add some yogurt and meat. The third way is to make your own dog food. Your choice depends on your level of comfort and the time you have to devote to your dog. For more on your dog's nutrition needs see Chapter 7.

Good training

Behavior problems do not arise because your dog is ornery or spiteful, and discipline is rarely the answer. Mental stagnation can also be a cause of unwanted behavior. Training on a regular basis, or doing something for you, makes your dog feel useful and provides the mental stimulation he needs. You can have your dog help you carry in groceries, take out the dirty laundry to the washing machine, carry your golf clubs to the car, bring them back into the house, pick things up off the floor that you have dropped, anything to make him feel useful.

Use your imagination to get your dog to help around the house, and you will be surprised by how useful he can become.

Dealing with Your Dog's Objectionable Behavior

Like beauty, objectionable behavior is in the eye of the beholder. Playful nipping or biting may be acceptable to some and not to others. Moreover, there are degrees of objectionable behavior. Getting on the couch in your absence is not nearly as serious an offense as destroying the couch in your absence.

Having worked with dogs for a lifetime, we are perhaps more tolerant of irritating behaviors than most. We know that dogs like to please and that most behaviors can be corrected with a little good training. What we do find objectionable, however, is, when visiting friends, having their untrained dogs jump up at us and scratching us in the process. Other critical negative behavior patterns include dogs that don't come when called, which can be dangerous, and dogs that don't stay when they are told.

All of these irritating behaviors can be trained away by the investment of a mere ten minutes a day, five times a week for around four weeks. It's such a small amount of time and energy to have a wonderful dog to be proud of. Trained dogs are free dogs — you can take them anywhere, and they are always welcome.

When you believe your dog has a behavior problem, you have several options.

- ✔ You can tolerate the behavior.
- ✔ You can spend more time with your dog in an effort to change the behavior.
- ✔ You can find a new home for the dog.
- ✔ You can take your dog for a one-way trip to the shelter or veterinarian.

Tolerating your dog's behavior problems

Considering the amount of time and energy that may be required to turn Buddy into the pet you always wanted, you may decide it is easier to live with his trying antics than to try to change him. Then you begin to consider the amount of time and energy that could be involved in dealing with your dog's annoying antics and you decide that you can live with them after all. You tolerate him the way he is, because you do not have the time, the energy, or the inclination to put in the required effort to change him.

TIP

A dog's home is his crate

One tool that aids in dealing with any kind of inappropriate behavior is a crate. Leaving Buddy in a crate when you are at work, saves you worrying about unwanted barking, housetraining, chewing, and digging. Properly trained to a crate, Buddy will think of it as his "den." He will always be safe in his crate. He can go anywhere with you, from the car to visiting friends. You can take him on holiday with you. He will be comfortable any time you have to leave him at the veterinarian, where dogs are kept in crates during treatment. (See Chapter 10 for more on training with a crate.)

Time is a factor everyone has to consider. Can you be disciplined enough to put aside ten minutes five times a week where you can work with Buddy in a place with no distractions, just concentrating on him? If so, you may be able to solve those annoying habits.

Behaviors you should not tolerate are those that threaten your safety or the safety of others, such as biting people or aggression. True aggression is defined as unpredictable biting — without warning — with the intent to draw blood (see Chapter 18 for more on aggression). You also should not tolerate behaviors that threaten the safety of your dog, such as chasing cars (see Chapter 4).

Trying to solve your dog's behavior problems

You have decided that you cannot live with such a dog and that you are going to work with him to be the pet you expected and always wanted. You understand this will require an investment of time and effort, perhaps even seeking expert help. But you are willing to work to achieve your goal — a long-lasting, mutually rewarding relationship. Good for you!

Obedience training, in and of itself, is not necessarily the answer. Still, when you train your dog, you are spending meaningful time with him, which in many cases is half the battle. Much depends on the cause of the problem.

For most of us, dog ownership is a compromise between tolerating and working with our dogs. There are certain behaviors we find objectionable, but realistically can't do anything about. As long as the joys of dog ownership outweigh the headaches, we put up with these behaviors.

Finding a new home for your dog

Your dog's temperament may be unsuitable to your lifestyle. A shy dog, or a dog with physical limitations, may never develop into a great playmate for active children. A dog that does not like to be left alone too long would not be suitable for someone who is gone all day. While some behaviors can be modified with training, others cannot, or the effort required would simply be too stressful for the dog.

In some instances, the dog and the owner are mismatched, and they need to divorce. The dog may require a great deal more exercise than the owner is able to give him and as a result is developing behavior problems. Whatever the reason, under some circumstances, placement into a new home where the dog's needs can be met is advisable and in the best interest of both dog and owner.

Going directly to the source

The easiest way to stop a behavior is by dealing with the need that brought it about in the first place rather than trying to correct the behavior itself. When your dog goes through teething, for example, you need to provide him with suitable chew toys. When your dog has an accident in the house, first ask yourself whether you have left him inside too long, or whether the dog is ill and a trip to the veterinarian is in order. If your dog is left in the yard by himself and continuously barks out of boredom, don't leave him out there. Your neighbors will thank you. When your dog needs more exercise than you can give him, consider a dogwalker or day care.

Every behavior has a time frame and a certain amount of energy attached to it. This energy needs to be expended in a normal and natural way. By trying to suppress this energy, or not giving it enough time to dissipate, you help cause a majority of behavior problems. Remember, a tired dog is a happy dog.

By using the Personality Profile in Chapter 2, you can easily find out where the energies lie with your dog. For example, is he high in prey drive? These dogs will need more exercise than dogs in other drives. They will be attracted to anything that moves quickly and will want to chase it. Finding an outlet for these behaviors, such as playing ball, throwing sticks, or hiding toys and having Buddy find them, goes a long way to exhausting the energies of this drive.

We recall an incident involving an English Bull Terrier who was left alone too much and who started tail spinning. The behavior escalated to the point that the dog became a complete neurotic. At that point, we suggested a new home and found one for the dog on a farm. The dog now had unlimited daily exercise and within a few weeks the tail-spinning behavior had completely disappeared.

The one-way trip to the pound

If all reclamation efforts have failed — you can't live with this dog and he can't be placed because he is dangerous or for some other reason — your final option is to put him to sleep. This option is not something to be considered lightly, and only when you have really tried to work it out and you truly have no other alternatives.

Incidentally, don't kid yourself about taking your dog to a shelter. Most are overwhelmed by the number of unwanted dogs and are able to find new homes for only a small percentage of these orphans. The sad fact is that we live in a throwaway society. Far too often, when the dog outgrows that cute puppy stage, out he goes.

Digging the Scene

One of the favorite pastimes of our Dachshunds is digging, or landscaping as we call it. They engage in this activity at every opportunity and with great zest. Because Dachshunds were bred to go after badgers, this behavior is instinctive, and trying to suppress it would probably make a neurotic nuisance out of the dog. For us, their digging is unrelated to the fact that our Dachshunds are obedience trained, housetrained, crate-trained, come when called (mostly), and stay when told.

Does that mean we have to put up with a yard that looks like a minefield? Not at all, but we do have to assume the responsibility for

- ✔ Expending the digging energy.
- ✔ Providing an outlet for it.
- ✔ Supervising the little darlings to make sure they don't get into trouble.

Expenditure of the energy involves exercise, and providing an outlet means taking them for walks in the woods where they can dig to their little hearts' content. Of course, you can always cover your yard with Astroturf or green cement!

The good news is that most so-called behavior problems are under your direct control; the bad news is that you have to get involved. The cure to digging is rather simple: Don't leave your dog unattended in the yard for lengthy periods.

In order to eliminate digging before it becomes an issue for Buddy and you, recognize that this behavior is part of prey drive. So all the tips we have given you about exhausting the behavior apply here. You can't make a dog dig until he is exhausted, but you can tire out your dog by playing ball or running with him so that he is too tired to dig!

Or, if you have Wirehaired Dachshunds, like we have, who dig regardless, you can provide a place where it is safe for them to dig and where they don't make craters in the lawn. Put up a small fenced area for them where they can dig. In our case, we walk them in the woods and allow them to dig there. Interestingly, our little guys dig under specific grasses to get at the roots and dirt. It obviously satisfies some nutritional need, and the fact that they have never had worms we attribute to the rotorooter effect of this daily intake of earth.

TECHNICAL STUFF

Understanding the reasons for digging

Although some breeds, such as the small terriers, have a true propensity for digging, all dogs will do it to some extent at one time or another. Take a look at some of the more common and sometimes comical reasons for digging.

✔ *Allelomimetic behavior,* or mimicking. In training, this practice is useful, but it may spell trouble for your gardening efforts. You plant, your dog digs up. Maybe you should do your gardening in secret and out of sight of your dog.

✔ Female dogs make nests for real or imaginary puppies

✔ To bury a bone and to dig up a bone

✔ To see what's there, because it's fun, or to find a cool spot

✔ Boredom, isolation, or frustration

Barking Up Any Tree

On the one hand, few things are more reassuring than knowing the dog will sound the alarm when a stranger approaches. On the other hand, few things are more nerve-wracking than the incessant barking of a dog. Dogs bark in response to a stimulus or because they are bored and want attention, any attention, even if it involves the owner being nasty to the dog. Therein lies the dilemma: You want the dog to bark, but only when you think he should.

Barking as a response

Dogs bark in response to some stimulus. Your dog is outside in the yard and some people walk by, so he barks. Barking is a natural response of defending his territory. Once the potential intruders have passed, he is quiet again. People passing are the stimulus that causes barking and once it has been removed, your dog stops.

If the people had stopped by the fence for a conversation, your dog would have continued to bark. To get him to stop, you have to remove your dog, or the people have to leave. Remove the stimulus from the dog or the dog from the stimulus. If you live in a busy area where this happens frequently, you may have to change your dog's environment. You may not be able to leave him in the yard for prolonged periods.

Your dog will also bark when he is in the house and someone comes to the door. After he has alerted you, tell your dog "thank you, that's enough," and have him sit at your side as you answer the door. If necessary, put him on leash so that you can control him.

He may also rush to the window and stand there and bark because he sees or hears something. Again, thank him for letting you know what's going on and tell him "that's enough." If he does not stop, go to him, take him away from the window and have him lie down in his corner.

Barking for no apparent reason

Your dog has a reason for barking, but it is not apparent to you. It can be due to any or all of the following:

- ✔ Anxiety
- ✔ Boredom
- ✔ Seeking attention because he is lonely

Theoretically, none of these reasons is difficult to overcome if you work to eliminate the potential causes. Spend more time exercising your dog. Spend more time training your dog. Don't leave your dog alone so long, and don't leave him alone so often.

As a practical matter, it's not that easy. Most people work for a living and the dog is left at home alone for prolonged periods. If you live in an apartment, your dog certainly can't bark all day. The stress on the dog is horrendous, not to mention the reaction of your neighbors.

Knowing a dog's motivation

Whatever you may think, Buddy does what he does for a reason. While the behavior may be unacceptable to you, to him it is the only way he can express his unhappiness and frustration. When he barks, or digs, or chews, the behavior in and of itself releases the stress that he is feeling and is self-rewarding. Excessive barking is often attention-seeking behavior, even if the consequences of the attention are unpleasant. For example, when you scold your dog for barking or, worse yet, physically punish him, he is still getting attention. All this means is that the energy of the drive has not been expended, and

you need to go back to his Personality Profile to figure out how your dog's energy can be channeled.

One good example of this is our little Labrador female, Anna Belle. She is a very high-energy dog in all three drives. Taking her to a friend's house, with four ponds and four dogs, Anna Belle runs for a couple of hours and swims to exhaustion, leaving her quiet and pliable at the end of the day. She is totally obedient, doesn't bark excessively, and doesn't seek attention. She is just plain tired and happy.

The most effective and least stressful methods for the dog that we know of is an electronic bark collar or one that sprays citronella as the dog barks. It takes the decision away from the dog as to whether to bark or not to bark. He no longer has to worry and can relax. Sounds contradictory, but it works.

Keeping your dog's barking to a minimum

One of the ways to keep your dog's barking to a minimum is to train your dog to bark on command. You then only give the command when you want him to bark. A good example of this would be when a stranger comes to the door. The beauty of this trick is that, when trained, you can stop your dog barking when you want to.

This command is really an easy and fun exercise to train. Stand with your dog on your left side with both of your feet lined up facing the same direction. Tell your dog to bark — a simple "bark" command will do — and slide your left foot over to touch your dog's right paw. Of course, the dog will look down at your foot and then up at you as if you have lost your mind. Then you bark yourself — make silly noises until your dog gives some verbal response. Give a treat immediately and tell Buddy how clever he is. The sound might not be much at first, but dogs catch on very quickly. Do this exercise a couple of times a day, and shortly you'll find Buddy barking along with you.

Capitalize on Buddy's normal barking behavior. For example, if you see someone walking toward your house, grab some treats, and just before Buddy starts to bark at someone outside, run up to him, line yourself up with your toes facing in the same direction, and as Buddy starts to bark, give your bark command. Then when he barks, tell him what a good boy he is and pop in the treat.

You can also use this trick to introduce a stop-barking command. Giving him the treat distracts him from barking. After you have gotten the response you want, then as you give the treat, quietly introduce the command, "quiet," making the sequence, "bark," "good boy," treat, and "quiet."

While you are training Buddy to do this, it helps to have a collar on him, so you can walk him away from the stimulation of whatever is making him bark, and distract him.

If Buddy is still barking too much, remember that the energy in his drive that feeds the barking has not been exhausted.

Chewing — The Non-Food Variety

The principal reasons that dogs chew are physiological and psychological. The first passes, the second does not, and both are a nuisance.

The physiological need to chew

As part of the teething process, puppies need to chew. They cannot help it. To get through this period, provide your dog with both a soft and a hard chew toy, such as a hard rubber bone or a real bone, as well as a canvas field dummy. Hard rubber Kong toys with a few pieces of kibble can keep a dog amused for a long time. Don't give him anything he can destroy or ingest, except food items. Carrots, apples, dog biscuits, or ice cubes are great to relieve the monotony, otherwise he will be impelled to find more interesting things to chew on, such as those new shoes you left lying around.

Make sure that your dog does not have access to personal articles, such as shoes, socks, and towels. Do not give him an old sock of yours as a toy — he can't tell the difference between an old pair and a new one. Think of it as good training for you not to leave things lying around the house.

A lonely dog will chew up anything in his path. Make sure that your dog gets enough attention from you — and that he gets some strong chew toys!

The psychological need to chew

Chewing after the dog has gone through teething is usually a manifestation of anxiety, boredom, or loneliness. This oral habit has nothing to do with being spiteful. Should your dog attack the furniture, baseboards, and walls, tip over the garbage can, or engage in other destructive chewing activities, use a crate to confine him when you can't supervise him. Confining him will save you lots and lots of money, and you won't lose your temper and get mad at the poor fellow. Even more important, he can't get into things that are a potential danger to him.

Rather than becoming angry at your dog for chewing up your prized possessions, give him some good solid chew toys. Use a crate or other means of confinement when you need to limit access to your personal items.

We want to emphasize that confinement is a problem-solving approach of last resort. Ideally, the dog is not left alone so long and so often that he feels the need to chew in order to relieve his boredom. Your dog doesn't need you to entertain him all the time, but extended periods of being alone can make your pet neurotic. All the problems in this chapter fall under the category of too much isolation.

Coping with Separation Anxiety

Separation anxiety is just that — your dog becomes anxious when you leave him. It is an emotional response to being left alone. Dogs that experience separation anxiety are usually high in pack drive and low in defense (fight) drive.

One solution to Buddy's boredom and loneliness is to get another dog. They can keep each other amused, and two dogs are more than twice the fun of one dog.

All the behavior problems discussed in this chapter can be the direct result of separation anxiety. To make matters worse, all too often the owner feeds into the behavior by making a big fuss before leaving the dog, who is left in an empty house in a state of high excitement.

If you have such a dog, get him accustomed to the routine of your arrivals and departures. Ignore the dog and, without saying or doing anything, walk out the door — just leave. Stay away for a short period. Return the same way, without saying anything, ignoring the dog for the first five minutes. What you want to accomplish is to take the emotional element out of your going and coming.

Many owners exacerbate the dog's separation anxiety by making a big fuss when they leave him, saying things such as, "Now don't worry. Mommy is going to be right back. You be good."

As your dog becomes used to being left for short periods, increase the time. Before long, your dog will view the separation as a normal part of a day and nothing to get excited about.

Soiling the House

House soiling after your dog has been housetrained and that is not marking behavior (see Chapter 10) can have a variety of causes. This activity is rarely a behavior problem, but is most frequently a result of one or more of the following:

- You have left your dog too long without giving him a chance to relieve himself. As the saying goes, accidents happen, and that's just what it was, an accident. You know your dog's endurance and schedule, so don't blame the dog when you for some reason are unable to adhere to it. You may have had to work late or some other unforeseen event prevented you from getting home on time. As long as it doesn't become a regular occurrence on your part, the behavior won't be a continuing problem.

✔ Your dog may have eaten something that disagreed with him, and he has an upset stomach. Abrupt dietary changes, such as changing dog foods, are the most common cause for an upset tummy. Any time you change your dog's diet, do it gradually, over a period of several days, so his system can get used to the new food.

✔ Giving treats at holiday times that your dog ordinarily doesn't get, such as turkey and gravy or pizza, can create havoc with his digestive system.

✔ Cystitis, a bladder infection, is more common among female dogs than male dogs, and may cause dribbling. You need to consult your veterinarian.

✔ As your dog ages, urinary incontinence may develop, and it can be treated with medication and homeopathic remedies.

✔ Chocolate can make your dog really sick. While containing several chemical agents that make it so good and tasty to us, these agents can be poisonous to Buddy. Be very careful to keep chocolate out of the way of your best friend. Dark chocolate is more poisonous than milk chocolate.

Cystitis is an inflammation of the bladder wall. It can be caused by a bacterial infection. It makes Buddy feel as if there is constant pressure on his bladder, and he will think that he has to urinate all the time, even after just relieving himself. When he does urinate, it can burn, which in turn causes him to spend a lot of time washing himself.

While not very dangerous in and of itself, left unattended cystitis can cause all sorts of problems as the bacteria can spread up into the kidneys. If you see any of the preceding symptoms, then a trip to your veterinarian is a must. A short course of the appropriate antibiotics cures this inflammation quickly.

Incontinence is caused by the slackening of the sphincter muscles that holds the urine in the bladder. This often happens as your dog ages. So many dogs are put to sleep for this perceived problem, which while not easy to live with, can be solved in several ways. Acupuncture is probably the best treatment and is very effective. If you can find a veterinarian trained in acupuncture, then visit and have a series of treatments to solve the problem. Many veterinarians today are trained in acupuncture and finding one who can help is not very difficult. A change in diet to a more natural diet (see Chapter 7) can often solve this problem. You can find many herbal and homeopathic remedies on the market specifically targeted at the kidney and bladder of older dogs. A good holistic veterinarian will be able to help you make the best choice for your dog.

While you are finding a veterinarian to help you, you still have to live with the soiling problem. Take a tablecloth that is plastic on one side and has a soft backing on it. Put this under your dog's blanket. This will save the furniture or floor, and both are easy to wash and keep clean. You can consider diapers, but they should be a last resort. Don't give up on that old friend — explore the alternatives and see how you can support Buddy in his old age.

Dribbling, or Submissive Wetting

Dogs that are high in defense flight and low in defense fight drives are notorious for submissive wetting behavior. (See Chapter 2 for more on your dog's drives.) This behavior usually occurs upon first greeting the dog. He will either squat or roll over on his back and dribble, dating back to his days as a puppy, when his mother would clean him.

When this does happen, do not scold your dog, because it only reinforces the behavior and actually makes it worse. By scolding him, you only make him act even more submissive, which brings on the wetting. Also, don't stand or lean over your dog or try to pick him up, as that, too, will make him act submissive and cause wetting.

Fortunately, submissive wetting is not difficult to solve. Follow these steps:

1. **When you come home, ignore your dog.**

   Don't approach your dog; let him come to you instead.

2. **Greet your dog without making eye contact and by offering the palm of your hand.**

   This step is important. The back of the hand transmits negative energy, and the palm of the hand transmits positive energy.

3. **Keep your mouth shut and let him sniff your palm.**

4. **Gently pet him under the chin, not on top of the head.**

5. **Do not reach or try to grab for the dog.**

 When friends visit you, they can help you manage your dog's wetting behavior. Tell your visitors when they arrive to ignore the dog and let him come to them. Instruct them about offering the palm of the hand and about not grabbing for the dog.

If you follow this routine, your dog will stop dribbling.

Suffering from Carsickness

Carsickness, which manifests itself in excessive drooling or vomiting, can be attributed to either of the following:

- True motion sickness
- A negative association with riding in a car

For obvious reasons, dogs that have a tendency to get carsick usually aren't taken for rides very often. And when they are, it's to the veterinarian. You can compare his reaction to that of a child who, every time it gets in the car, goes to the doctor for a shot. It doesn't take many repetitions before your dog makes an unpleasant association with your car.

Some dogs get sick in vans because they *can't* see out of the window, and others get sick in cars because they *can* see out of the window. Whatever the reason for the dog's reaction, you can create a pleasant association with the car. When working with your dog to make car rides a positive thing, you can tell how well he is taking to the car and how much time you need to spend at each sequence.

Throughout this remedial exercise, maintain a light and happy attitude. Avoid a solicitous tone of voice and phrases such as, "It's all right. Don't worry. Nothing is going to happen to you." These reassurances validate the dog's concerns and reinforce the behavior.

1. **Open all the doors and, with the engine off, coax your dog into the car.**

   If he doesn't want to go in, pick him up and put him in the car. After he is in the car (no matter how he got there), give him a treat, tell how proud you are of him, and immediately let him out again. Repeat this step until he is comfortable getting into the car on his own.

2. **After your dog is comfortable willingly getting into the car, close the doors on one side of the car, keep the engine shut off, and coax your dog into the car again.**

3. **When he is comfortable with Step 2, tell your dog to get in the car, give him a treat, and close the doors.**

   Let him out again and give him a treat. Repeat until he readily goes into the car, and you can close the doors for up to one minute.

4. **Tell your dog to get into the car, get in yourself, close all the doors, and start the engine.**

   Give your dog a treat. Turn off the engine and let him out.

5. **Now it's time for a short drive, no more than once around the block.**

   Increase the length of the rides, always starting and ending with a treat.

Ginger cookies are an excellent treat. Ginger calms your dog's stomach.

Eating Stools (Coprophagy)

Halitosis is one thing, but no one wants to be greeted by a canine companion who is in the habit of eating stools. Some dogs eat their own, those of other dogs, or those of other animals, such as cats, horses, and cows. Cat stools seem to be especially attractive and are particularly enticing when frozen.

Without a doubt, this behavior is decidedly undesirable. Eating stools, too, can be caused by boredom or, as is more often the case, by dietary deficiencies. Unable to assimilate protein because his food is lacking the correct digestive enzymes, vitamins, and minerals, your dog eats stools that contain these ingredients (see Chapter 7 for more on the importance of these elements to your dog's diet). As unappealing as this behavior may be, it is something that dogs do — don't freak out that your dog is wacko.

To solve the problem, experiment by adding some raw food to your dog's diet, as well as digestive enzymes. Better yet, try feeding the Healthy Dog Diet, described in Chapter 7, and the behavior should disappear. Should the behavior persist, consult your veterinarian who then will run some blood tests to see if there are any health-related problems related to this behavior.

Early on in our career, we received a call concerning coprophagy that went something like this: "My dogs are eating their stools. I have consulted my veterinarian, and the food supplements he prescribed did not work. I then consulted a dog behavior counselor, and he told me to sprinkle Tabasco sauce on the stools. That stopped the dogs for a while, but now they have developed a taste for Tabasco and are right back at it again. Can you help?"

We advised the individual that while he was out in the yard sprinkling Tabasco on the stools, cleaning up after the dogs would probably be just as easy, thereby precluding the dogs from doing their own cleaning up. Two weeks later, we got another call. "It works! They are no longer eating stools."

Chapter 7

Feeding Your Dog

*Y*our dog's behavior, happiness, health, longevity, and overall well being are inextricably intertwined with what you feed him. Dogs, just like everyone else, have specific nutritional requirements that need to be met. And to complicate matters, the needs of dogs vary. For example, even though your first dog may have done wonderfully well on Barfo Special Blend, the same food may be completely wrong for Buddy. Every dog has his own nutritional needs that may be quite dissimilar to those of the dog next door. What your dog eats has a tremendous impact on his health and his trainability.

We are not trying to turn you into an expert on canine nutrition, but you should know some basic concepts. If you do want to become an expert on feeding your dog, see *The Holistic Guide for a Healthy Dog,* 2nd Edition, by Wendy Volhard and Kerry Brown, DVM (IDG Books Worldwide, Inc., 2000).

You should also know the most common and most visible symptoms of nutritional deficiencies. Recognizing these deficiencies saves you a great deal of money in veterinary bills because you can make the necessary adjustments to your dog's diet.

Finding the Right Food for Your Dog

Not all dog foods are alike; there are enormous quality differences. The cliché "garbage in, garbage out" applies with terrifying validity. So many choices are available today that trying to make an informed decision can become an overwhelming task. We are going to tackle the job by the process of elimination. Two commonly used criteria immediately come to mind: advertising and price.

In choosing a food for your dog, forget about advertising and price. They are not valid criteria for selection. You need to make the decision based on what is in the food and on your dog's nutritional requirements.

✔ Forget about what the ad says about how good this food is for your dog. It may be okay for Buddy, but perhaps it is not. You have to look at what's in the food.

✔ Forget about price. This works both ways. Just because one brand of food costs more doesn't necessarily mean it's better than a less expensive variety.

Following is a quick checklist to help you determine whether Buddy is getting what he needs. Note that for each item, Buddy is the source of your information, not an advertisement.

✔ He doesn't want to eat the food.

✔ He has large, voluminous stools that smell awful.

✔ He has gas.

✔ His teeth get dirty and brown.

✔ His breath smells.

✔ He burps a lot.

✔ He constantly sheds.

✔ He has a very dull coat.

✔ He smells like a dog.

✔ He is prone to ear and skin infections.

✔ He has no energy or is hyperactive.

✔ He easily picks up fleas.

✔ He easily picks up worms and has to be wormed frequently.

✔ His immune system is impaired.

All of the above happen occasionally with any dog — but only occasionally. When several of the items on the list occur frequently or continuously, it's time to find out why.

Reading labels and making choices

On the back of every dog food package is information that helps you decide which food is right for your dog. The information lists the ingredients in order of weight, beginning with the heaviest item. The package contains the guaranteed analysis for crude protein, fat, fiber, moisture, ash, and often calcium, phosphorus, and magnesium ratios. The label may also state that the food is nutritionally complete or provides 100 percent nutrition for the dog. To make this claim, the food has to meet the nutrient requirements of the Association of American Feed Control Officers (AAFCO) — a guarantee that some form of testing, usually anywhere from two to six weeks, has been done on the product.

A dog food company must also list its name and address and give its telephone number, plus the date of manufacture, the weight of the product in the package, and usually the life stage for which the food is intended. It can be puppy, maintenance, adult, performance, old age, or light food for overweight dogs.

The saying "You get what you pay for" isn't necessarily true with dog food. There is a surprisingly small difference between good and not-so-good food, and some not-so-good foods are higher priced than good foods!

A high-quality food is labeled *performance* and lists an animal protein in the first two or three ingredients — usually two kinds (chicken and lamb, chicken and fish, beef and chicken, and so on).

Although these foods are marketed primarily for working or breeding animals, they are the best-quality foods on the market for all dogs. Performance foods also contain the correct quantity of fats and oils needed for energy, good coat, and skin. Performance foods don't contain soy, which dogs can't digest.

The next category of dog food is called *Super Premium 1,* and it usually contains an animal protein first, followed by several grains. Although it provides energy for your dog from high fat levels, it's not as good as the performance foods because it contains less animal protein.

Premium foods do contain a high level of protein, but you need to look at the source because the protein can come from grains and not animal protein. These foods may also contain soy.

Foods listed as *Regular, Econo, Low Protein,* or *Light (Lite)* are full of grains and are guaranteed to make your dog into a couch potato. They are animal protein deficient and, although marketed for the older dog, in our opinion should be taken off the market. They produce voluminous smelly stools, caused by the inability of the dog to break down and digest this food. Dogs fed this diet for any length of time show classic signs of animal protein deficiencies, listed later in the chapter.

Giving meat to a carnivore

Your dog is a carnivore and not a vegetarian. He needs meat. His teeth are quite different from ours — they are made for ripping and tearing meat. They do not have flat surfaces for grinding up grains. His digestion starts in his stomach and not in his mouth. All the enzymes in his system are geared toward breaking down meat and raw foods. There is no doubt about it, Buddy is a carnivore, and he needs to eat meat to stay healthy.

Your dog's body, as well as yours, is made up of cells, a lot of them. Each cell needs 45 nutrients to function properly. The cells need the following:

- Protein, consisting of 9 to 12 essential amino acids
- Carbohydrates
- Fat
- Vitamins
- Minerals
- Water

All these nutrients need to be in the correct proportion for the necessary chemical reactions of digestion, absorption, transportation, and elimination to occur. If the cells are going to be able to continue to live, the exact composition of the body fluids that bathe the outside of the cells needs to be controlled from moment to moment, day by day, with no more than a few percentage points variation.

These nutrients are the fuel, which is converted into energy. Energy produces heat and how much heat is produced determines the ability of your dog to control his body temperature. Everything your dog does, from running and playing, to working and living a long and healthy life, is determined by the fuel you provide and the energy it produces.

The term *calorie* is used to measure energy in food. Optimally, every dog will eat the quantity of food he needs to meet his caloric needs. The food you feed must provide sufficient calories so your dog's body can achieve the following:

- Produce energy to grow correctly
- Maintain health during adulthood
- Reproduce
- Grow into a quality old age

Keeping your dog rich in protein

The back of dog food packages tell you how much protein is in the food. How much protein is in dog food is important, but even more important is the source.

The manufacturer has choices as to what kind of protein to put into the food. The percentage of protein on the package generally is a combination of proteins found in plants or grains, such as corn, wheat, soy, and rice, plus an animal protein, such as chicken, beef, or lamb.

By law, the heaviest and largest amount of whatever ingredient contained in the food has to be listed first. By looking at the list of ingredients, you can easily discover the origin of the protein. For example, if the first five ingredients listed come from four grains, the majority of the protein in that food comes from grains. The more grains in a dog food, the cheaper it is to produce. We wonder what Buddy thinks of such a food.

The activity level of your dog is likely to correspond with the amount of animal protein he needs in his diet. The busy little Jack Russell is apt to need more animal protein than a pooch that spends his time lying around the house.

It has also been our experience that the majority of the Working breeds, Sporting breeds, Toys, and Terriers need extra animal protein in their diets. Dogs that lead a couch potato existence can survive on food with more plant than animal protein.

One more thing you need to know about protein: *Amino acid* is the name given to the building blocks of protein, and when they are heated, they are partially destroyed. All dry and canned commercial dog food is heated in the manufacturing process. So commercial food contains protein that is chemically changed by heat and therefore deficient in amino acids. We show you how to compensate for that at the end of the chapter.

Animal protein deficiencies

When Buddy does not get enough raw animal protein as part of his diet, or there is an imbalance of his nutrients, one or more of the following may occur:

- Chronic skin and/or ear infections
- Reproductive system, heart, kidney, liver, bladder, thyroid and adrenal glands may be compromised
- Some kind of epilepsy or cancers
- Spinning or tail chasing
- Aggression
- Timidity
- Lack of pigmentation
- Excessive shedding
- Gastrointestinal upsets, vomiting, or diarrhea
- Poor appetite
- Impaired ability to heal from wounds or surgery, such as spaying and neutering
- Weakened immune system that cannot properly tolerate vaccines

This is only a short list of the more common symptoms associated with an animal-protein deficiency.

Food for Growth at Critical Times

In contrast to humans, dogs grow *fast*. During the first seven months of Buddy's life, his birth weight increases anywhere from 15 to 40 times, depending upon his breed. By one year of age, his birth weight increases 60 times and his skeletal development is almost complete. For strength and proper growth to occur, he needs the right food. He also needs twice the amount of food of an adult while he is growing, especially during growth spurts. Nutritional deficiencies at an early age, even for short periods, can cause problems later on.

The most critical period for a puppy is between 4 and 7 months, the time of maximum growth. His little body is being severely stressed as his baby teeth drop out and his adult teeth come in. He is growing like a weed, and at the same time his body is being assaulted with a huge number of vaccines. During this time of growth, Buddy needs the right food so that his immune system can cope with all these demands and onslaughts.

To find out how you can protect him as best as possible, you need to take a look at different dog foods to find the ones that best meet the criteria for young Buddy's growth. We give you some ideas of which foods to choose and what to add to them to make up for the deficiencies caused in processing.

Deciphering puppy food labels

Puppy foods do contain more protein than adult or maintenance foods. Manufacturers know that puppies need more protein for growth. Nonetheless, you still need to know the source of the protein — that is, animal or plant.

Look for a puppy food that has two animal proteins in the first three ingredients — or better yet, one that lists animal protein as its first two ingredients.

Once you have selected a food for young Buddy on the basis of its protein percentage, your job isn't quite done yet. You have to check a few other items.

Going easy on the carbohydrates

Your dog also needs carbohydrates found in grains and some vegetables for proper digestion. Through the digestive process, carbohydrates are broken down first into starch and then into simple sugars and into glucose, necessary for energy and proper functioning of the brain. Carbohydrates are also needed for stool formation and correct functioning of the thyroid gland.

Dogs do not need many carbohydrates to be healthy, and a diet low in carbo-hydrates and high in protein is an ideal diet. Oats, barley, and brown rice are carbohydrates that contain a lot of vitamins and minerals. They also contain protein and fat. Corn is popular because of its low price. Other sources of carbohydrates are vegetables, especially root vegetables.

Soy is another carbohydrate that is found in some foods. Soy admittedly is high in protein, but it binds other nutrients and makes them unavailable for absorption. We recommend that you stay away from dog foods containing soy. It is best fed to those species of animals with gizzards, such as birds, that can break it down. Soy burgers may be a healthy food choice for people, but not for Buddy.

Carbohydrates have to be broken down for the dog to be able to digest them. Dog food companies use a heat process to do so, and therein lies a problem. The heat process destroys many of the vitamins and minerals contained in carbohydrates. The question that comes immediately to mind is, "Where do dogs in the wild get the grains and vegetables they need?" The answer is from the intestines of their prey, all neatly predigested.

Knowing the value of fats — in moderation

Fat is either saturated or polyunsaturated, and your dog needs both. Saturated fat comes from animal sources, and polyunsaturated fat comes from vegetable sources. Together they supply the essential fatty acids (EFA) necessary to maintain good health.

In the manufacturing of the majority of dog foods, fat is sprayed on as the last ingredient. Fat makes the dog food palatable, like potato chips and French fries.

Saturated fat comes from animal sources and is used for energy. For dogs that get a great deal of exercise or participate in competitive events, the food has to be high in animal fat. Not enough animal fat in your dog's diet can create

- Lack of energy
- Heart problems
- Growth deficits
- Dry skin
- Cell damage

On the other hand, too much animal fat in the diet creates

 ✔ Obesity

 ✔ Mammary gland tumors

 ✔ Cancer of the colon and rectum

Polyunsaturated fat is found in vegetable sources, such as flax seed oil, safflower oil, wheat germ oil, olive oil, and corn oil. Your dog needs polyunsaturated fat for healthy skin and coat. Too little of this fat can produce skin lesions on the belly, thighs, and between the shoulder blades. If your dog has a dry coat, you may need to add oil to his food.

Linoleic acid is one of the three essential fatty acids that have to be provided daily in your dog's food. Safflower and flax seed oil provide the best source of linoleic acid and are the least allergenic. These oils are better than corn oil, which contains only a tiny amount of linoleic acid.

Lack of polyunsaturated fat in your dog's diet can cause

 ✔ Coarse, dry coat

 ✔ Improper growth

 ✔ Skin lesions on the belly, inside the back legs, and between the shoulder blades

 ✔ Thickened areas of skin

 ✔ Horny skin growths

 ✔ Skin ulcerations and infections

 ✔ Poor blood clotting

 ✔ Extreme itching and scratching

Look for food that contains both animal and vegetable oils.

What else is in this food?

The dog food manufacturer has choices on how to preserve the fat in food to prevent it from becoming rancid, such as using the chemicals BHA, BHT, ethoxyquin, or propyl gallate. If a fat is preserved with these chemicals, it has a long shelf life and is little affected by heat and light. Even so, many dog owners would prefer not to feed these chemicals to their dogs, especially ethoxyquin. (Check out the nearby sidebar for more info on these chemicals.)

A manufacturer can also use natural preservatives, such as vitamins C and E. Vitamin E is listed as tocopherol. The down side to natural preservatives is a shorter shelf life, no more than six months.

Common chemicals used in dog foods

When you're reading dog food packages, it's sometimes hard to tell what is a preservative and what is not. Following is a list of the more common chemicals seen on the packages:

✔ **Antioxidants.** Used to preserve the fats in the food. These are BHA, BHT, ethoxyquin, and propyl gallate. Ethoxyquin has been linked to birth defects and immune disorders, so you may want to stay away from products that contain it.

✔ **Mold inhibitors.** Used to retard the growth of molds and yeast. These are potassium salts, sodium or calcium proprionate, sodium diacetate, sorbic acid, and acetic or lactic acid.

✔ **Sequestrants.** Used to prevent physical or chemial changes to the color, odor, flavor, or appearance of the food. These are sodium, potassium or calcium salts, and citric, tartaric, or pyrophosphoric acids.

✔ **Humectants.** Used to prevent food from drying out or getting too moist. These are calcium silicate, propylene glycol, glycerine, and sorbitol.

✔ **Texturizers.** Not preservatives as such but used in meats to maintain their texture and color. The most common are sodium nitrite and sodium nitrate.

Note that natural preservatives are vitamins C and E. Vitamin E is often listed as *tocopherol*.

What else is not in this food?

Vitamins are needed in your dog's food to release the nutrients and enzymes from the ingested food so that the body can absorb and use them. Without vitamins, your dog can't break down food and use it.

Because vitamins begin to break down when you open your dog food bag and expose the food to the elements, close the food up tightly and keep it away from light. Doing so helps to retain the quality of the contents.

In researching *The Holistic Guide for a Healthy Dog,* we called dog food manufacturers to ask them their source of vitamins and how they protected them against destruction from the heat process. Their responses were astonishing. They acknowledged awareness of the problem, and, to overcome it, they added more vitamins to the food to make up the difference. Of course, this is nonsense. If vitamins are destroyed by heat, it doesn't make any difference how much you put in the food. They will still be destroyed.

We also learned that most of the finished products were not tested. In other words, vitamins and minerals go into the food, but what actually reaches your dog seems as much a mystery to some of the manufacturers as it is to us.

Vitamins are not only lost in the manufacturing process, but also begin to deteriorate as soon as you open up your dog food bag and expose the food to light and air. Vitamins B and C are particularly sensitive to exposure. Vitamin C is needed for healthy teeth and gums. In the old days, sailors often suffered from a vitamin C deficiency due to the lack of fresh fruits and vegetables while at sea. This malady is called scurvy and results in weakness, anemia, spongy and inflamed gums, and dirty teeth. The same thing happens to the vitamin C – deficient dog.

Two types of vitamins exist — water soluble and fat soluble. Water-soluble vitamins are B and C. Any excess is filtered through the kidneys and urinated out between four to eight hours after ingestion. For this reason, these vitamins must be present in each meal. Vitamins A, D, E, and K are fat soluble and stored in the fatty tissues of the body and the liver. Your dog needs both types.

A fairly common misconception is that dogs don't need extra vitamin C because they produce their own. Although they do produce their own vitamin C, they do not produce enough, especially in our polluted environment.

Vitamin C strengthens the immune system, speeds wound healing, helps the function of the musculoskeletal system, and is needed whenever the dog gets wormed, is given drugs of any kind, or is put under any kind of stress. A lack of vitamin C in the diet commonly results in urinary tract infections, cystitis, and limps.

Vitamin B, which is made up of a number of individual parts, is called vitamin B-complex. Also water-soluble and fragile, vitamin B is needed for energy and to promote biochemical reactions in the body that work with enzymes to change the carbohydrates into glucose, as well as to break down protein. Because not enough of either is contained in any processed dog food to meet our criteria for raising Buddy, you have to add these vitamins to his diet. We use the carefully tested vitamins from PHD Products with our own dogs.

Adding minerals

Minerals make up less than two percent of any formulated diet, and yet they are the most critical of nutrients. Although your dog can manufacture some vitamins on his own, he is not able to make minerals. They are needed

- ✔ So that the body fluids are composed correctly
- ✔ For formation of blood and bones
- ✔ To promote a healthy nervous system
- ✔ To function as coenzymes together with vitamins

Because between 50 and 80 percent of minerals are lost in the manufacturing process, we recommend that you add extra minerals to your dog's food.

We add the product Wellness, manufactured by PHD Products, to our dogs' daily diet. Wellness provides an herbal vitamin/mineral mix from natural sources and contains all those vitamins and minerals that are lost in the processing of commercial food. It supplies Buddy with the necessary tools needed to absorb and break down his food and protects him from viruses and bacteria found in his environment.

Quenching his thirst — keeping fresh water around

Your dog should have access to fresh water in a clean, stainless steel bowl at all times. The exception is when the puppy is being housetrained, when you should limit access to water after 8:00 p.m. so that the puppy will last through the night.

Water is the most necessary ingredient dogs need on a daily basis. Without water, your dog will die. If a dog has adequate water, he can live for three weeks without food, but he can live only a few days without water. Water is used by the dog for digestive processes, in breaking down and absorption of nutrients, as well as maintenance of body temperature. Water helps to detoxify the body and transport toxic substances out of the body through the eliminative organs. Water is also used to keep the acid levels of the blood constant.

The kind of food you feed your dog determines how much water your dog needs. Kibble contains about 10 percent moisture, and your dog needs about a quart of water for every pound of food he eats. A dog fed only canned food, which is around 78 percent moisture, needs considerably less water. If fed raw foods, a dog may drink less than a cup of water a day because sufficient water is contained in the food.

City water systems usually provide water free from parasites and bacteria by using chemicals such as chlorine, aluminum salts, soda, ash, phosphates, calcium hydroxides, and activated carbon. According to a study reported in *Consumer Reports* in 1990, the main contaminants remaining are lead, radon, and nitrates. Lead comes from water pipes in houses built early in the last century. Radon is a by-product of uranium found in the Earth's crust and is more prevalent in water from wells and ground water in the northeast, North Carolina, and Arizona. Water from lakes and rivers is less contaminated with radon. Nitrates come from ground water sources and contain agricultural contaminants.

Note also that the more alkaline the food is, the more water Buddy will drink to maintain his correct acid/alkaline balance. If Buddy is drinking too much water, a change in diet to a more acidic food (one containing more animal protein) may be in order. If Buddy still continues to drink a large amount of water, it could be the beginnings of a kidney or bladder infection. When in doubt, visit your veterinarian for a checkup.

Digesting information

According to a Swedish study, raw foods pass through a dog's stomach and into the intestinal tract in 4 1/2 hours. So after that time span, the dog is already receiving energy from that food. Raw foods are the most easily digested by the dog.

Semi-moist foods — the kind that you can find in boxes on the supermarket shelf and shaped like hamburgers or the kind that are in rolls like sausages — take almost nine hours to pass through the stomach.

Dry foods take between 15 and 16 hours, so if you choose to feed Buddy any kind of dry processed dog food, it will be in his stomach from morning 'til night.

The following sections provide some insight into the food processing issue.

Canned food

Ingredients in canned foods are measured in wet weight rather than dry weight (which is how kibble is measured). The ingredients listed on the label reflect the actual amount of raw ingredients that went into the can. Canned food lists protein as 8 to 10 percent, which is less than that found in kibble, but the protein is calculated differently. A simple and approximate way to compare the two is to double the amount of protein listed on the can to compare it with kibble. A listing of 10 percent protein on the canned food label equals around 20 percent on the kibble package.

Canned food comes in different price ranges and in many qualities. Some canned foods contain only meat protein, and others contain primarily cereal grains. Some come in a stew form. In judging the quality of these foods, look for the AAFCO statement on the can. That statement assures you that the food has gone through some kind of testing.

Feeding canned food is much more expensive than feeding dry food because the moisture content in the can is around 78 percent, so you're paying for only 22 percent of dry ingredients.

Canned food is processed at a very high temperature that kills bacteria and viruses. Also, canned food contains fewer preservatives than kibble. Many dogs like their kibble pepped up with a bit of canned food, but it contains little nutritive value because the heat processing effectively kills the vitamins and minerals in the food, as well as changes the amino acids in the protein.

Semi-moist food

Semi-moist food, although consumer friendly, contains sweeteners or preservatives to give it a long shelf life. Coloring is added to make it look appetizing. As a sole diet for dogs, it may cause digestive upsets because of its ingredients and high preservative content. The moisture content ranges from 20 to 25 percent. There are some natural semi-moist foods. One comes in the shape of a large sausage, and small pieces can be cut off for treats. Dogs fed these products exclusively on a regular basis may develop digestive problems.

Sugar is commonly listed as the fourth or fifth ingredient in these foods. The chemical name for sugar is *dextrose*. Sugar stimulates the pancreas to produce insulin, which is needed to break down carbohydrates and sugar in the food. The pancreas has to work overtime to produce enough insulin to break down this food, setting the stage for diseases of the pancreas, which can cause not only digestive upsets but behavioral problems as well. Hyperactivity is the most common of the behavioral problems.

Raw food

Our years with dogs have made it abundantly clear to us that feeding a balanced raw diet — which emulates what the wolf eats in the wild — is the best and most efficient way to feed a dog. A correctly formulated raw diet provides all the known nutrients in a form the dog can quickly digest and turn into energy. Dogs fed this way live longer and are much healthier than their counterparts who are fed commercial foods.

We have always felt that many disease states, including musculoskelatal disorders (such as hip dysplasia), are certainly exacerbated — if not actually caused by — poor nutrition. Our belief along these lines has since been confirmed by veterinarian Marc Torel and scientific journalist Klaus Dieter Kammerer in their book, *The Thirty Years War: 1966-1996* (Transanimal Publishing House, 1997).

Many raw diets are available for you to choose from, but making the correct choice is even more difficult than comparing commercial dog foods. We apply the same criteria to the examination of raw food diets as we do to commercial foods: Both should be clinically tested and provide a balanced diet for a dog. Diets, especially homemade ones, be they raw or cooked, that do not meet these criteria can do more damage to your dog than commercial dog food.

There are other considerations as well. Feeding raw meat or raw chicken to a dog can cause digestive upsets if the meat contains a high level of bacteria in the form of e-coli or salmonella. Although a dog that has been fed raw foods for a long time can easily deal with both of these bacteria, a sick dog or a dog just being transferred over to a raw diet may become sick.

The reason is that the dog's digestive system is not the same as a human's. The dog's stomach acid is very strong, and in a healthy dog, this acid kills any bacteria that enter it. A sick dog, or a dog switching over to a raw diet, needs a transition diet to rebuild that stomach acid to the point where it can deal with either e-coli or salmonella. After the transition diet is followed, you need to use a simple method of killing bacteria the first time meat is used: Put either the meat or chicken into a sieve in the sink, pour boiling water over it, and cool it before feeding. Doing so kills the bacteria. After doing this for a couple of weeks, the stomach acid will be strong enough to deal with the bacteria themselves without problems, and the raw meat can be introduced.

Enzymes and enzyme robbing

Enzymes make a body tick. They are already contained in the body and are made through what you feed your dog.

When semi-moist food or dry food sits in the dog's stomach, it does so because there are not enough enzymes in the stomach to break it down. Remember, a dog's stomach is designed to deal with raw foods.

So the stomach sends a message to the brain: "Hey, brain, we need some more enzymes down here." The brain responds, "Okay, okay, but I need some time." It then gathers enzymes from the heart, the liver, the kidneys, and other parts of the body to be transported to the stomach. In the meantime, the food sits there until enough enzymes are collected for digestion. This process is called enzyme robbing.

A dog's vital internal organs — his heart, liver, and kidneys — need the enzymes that they contain to function at their best. When a dog consumes semi-moist and dry foods, some of these enzymes must be diverted to the stomach to aid in digestion. Ultimately, the dog's vital organs lose out.

Robbing various organs in the body of the enzymes that they themselves need to function correctly can have a detrimental effect on those organs. If a dog has a predisposition for problems in his heart, kidneys or liver disease, such enzyme loss can hasten that disease and reduce the dog's life span.

Feeding Buddy

Over 30 years of breeding, raising, working, and living with dogs of several breeds have had a profound effect on our way of thinking. Even so, we are realists. You are a busy person and may not even cook for yourself, much less be concerned about what goes into your dog. Fortunately, you can take some shortcuts to safeguard your dog's health.

This section provides you with three options for feeding Buddy — from using a beefed-up version of commercial dog food, to using an easy alternative to making your own, to making your own. Only you can decide which option is best for your life style and your level of comfort.

Option 1: Beefed-up commercial food

All quantities are for a 50-lb dog. Adjust according to your dog's weight. For a 25-lb dog, halve the recipe. For a 75-lb dog, halve the recipe and add that to the 50-lb diet. When calculating the amount for the weight of your dog, err on the side of too little, rather than too much. Some dogs eat more than their weight indicates, and some dogs less. Use common sense and keep all ingredients in proportion.

Feed the following twice a day:

> 1 ½ cups Performance Food (PHD)
>
> ¼ tsp. vitamin C (PHD)
>
> 1 vitamin B-complex (PHD)
>
> ⅛ tsp. vitamin/mineral mix (Wellness from PHD)
>
> ¼ cup of beef (hamburger, 85 percent fat free), or ⅔ meat and ⅓ beef liver for a total of ¼ cup. You can also use chicken and chicken livers.
>
> 2 Tbsp. fresh vegetables
>
> 2 Tbsp. fresh or dried fruit

To the morning meal, add one Amino Acid Complex tablet (Nature Most), and, four times a week, one large egg cooked with shell for five minutes.

Once a week substitute cottage cheese for the meat on one day, and unflavored yogurt containing acidophillus on another day.

Chop the vegetables in a food processor or parboil them to make it easier for your dog to digest the cellulose.

For treats, try carrot sticks, dried liver, broccoli, raisins, parsnips, lettuce, bananas, prunes, cucumbers, or any fruit or vegetable in season.

Option 2: Natural Diet Foundation formula

The NDF formula, available from PHD, is the same as our homemade diet, except that it's dehydrated. This carefully formulated diet meets the needs of dogs of different breeds, of different ages, and living in different climates. It was clinically tested prior to marketing. Since no heat is used in the processing of the food, all the vitamins and minerals are unaltered by the food processing. It uses only human-grade ingredients and is the next best thing to making your own.

For the morning meal, all you add is water, yogurt, and vegetables. For the evening meal, all you add is meat. Directions for amounts to feed are on the package.

Option 3: Wendy Volhard's Natural Diet recipe

Making your own dog food is becoming a popular option, although it's hardly a new one. Every dog alive today can trace its ancestry back to dogs that were raised on homemade diets. The dog food industry, in comparison to dogs themselves, is young — maybe 50 to 60 years — although canned meat for dogs was sold at the turn of the 20th century. Originally, the commercial foods were made to supplement homemade food.

Why make your own?

Many dogs do not thrive on commercially prepared rations. They exhibit disease states, often mistaken for allergies, which are deficiency diseases caused by feeding cereal-based foods. A dog in his natural state would eat meat. His prey would be that of a grass-eating animal — an herbivore. Along with the internal organs and the muscle meat, he would eat the predigested grasses and plants of the carcass. Those grasses and plants would consist of no more than 20 to 25 percent of his total diet. He would raid nests from ground-breeding birds and eat the eggs, and he would catch the occasional insect. He would maybe forage on certain weeds and grasses and eat berries and fruit.

In formulating the Natural Diet, we stayed within these boundaries — with the exception of the insects. Although domestication has changed the appearance of many dogs through selective breeding, the digestive tract of the dog remains substantially the same as it always was. We really do have a wolf in our living rooms.

The Natural Diet consists of two meals. One is a cereal meal plus supplements, which makes up 25 percent of the total diet. The other half is a raw meat meal plus supplements, which is 75 percent of the total diet. In separating these meals — both of which are balanced — the digestive system uses enzymes present in the stomach and intestines to efficiently and quickly break down the food. It decreases the load on the digestive organs, which are maintained in a healthy state for a longer period of time.

For more information on how to make your own food, read *The Holistic Guide for a Healthy Dog,* 2nd Edition, by Wendy Volhard and Kerry Brown, DVM (IDG Books Worldwide, Inc., 2000).

Benefits of the Natural Diet

The advantages of feeding the Natural Diet are many. Health and longevity are increased, there is resistance to disease, and the diet can be tailored to individual needs. This is beneficial for some breeds of dogs, especially imported dogs or relatives of imported dogs, who have difficulty in digesting corn contained in the majority of prepared commercial diets. The diet allows individual ingredients to be substituted as necessary. Dogs are able to digest and utilize the Natural Diet, and stool volume is less than the 25 percent. The diet contains a lot of moisture in the natural ingredients, and therefore the dog drinks little water. Young dogs raised on this diet grow more slowly than dogs raised on commercial food and have fewer musculoskeletal problems. Fleas, ticks, and worms are almost unheard of on the Natural Diet. Skin, ear, and eye problems are rare, and so is bloat. Teeth rarely, if ever, have to be cleaned. Overall vitality and energy are unequaled. And dogs love to eat it.

Transferring to the Natural Diet

Unless your dog is already used to a raw diet, you need to put him on the following short-term transitional meal plan to avoid digestive upsets that may come from the switch to the Natural Diet.

Note: This diet is for a 50-pound dog. Adjust it according to your dog's weight. And make sure that fresh water is always available to your dog.

Day 1: No food. At mealtime, feed 2 tsp. honey mixed with a cup of lukewarm water.

Day 2: In the morning, give honey and water as in Day 1. In the evening, give 1 cup yogurt or kefir and 2 tsp. honey.

Day 3: In the morning, give 1 cup yogurt or kefir and 2 tsp. honey. In the evening, give 1 cup yogurt or kefir, 2 tsp. honey, and 1 tsp. dry or 2 Tbsp. fresh herbs.

Day 4: In the morning, give 2 cups yogurt or kefir, 2 tsp. honey, 1 Tbsp. dry or 2 Tbsp. fresh herbs, and ½ ounce (dry weight) cooked oatmeal. In the evening, give 1 cup yogurt or kefir, 2 tsp. honey, 1 tsp. dry to 2 Tbsp. fresh herbs, 2 ounces (dry weight) cooked oatmeal, and 1 garlic capsule.

Day 5: In the morning, give ½ normal ration of cereal and supplements as listed in the Natural Diet chart shown in Table 7-1. In the evening, give ½ normal ration of meat meal as listed on the Natural Diet chart.

Day 6: In the morning, give the normal amount of food as listed for Days 1–6 in Table 7-1. In the evening, give the normal amount of food as listed on Days 1–6 in Table 7-1.

Now your dog should be ready to follow the full Natural Diet listed in Table 7-1.

Table 7-1	Natural Diet — 50-Pound Dog
Breakfast (days 1–6)	*Dinner (days 1–6)*
3 oz. grain mix (dry)	12 oz. meat (days 1–5)
2 tsp. molasses	2 ½ oz. liver (days 1–5)
2 tsp. safflower oil	14 oz. cottage cheese (day 6)
200 IU Vitamin E	200 mg Vitamin C
200 mg Vitamin C	1 tsp. cod liver oil
50 mg Vitamin B Complex	1 Tbsp. apple cider vinegar
1 ¼ egg, small (4 times per week)	½ tsp. kelp
½ cup yogurt or kefir	1 tsp. brewer's yeast
	1 ½ garlic capsule (325 mg)
	2 ½ bone meal
	2 Tbsp. wheat germ
	3 Tbsp. wheat bran
	2 tsp. dry herbs
	2 Tbsp. fruit (alternate days)
Breakfast (day 7)	*Dinner (day 7)*
2 ⅓ oz. grain mix (dry)	Fast
200 mg Vitamin C	
50 mg Vitamin B Complex	
1 cup yogurt or kefir	
4 tsp. honey	

Give your dog a bone

Once or twice a week, give your dog a bone as a special treat. They love large beef bones, raw chicken necks, and the tips off chicken wings. If you're not sure about how long these things have been in the supermarket case, douse them with boiling water to kill any bacteria before feeding. The side benefit of feeding bones is that your dog has beautiful, pearly white teeth that don't need to be cleaned. Feeding too many bones, however, will give him constipation and hard, chalky stools. Be careful, too, to give your dog only large bones that can't splinter.

When you give your dog a bone, leave him alone. Dogs get possessive about their bones. Bones are one of the few items that may cause Buddy to growl at you if you try to take one away from him. It is a very special treat, and he wants to be in a place to relax and enjoy it. Let him go to his crate, which is the perfect place for him to enjoy his bone in peace. It will get him away from other dogs or cats in the family, the children, and you. Give him a few hours just to indulge himself. Let him be a dog. After a few days of chewing a fresh bone, it loses its magic, and most dogs will allow the kids, other dogs, or you to pick them up or handle them.

Chapter 8

Choosing a New Dog

- -

In This Chapter

▶ Choosing the right breed for you

▶ Knowing when to use a breeder

▶ Testing your future puppy

▶ Knowing when to go to a shelter

- -

*E*ven if you already have a dog, this chapter gives you additional insights into what you have chosen and will definitely help you with selecting your next dog.

Getting a dog or puppy on impulse is rarely a good idea. Remember that dogs, like cars, were designed for a particular function. You need to decide what you want: a Corvette or a Suburban, a Fox Terrier or a Newfoundland. You need to research exactly what you want so that you understand the commitment required for the particular dog you have selected.

When the various breeds were originally developed, there was a greater emphasis on the ability to do a job, such as herding, guarding, hunting, drafting, and the like, than on the dog's appearance. If a particular breed interests you, find out first what the dog was bred to do. There are so many different breeds to choose from and if there is a secret to getting that "perfect puppy," it lies in doing your homework.

The ideal source for this homework is *The Complete Dog Book,* 19th Edition (published by IDG Books Worldwide, Inc.), the official publication of the American Kennel Club. The book describes in detail the behavioral characteristics of the 148 breeds recognized by the American Kennel Club. In this chapter, we list some of the reasons for having a dog in the first place. Many dogs are readily trained to satisfy most of these reasons. Still, the more specific the task, such as hunting, herding, or protecting, the greater the need to select a dog bred for that task. Trying to train a protection dog into a hunting dog, and vice versa, is not worth the aggravation, and often times it can't be done at all.

The Match Game: What Kind of Dog Is for You?

The well-trained dog begins with some idea of what role the dog is expected to play in your life and then selecting a dog that is suitable for the job. Some of the reasons for selecting a dog follow:

- Companionship
- Playmate for the kids
- Protection
- A special activity, such as hunting, herding, breeding, or showing
- Status symbol
- A combination of the above

Some dogs are able to fill all of these expectations, while others have more limited talents.

 When choosing a dog or puppy, consider the amount of time you can (or are willing) to devote to exercising with your dog. Some breeds are more demanding in this respect than others — and if you fail to take an active role, your dog will not be a happy pet. Remember that all dogs, at a minimum, need to take two 20-minute walks each day.

You also need to take into account your own lifestyle and circumstances. For most of us, this means a dog that can satisfy your need for companionship, is easily trained, and doesn't require a lot of upkeep.

Distinguishing between breeds

Everyone has his or her own preference concerning dog breeds, and there is an enormous choice, from the four-pound Yorkshire Terrier to the 200-pound Mastiff. Many dogs, such as Poodles and Schnauzers, come in different sizes. Others have a smaller version that is similar in appearance, such as Collies and Shelties, or Doberman Pinschers and Miniature Pinschers, or German Shepherds and Corgis, or Greyhounds and Whippets. (See Figure 8-1.)

Getting a dog for a status symbol usually means one of the guarding or rarer breeds, and often these represent some special challenges. If you want a rare breed, first find out why the breed is rare, and if there are any potential drawbacks to owning this type of dog. They may be rare because they are not suitable as a pet in an urban or suburban environment, or because of health problems, or just because the "taking care of" part of having the dog is too demanding. For example, the Komondor, a Hungarian herding dog dating back more than a thousand years, is an impressive and handsome dog, but he has a heavily matted coat, giving him the appearance of an unmade bed. Taking care of this coat requires real dedication.

Conversely, one of the most popular dogs, and first in American Kennel Club registrations, is the Labrador Retriever. The reason is simple — the Lab is a good multi-purpose dog that can serve as a companion and playmate for the kids, is naturally protective, generally enjoys good health, makes a good guide dog, and with little time and effort can be transformed into a well-trained dog. Many of the Sporting dogs, such as the Flat-Coated Retriever, the Golden Retriever, and the English Springer Spaniel, meet these same criteria. And so do the Bernese Mountain Dogs, the Doberman Pinschers, and the Newfoundlands from the Working Group, and the Border Collie, the Shetland Sheepdog, and the Welsh Corgis from the Herding Group.

Breeds with long hair require more upkeep than those with short hair. It's pretty obvious when you think about it, but often completely overlooked when selecting a puppy or dog.

Poodles and Terriers don't shed like other dogs, but have to be groomed regularly (see Figure 8-2). Unless you are willing to spend the time and effort learning how to do it yourself, this means periodic visits to a professional groomer, an expensive proposition. These breeds may be a good alternative to individuals who are allergic to dogs that shed.

Figure 8-1:
A Terrier is one of many fine breeds to choose from.

Photo courtesy of Winter/Churchill aka dog photo,com

Figure 8-2:
Breeds such as Poodles and Terriers require regular grooming.

Some breeds, such as terriers and some of the herding dogs, bark a lot more than others. If you live in an apartment, such a dog would not be a good choice.

How much time do you have?

In selecting a dog or puppy be aware of the time factor. How much exercise does this particular breed require and are you in a position to give it to your dog? Some breeds require less exercise than others, but all require two daily 20-minute walks, at a minimum, and some, such as the Sporting breeds, much more. Just letting the dog out in a backyard is not sufficient.

In the selection process, you need to remind yourself continuously that your dog is going to be with you anywhere from 8 to 16 years. And the older he or she gets, the more important regular exercise becomes.

How much time do you have available to devote to training that cute little bundle of fur? If you have little, or no more that 10 to 15 minutes a day, then you need to select a breed that is easily trained and doesn't require much exercise.

Stonehenge and your dog

Why do the breed standards for many dogs sound so similar when describing the dog's temperament? Because so many of them were written by the same man. In 1874, J.H. Walsh, under the pen name of Stonehenge, published *The Dog: Its Varieties and Management in Health,* the first major effort to describe the more than 60 breeds recognized at that time.

Today's equivalent would be *The Complete Dog Book: Official Publication of the American Kennel Club.* The Flat-Coated Retriever is described in the official standard for the breed as follows: "As a family companinion he is sensible, alert and highly intelligent; a lighthearted, affectionate and adaptable friend." The Golden Retriver is "[f]riendly, reliable and trustworthy." The English Springer Spaniel is "friendly, eager to please, quick to learn and willing to obey."

The Bernese Mountain Dog is "self-confident, alert and good-natured . . ." The Doberman Pinscher, although not one of Stonehenge's original 60, is portrayed as "[e]nergetic, watchful, determined, alert, fearless, loyal and obedient." The Newfoundland is all of the above and "the traditional children's protector and playmate."

The Border Collie is "intelligent, alert and responsive," the Shetland Sheepdog is "intensely loyal, affectionate, and responsive to its owner," and the Welsh Corgi is "[e]ven-tempered, loyal, affectionate, and adaptable."

In short, all these dogs are affectionate, intelligent, loyal, and easy to train.

Knowing What Breed You Need

A good place to start is *The Complete Dog Book,* by the American Kennel Club, a tremendous resource. It describes in detail the 148 different breeds recognized by that organization. In addition to the breed's history and physical features, the descriptions often include a discussion of the breed's special qualities. For example, the description of the Labrador Retriever (see Figure 8-3) states: "Today's Labrador Retriever has several important roles in society. Its fine temperament and dependability have established its reputation as an excellent breed for guiding the blind, for search and rescue work, and, of course, for rounding out the family."

Having been the proud owners of a lovely Lab, we can attest to the accuracy of this profile.

Another wealth of information can be found at dog shows where you can see most of these dogs and talk to their owners.

Figure 8-3:
The
dependable
Labrador
Retriever.

Photo courtesy Ed Camelli

To help you get the dog you want, we have devised the Volhard Puppy Aptitude Test (PAT), which is covered a little later in this chapter and which is amazingly accurate in predicting inherited behavioral tendencies and how the puppy will turn out as an adult. In the explanation of PAT, we detail — on the basis of the puppy's score — the predicted behavioral tendencies of the puppy as an adult dog. This information, in turn, will tell you whether or not that particular puppy is suitable for your purposes. The scores of the puppies are also a good indicator of the ease or difficulty for training a particular puppy for a specific task.

Going the Breeder Route

Once you have done your research and you have decided on the breed that is most suited to your life-style and expectations, it is time to choose a breeder. You can meet breeders at dog shows, through the local newspaper, or popular dog magazines, such as *American Kennel Club Gazette, Dog World,* or *Dog Fancy.* Anyone can call him- or herself a *breeder,* whether he or she has bred one litter or has been breeding for 20 years. Whether a first-timer or an experienced breeder, the difference doesn't necessarily have anything to do with the quality or price of the puppies.

As a general rule, here are some of the criteria you want to follow in selecting a breeder:

- ✔ Choose an experienced breeder, one who has had several litters and who knows his breed.

- ✔ Choose a breeder who has shown his dogs and has done some winning, which is a fairly good indication that his or her dogs conform to the standard of the breed and will grow up resembling the dogs that attracted you to the breed in the first place.

- ✔ Choose a breeder who is using our Puppy Aptitude Test. If he or she hasn't heard of it, show it to him; avoid one that says "I don't believe in that."

- ✔ Choose a breeder whose dogs are certified by the applicable registries against breed-related genetic disorders, such as eye problems, hip dysplasia, and the like.

- ✔ Choose a breeder where you can interact with adult dogs, and get some idea how long they live.

- ✔ Choose a breeder where the dogs are well housed and everything is clean.

The majority of breeders today show a great willingness to have their puppies tested, and are interested in the results. It shows them the inherited behaviors of their breeding stock, valuable information for future breedings. The results make it easier for them to place the right puppy into the right home where people will be happy with it. After all, no breeder wants a puppy returned when it is 8 months old and may have been ruined by being improperly raised.

Puppy testing is permitted by most breeders, as it gives them useful information for breeding future litters. Test results also help breeders "match" their puppies with interested buyers. A good breeder wants every dog he sells to have a happy life in a good home.

Always interact with a puppy individually, away from its littermates. Whatever you do, don't try to pick a puppy by examining the entire litter together — you will not be able to pick the right one for you.

Testing Your Puppy

The purpose of the Volhard Puppy Aptitude Test (PAT) is to enable you to select the right dog for the right home. The closer the match, the easier it will be for you to train the dog. Conversely, a serious mismatch can mean difficulty training the dog — to the point where, ultimately, the dog has to be placed in a new home or winds up at the shelter.

Some of the tests we used to create PAT were developed as long ago as the 1930s for dogs bred to become guide dogs. Then in the 1950s, studies were conducted on puppies to see how quickly they could learn. These studies were actually done to identify children's learning stages.

The ideal age to test the puppy is at 49 days of age when the puppy is neurologically complete and it has the brain of an adult. With each passing day after the 49th day, the responses will be tainted by prior learning.

More tests were developed by Clarence Pfaffenberger and, most notably, William Campbell, to determine if pups could be tested for dominance and submission. These tests proved that it was indeed possible to predict future behavioral traits of adult dogs by testing puppies at 49 days of age. Testing before or after that age, affected the accuracy of the test, depending on the time before or after the 49th day.

We took these tests, added some of our own, and put together what is now known as PAT. PAT uses a scoring system from 1-6 and consists of ten tests. The tests are done consecutively and in the order listed. Each test is scored separately, and interpreted on its own merits. The scores are not averaged, and there are no winners or losers. The entire purpose is to select the right puppy for the right home.

The test covers these areas:

- **Social attraction:** Degree of social attraction to people, confidence, or dependence.
- **Following:** Willingness to follow a person.
- **Restraint:** Degree of dominant or submissive tendency, and ease of handling in difficult situations.
- **Social dominance:** Degree of acceptance of social dominance by a person.
- **Elevation dominance:** Degree of accepting dominance while in a position of no control, such as at the veterinarian or groomer.
- **Retrieving:** Degree of willingness to do something for you. Together with social attraction and following, a key indicator for ease or difficulty in training.
- **Touch sensitivity:** Degree of sensitivity to touch and a key indicator to the type of training equipment required.
- **Sound sensitivity:** Degree of sensitivity to sound, such as loud noises or thunderstorms.
- **Sight sensitivity:** Degree of response to a moving object, such as chasing bicycles, children, or squirrels.
- **Stability:** Degree of startle response to a strange object.

Monitoring the test

Here are the ground rules for performing the test:

- ✔ The testing is done in a location unfamiliar to the puppies. This does not mean they have to taken away from home. A 10-foot square area is perfectly adequate, such as a room in the house where the puppies have not been.
- ✔ The puppies are tested one at a time.
- ✔ There are no other dogs or people, except the scorer and the tester, in the testing area.
- ✔ The puppies do not know the tester.
- ✔ The scorer is a disinterested third party and not the person interested in selling you a puppy.
- ✔ The scorer is unobtrusive and positions himself or herself so he or she can observe the puppies' responses without having to move.
- ✔ The puppies are tested before they are fed.
- ✔ The puppies are tested when they are at their liveliest
- ✔ Do not try to test a puppy that is not feeling well.
- ✔ Puppies should not be tested the day of or the day after being vaccinated.
- ✔ Only the first response counts.

During the Puppy Aptitude Test, watch the puppy's tail. It will make a difference in the scoring whether the tail is up or down.

During the testing, make a note of the heart rate of the pup, which is an indication of how it manages stress, as well as its energy level. Puppies come with high, medium, or low energy levels. You have to decide for yourself the level that suits your lifestyle. Dogs with high energy levels need a great deal of exercise and will get into mischief if this energy is not channeled in the right direction.

The tests indicating the heart rate of the puppy are the restraint and elevation tests. With your hand on the puppy's chest for both tests, note whether the heart races or beats quietly. This heart rate is a comparison of the litter as a whole. Heart rates among breeds can differ. You will be surprised by the variation in beats per minute between puppies. When you feel a heart racing, make a note of it on your testing sheet. A racing heartbeat can indicate a high-energy puppy, but also one that stresses. A slow heartbeat would indicate a pup less prone to stress, but may mean that it is not very energetic either.

"Don't worry, he'll grow out of it." Famous last words — and it won't happen. You see what you get and you get what you see. If the puppy has a noticeable structural flaw now, he will have that same flaw as an adult dog.

Finally, look at the overall structure of the puppy. You see what you get at 49 days age. If the pup has strong and straight front and back legs, with all four feet pointing in the same direction, it will grow up that way, provided you give it the proper diet and environment in which to grow. If you notice something out of the ordinary at this age, it will stay with the puppy for the rest of its life; he will not grow out of it.

Testing and scoring your puppy

The tests are simple to perform, and anyone with some common sense can do them. You can, however, elicit the help of someone who has tested puppies before and knows what they are doing. During testing, maintain a positive, upbeat, and friendly attitude toward the puppies. Try to get each puppy to interact with you to bring out the best in him or her. Make the test a pleasant experience for the puppy.

Note: Included in each of the following tests are the responses you'll see and the score assigned to each particular response. You will see some variations and will have to make a judgment on what score to give them.

Test 1: Social attraction

The owner or caretaker of the puppy places it in the test area about four feet from the tester and then leaves the test area. The tester kneels down and coaxes the puppy to come to him or her by encouragingly and gently clapping hands and calling. The tester must coax the puppy in the opposite direction from where it entered the test area. *Hint:* Lean backward, sitting on your heels instead of leaning forward toward the puppy. Keep your hands close to your body encouraging the puppy to come to you, instead of you trying to reach for the puppy.

Here's how to score your puppy:

Came readily, tail up, jumped, bit at hands	1
Came readily, tail up, pawed, licked at hands	2
Came readily, tail up	3
Came readily, tail down	4
Came hesitantly, tail down	5
Didn't come at all	6

Test 2: Following

The tester stands up and slowly walks away encouraging the puppy to follow. *Hint:* Make sure the puppy sees you walk away and get the puppy to focus on you by lightly clapping your hands and using verbal encouragement to get the puppy to follow you. Do not lean over the puppy.

Here's how to score your puppy:

Followed readily, tail up, got underfoot, bit at feet	1
Followed readily, tail up, got underfoot	2
Followed readily, tail up	3
Followed readily, tail down	4
Followed hesitantly, tail down	5
Did not follow or went away	6

Test 3: Restraint

The tester crouches down and gently rolls the puppy on its back and holds it on its back for 30 seconds. *Hint:* Hold the puppy down without applying too much pressure. The object is not to keep it on its back but to test its response to being placed in that position.

Here's how to score your puppy:

Struggled fiercely, flailed, bit	1
Struggled fiercely, flailed	2
Settled, struggled, settled with some eye contact	3
Struggled, then settled	4
No struggle, no eye contact	5
No struggle, strained to avoid eye contact	6

Test 4: Social dominance

Let the puppy stand up or sit and gently stroke it from the head to the back while you crouch beside it. See if it will lick your face, an indication of a forgiving nature. Continue stroking until you see a behavior you can score. *Hint:* When you crouch next to the puppy avoid leaning or hovering over the puppy. Have the puppy at your side with both of you facing in the same direction.

Here's how to score your puppy:

Jumped, pawed, bit, growled	1
Jumped, pawed	2
Cuddled up to tester and tried to lick face	3
Squirmed, licked at hands	4
Rolled over, licked at hands	5
Went away and stayed away	6

Test 5: Elevation dominance

The tester cradles the puppy with both hands, supporting the puppy under its chest, and gently lifts it two feet off the ground and holds it there for 30 seconds.

Here's how to score your puppy:

Struggled fiercely, tried to bite	1
Struggled fiercely	2
Struggled, settled, struggled, settled	3
No struggle, relaxed	4
No struggle, body stiff	5
No struggle, froze	6

Test 6: Retrieving

The tester crouches beside the puppy and attracts its attention with a crumpled up piece of paper. When the puppy shows some interest, the tester throws the paper no more than four feet in front of the puppy encouraging it to retrieve the paper.

Here's how to score your puppy:

Chased object, picked it up, and ran away	1
Chased object, stood over it, and did not return	2
Chased object, picked it up, and returned with it to tester	3
Chased object and returned without it to tester	4
Started to chase object, lost interest	5
Does not chase object	6

Test 7: Touch sensitivity

The tester locates the webbing of one of the puppy's front paws and presses it lightly between his index finger and thumb. The tester gradually increases pressure while counting to ten and stops when the puppy pulls away or shows signs of discomfort.

Here's how to score your puppy:

8-10 count before response	1
6-8 count before response	2

5-6 count before response	3
3-5 count before response	4
2-3 count before response	5
1-2 count before response	6

Test 8: Sound sensitivity

The puppy is placed in the center of the testing area and an assistant stationed at the perimeter makes a sharp noise, such as banging a metal spoon on the bottom of a metal pan.

Here's how to score your puppy:

Listened, located sound, and ran toward it barking	1
Listened, located sound, and walked slowly toward it	2
Listened, located sound, and showed curiosity	3
Listened and located sound	4
Cringed, backed off, and hid behind tester	5
Ignored sound and showed no curiosity	6

Test 9: Sight sensitivity

The puppy is placed in the center of the testing area. The tester ties a string around a bath towel and jerks it across the floor, two feet away from the puppy.

Here's how to score your puppy:

Looked, attacked, and bit object	1
Looked and put feet on object and put mouth on it	2
Looked with curiosity and attempted to investigate, tail up	3
Looked with curiosity, tail down	4
Ran away or hid behind tester	5
Ignores, shows no curiosity	6

Test 10: Stability

An umbrella is opened about five feet from the puppy and gently placed on the ground.

Here's how to score your puppy:

Looked and ran to the umbrella, mouthing or biting it	1
Looked and walked to the umbrella, smelling it cautiously	2
Looked and went to investigate	3
Sat and looked, but did not move toward the umbrella	4
Ran away from the umbrella	5
Showed no interest	6

Figuring out what the scores mean

The scores are not added up, and the results are not based on a cumulative score. Instead, the scores are interpreted as follows:

Mostly 1s

- ✔ Strong desire to be pack leader and is not shy about bucking for a promotion.
- ✔ Has a predisposition to be aggressive to people and other dogs and will bite.
- ✔ Should only be placed into a very experienced home where the dog will be trained and worked on a regular basis.

Mostly 2s

- ✔ Also has leadership aspirations.
- ✔ May be hard to manage and has the capacity to bite.
- ✔ Has lots of self-confidence.
- ✔ Should not be placed with an inexperienced owner.
- ✔ Too unruly to be good with children and elderly people, or with other animals.
- ✔ Needs strict schedule, loads of exercise and lots of training.
- ✔ Has the potential to be a great show dog with someone who understands dog behavior.

Stay away from the puppy with a lot of 1s or 2s. It has strong leadership aspirations and may be difficult to manage. This puppy needs an experienced owner. Not good with children.

Mostly 3s

> ✔ Can be a high-energy dog and may need lots of exercise.
>
> ✔ Good with people and other animals.
>
> ✔ Can be a bit of a handful to live with.
>
> ✔ Needs training, does very well at it, and learns quickly.
>
> ✔ Great dog for second-time owner.

Mostly 4s

> ✔ The kind of dog that makes the perfect pet.
>
> ✔ Best choice for the first-time owner.
>
> ✔ Rarely will buck for a promotion in the family.
>
> ✔ Easy to train, and rather quiet.
>
> ✔ Good with elderly people, children, although may need protection from the children.
>
> ✔ Choose this pup, take it to obedience classes, and you'll be the star, without having to do too much work!

The puppy with mostly 3s and 4s can be quite a handful, but should be good with children and does well with training. Energy needs to be dispersed with plenty of exercise.

Mostly 5s

> ✔ Fearful, shy, and needs special handling.
>
> ✔ Will run away at the slightest stress in its life.
>
> ✔ Strange people, strange places, different floor or ground surfaces may upset it.
>
> ✔ Often afraid of loud noises and terrified of thunderstorms.
>
> ✔ When you greet it upon your return, may submissively urinate.
>
> ✔ Needs a very special home where the environment doesn't change too much and where there are no children.
>
> ✔ Best for a quiet, elderly couple.
>
> ✔ If cornered and cannot get away, has a tendency to bite.

This puppy will do well in a quiet, stable, and predictable environment. Basic training and a controlled setting will build up its confidence.

Mostly 6s

- So independent that he doesn't need you or other people.
- Doesn't care if it is trained or not — it is its own person.
- Unlikely to bond to you, since it doesn't need you.
- A great guard dog for gas stations!
- Do not take this puppy and think you can change it into a lovable bundle — you can't, so leave well enough alone.

Avoid the puppy with several 6s. It is so independent it doesn't need you or anyone. It is its own person and unlikely to bond to you.

Interpreting the results

Few puppies will test with all 2s or all 3s — there will be a mixture of scores.

For that first time, wonderfully easy to train, potential star, look for a puppy that has quite a few 4s and 3s. Don't worry about the score on touch sensitivity — you can compensate for that with the right training equipment.

Think with your head, not your heart, when selecting the puppy for you. Don't forget that you are choosing a companion that will be with you for up to 16 years. This is not a decision to make in haste. Give yourself the time you need to reflect on the puppies you are attracted to, and how you expect each of them to fit into your lifestyle.

Avoid the puppy with a score of 1 on the restraint and elevation tests. This puppy will be too much for the first-time owner.

It's hard not to become emotional when picking a puppy — they are all so cute, soft, and cuddly. Remind yourself that this dog is going to be with you for 8 to 16 years. Don't hesitate to step back a little to contemplate your decision. Sleep on it and review it in the light of day.

It's a lot more fun to have a good dog, one that is easy to train, one you can live with, and one you can be proud of, than one that is a constant struggle.

When a Dog from a Shelter Is a Good Choice

Don't overlook an animal shelter as a source for a good dog. Not all dogs wind up in a shelter because they are bad. After that cute puppy stage, when the dog grows up, it may become too much for its owner. Or, there may have been a change in the owner's circumstances, forcing him or her into having to give up the dog.

Most of the dogs waiting to be adopted are housetrained and already have some training. If the dog has been properly socialized to people, he will be able to adapt to a new environment. Bonding with a new owner may take some time, but once accomplished, you will have a devoted companion.

There are lots of loving, lovable dogs waiting to be adopted at animal shelters all over the country. Some people give up their dogs when they learn that dog ownership is more demanding than they expected. Others may have to move to a place where they cannot keep a dog. Many shelter dogs are just waiting to prove their pet potential.

While you can't use the entire puppy test at a shelter, there are some tests that will give you a good indication of what to look for.

- **Restraint:** Try putting the dog into a down position with some food, and then gently rolling him over and see what happens. If the dog jumps up and runs away or tries to bite you, this is not the dog for you. Rather, look for a dog that turns over readily, but squirms around a bit. Apply just enough pressure to keep the dog on his back; ease up if he struggles too much. Intermittent squirming is okay; constant squirming is not okay.

- **Social dominance:** Directly after the restraint test, if the dog didn't struggle too much and if you think it's safe, try sitting the dog and just stroking him, getting your face relatively close to him while talking to him softly, to see if he licks you and forgives you for the upside down experience. A dog that wants to get away from you is not a good candidate.

- **Retrieving:** Crumple up a small piece of paper and show it to the dog. Have him on your left side with your arm around him and throw the paper with your right hand about six feet, encouraging the dog to get it and bring it back. You are looking for a dog that brings the paper back to you.

Guide dog trainers have the greatest faith in this last test. A dog that retrieves nearly always works out to be a guide dog because it indicates a willingness to please the owner. Other organizations that use dogs from a shelter, such as those who use dogs to sniff out contraband or drugs, and police departments, place almost sole reliance on this test. They know that if a dog brings back the object, they can train him to do almost anything.

Wherever you get your dog, be it from a pet store or from friends, use the three preceding tests to get a clear indication of what will be involved in training the dog. By the way, it's not too late to use these tests with the dog you already have. It just might explain some of your dog's behaviors.

Chapter 9

Surviving the Puppy Period

. . . .

. . . .

*E*veryone wants a super puppy, one that is well behaved and listens to every word we say — a Lassie or perhaps even a Beethoven. Of course, heredity plays a role but not nearly as much as early upbringing and environment.

From birth until maturity, your dog goes through a number of developmental stages. What happens during these stages has a lasting effect on how your dog turns out, his ability to learn, his outlook on life, and his behavior.

The many scientists and behaviorists who've studied dog behavior over the last century have made important discoveries about these developmental stages and how they relate to a dog's ability to grow into a well-adjusted pet. These stages are called *the critical periods*, and what happens or doesn't happen during that time determines how the pup turns out as an adult and how he responds to your efforts to train him.

The first two critical periods are from birth to 49 days. During this time, the puppy needs his mother and the interaction with his littermates (see Figure 9-1). He also needs to have interaction with humans. Although these particular periods are not within your control, we briefly describe in this chapter what happens during the weaning period when the puppy learns to learn. And we also deal with the periods that follow and how they relate to training.

Photo courtesy Mary Bloom

Figure 9-1:
A mother
and her
litter.

Understanding Your Puppy's Socialization Needs

At about the 49th day of life, when the puppy's brain is neurologically complete, that special attachment between the dog and his owner, called *bonding,* begins. It is one of the reasons why this is the ideal time for puppies to leave the nest for their new homes so that bonding with the new owner or family can take place.

Bonding to people becomes increasingly difficult the longer a puppy remains with its mother or littermates. The dog also becomes more difficult to train. With each passing day, the pup loses a little of its ability to adapt to a new environment.

In addition, with delay there is the potential for built-in behavior problems.

- The pup may grow up being too dog-oriented.
- The pup will probably not care much about people.
- The pup may be difficult to teach to accept responsibility.
- The pup may be more difficult to train, including housetraining.

The weaning period: Weeks 3-7

You must also be wary of taking a puppy away from the mother too soon, because it deprives the puppy of important lessons. Between three to seven weeks of age, the mother teaches her puppies basic doggy manners. She communicates to the puppies what is acceptable and what is unacceptable behavior.

For example, after the puppies' teeth have come in, nursing them becomes a painful experience, so she teaches them to take it easy. She does whatever it takes, from growls to snarls and even snaps, and continues this lesson throughout the weaning process when she wants the puppies to leave her alone. After just a few repetitions, the puppies get the message and respond to a mere look or a curled lip from mother. The puppy learns dog language, or lip reading, as we call it, and learns bite inhibition, an important lesson.

The puppies also learn from each other. While playing, tempers may flare because one will have bitten another one too hard. The puppies learn from these exchanges what it feels like to be bitten and, at the same time, to inhibit biting during play (see Figure 9-2). Those that have not had these lessons may find it difficult to accept discipline while growing up.

Figure 9-2:
Puppies at
play.

Puppies separated from their canine family before they have had the opportunity for these experiences tend to identify more with humans than with other dogs. To put it simply, they don't know they are dogs, and they tend to have their own sets of problems, such as the following:

- ✔ Mouthing and biting their owner
- ✔ An unhealthy attachment to humans
- ✔ Aggression toward other dogs
- ✔ Nervousness
- ✔ Excessive barking
- ✔ Difficulty with housetraining
- ✔ A dislike of being left alone

Getting to know everyone: Weeks 7-12

Your dog is a social animal. To become an acceptable pet, the pup needs to interact with you and your family, as well as other humans and dogs during the seventh through the twelfth week of life. If denied these opportunities, your dog's behavior around other people or dogs may be unpredictable — your dog may be fearful or perhaps even aggressive. For example, unless regularly exposed to children during this period, a dog may be uncomfortable or untrustworthy around them.

Socializing your puppy is critical for it to become a friendly adult dog. When your puppy is developing, expose it to as many different people as possible, including children and older people (see Figure 9-3). Let it meet new dogs too. These early experiences will pay off big time when your dog grows up.

Your puppy needs the chance to meet and to have positive experiences with those persons and activities that will play a role in its life.

- ✔ You are a grandparent whose grandchildren occasionally visit — have your puppy meet children as often as you can.
- ✔ You live by yourself, but have friends visit you — make an effort to let your puppy meet other people, particularly members of the opposite sex.
- ✔ You plan to take your dog on family outings or vacations — introduce riding in a car.

We've been fortunate in that we've been able to take our puppies to our training camps. The wealth of experience they gained from the week-long exposure to other dogs and people has made it easy for us to take our dogs anywhere. As a result, they get along with people and dogs — and are ambassadors for all dogs.

Figure 9-3:
Allow your children to bond with your puppy early.

Photo courtesy of Mary Bloom

Socialization with other dogs is equally important, and should be the norm rather than the exception. It also needs to occur on a regular basis. Ideally, the puppy has a mentor, an older dog who can teach it the ropes. We have been fortunate enough in always having had a mentor dog who supervised the upbringing of a new puppy, making our task that much easier.

Puppies learn from other dogs, but can only do so if they have a chance to spend time with them. Make a point of introducing your young dog to other puppies and adults on a regular basis. In the ideal situation, the puppy will have a mentor, an older dog who can teach it the ropes.

If you plan on taking your puppy to obedience class or dog shows or ultimately using the dog in a breeding program, it needs to have the chance to interact with other dogs. Time spent now is well worth the effort — it will build his confidence and make your job training him that much easier.

This is also a time when your puppy will follow your every footstep. Encourage this behavior by rewarding the puppy with an occasional treat, a pat on the head or a kind word.

Suddenly he is afraid: Weeks 8-12

Weeks 8 through 12 are called the *fear imprint period.* During this period, any painful or particularly frightening experience leaves a more lasting impression on your pup than if it occurred at any other time in his life. If the experience is sufficiently traumatic, it could literally ruin your pup for life.

During this time, avoid exposing the puppy to traumatic experiences. For example, elective surgery, such as ear cropping, should be done, if at all, before 8 weeks or after 11 weeks of age. When you need to take your puppy to the veterinarian, have the doctor give the puppy a treat before, during, and after the examination to make the visit a pleasant experience. Although you should stay away from stressful situations, do continue to train your puppy in a positive and non-punitive way.

During the first year's growth, you may see fear reactions at other times. Do not respond by dragging your puppy to the object that caused the fear. On the other hand, don't pet or reassure the dog — you may create the impression that you approve of this behavior. Rather, distract the puppy with a toy or a treat to get his mind off whatever scared him and go on to something pleasant. Practice some of the commands you have already taught him so he can focus on a positive experience. After a short time, sometimes up to two weeks, the fearful behavior will disappear.

Now he wants to leave home: Beyond 12 weeks

Sometime between the fourth and eighth months, your puppy begins to realize that there is a big, wide world out there. Up to now, every time you called, Buddy willingly came to you. But now he may prefer to wander off and investigate. Buddy is maturing and cutting the apron strings. This is normal. He is not being spiteful or disobedient, just becoming an adolescent.

While he's going through this phase, it is best to keep Buddy on a leash or in a confined area until he has learned to come when called. Otherwise, not coming when called becomes a pattern — annoying to you and dangerous to the dog. After this activity becomes a habit, it is difficult to break; prevention is the best cure. Teaching your dog to come when called is much easier before he has developed the habit of running away.

When you do need to gather in a wandering Buddy, do not, under any circumstances, play the game of chasing the dog. Instead, run the other way and get your dog to chase you. If that doesn't work, kneel on the ground and pretend you have found something extremely interesting, hoping your puppy's curiosity brings him to you. If you do have to go to the pup, approach slowly until you can calmly take hold of the collar.

During this time your puppy also goes through teething and needs to chew — anything and everything. Dogs, like children, can't help it. If one of your favorite shoes is demolished, try to control yourself. Puppies have the irritating habit of tackling many shoes, but only one from each pair. Look at it as a lesson to keep your possessions out of reach. Scolding will not stop the need to chew, but it may cause your pet to fear you.

Your job is to provide acceptable outlets for this need, such as chew bones and toys. Our dogs' favorites are marrow bones, which you can get at the supermarket. These bones provide hours of entertainment for any dog, and they keep their teeth clean. There are also artificial versions. Kong toys are also a great favorite. All these things come in different sizes appropriate to the size of your dog. Just be sure that they are large enough so he can't accidentally swallow them.

Stay away from soft and fuzzy toys. Chances are, your dog will destroy them and may ingest part of them. We personally also don't like any items that have been treated with various chemicals or items that become soft and gooey with chewing because they can be swallowed by the dog and get stuck in the intestines. Tennis balls are fine for supervised play and retrieving but not as a chew toy. We've heard too many horror stories about dogs getting them stuck in the back of their mouths.

When Buddy is going through this stage, you may want to consider crating him when he is left alone. Doing so will keep him and your possessions safe, and both of you will be happy. Crating him during this growth spurt helps with his housetraining, too. With all the chewing he is doing during his teething, accidents sometimes happen. (Turn to Chapter 10 for more on housetraining.)

Managing the Terrible Twos

The adolescent stage of your dog's life, depending on the breed, takes place anywhere from 4 months to 2 years and culminates in sexual maturity. Generally, the smaller the dog, the sooner he matures. Larger dogs enter (and end) adolescence later in life.

Adolescence is a time when the cute little puppy can turn into a teenage monster. He starts to lose his baby teeth and his soft, fuzzy puppy coat; he goes through growth spurts and looks gangly, either up in the rear or down in front; he is entering an ugly-duckling stage.

Depending on the size of the dog, 40 to 70 percent of adult growth is achieved by 7 months of age. If you have one of the larger breeds, you'd better start training now, before the dog gets so big that you can't manage him.

As Buddy is beginning to mature, he starts to display some puzzling behaviors, as well as some perfectly normal but objectionable ones.

Surviving the juvenile flakies

We use the term *juvenile flakies* because it most accurately describes what is technically known as a second fear imprint period. Juvenile flakies are apprehension or fear behaviors that are usually short-lived. They are caused by temporary calcium deficiencies related to a puppy's periodic growth spurts.

The timing of this event (or events) is not as clearly defined as the first fear imprint period and coincides with growth spurts; hence it may occur more than once as the dog matures. Even though he may have been outgoing and confident before, your puppy now may be reluctant to approach someone or something new and unfamiliar, or he may suddenly be afraid of something familiar.

Fear of the new or unfamiliar has its roots in evolution. In a wolf pack, once the pups become 8 to 10 months of age, they are allowed to come on a hunt. The first lesson they have to learn is to stay with the pack; if they wander off, they might get lost or into trouble. They also have to develop survival techniques, one of which is fear. The message to the puppy is "if you see or smell something unfamiliar, run the other way."

Apprehension or fear of the familiar is also caused by growth spurts. At this point in a puppy's life, hormones start to surge. Hormones can affect the calcium uptake in the body, and, coupled with growth, this can be a difficult time for the growing puppy.

Puppy discovers sex

Sometime during this four-month to two-year period, depending on the size of your dog, the puppy will discover sex, and you will be the first to know about it.

Being patient with the flakies

One day, when our Dachshund, Manfred, was 6 months old, he came into the kitchen after having been outside in the yard. Then he noticed on the floor, near his water bowl, a brown paper grocery bag. He flattened, looked as though he had seen a ghost, and tried to run back out into the yard.

If Manfred was going through a growth spurt at this time, which would be normal at 6 months, he could be experiencing a temporary calcium deficiency, which in turn would produce his fear reaction.

He had seen brown paper grocery bags many times before, but this one was going to get him. We reminded ourselves that he was going through the flakies and ignored the behavior.

Should you observe something like this with your puppy, do not try to drag him up to the object in an effort to "teach" the puppy to accept it. If you make a big deal out of it, you create the impression that there is a good reason to be afraid of whatever triggered the reaction. Leave the puppy alone, ignore the behavior, and it will pass.

When our Landseer Newfoundland, Evo, was almost 2, he fell in love. He had always enjoyed playing with other dogs. He is generally well behaved and gets along with people and all the dogs he has met. We took him to a training facility where we were to meet up with friends who had just adopted an 11-month-old female Labrador Retriever named Indy. Evo was very sweet with her, and at first they played nicely together, chasing and batting at each other with their paws. All of a sudden, a strange look came over Evo's face, and with his face crinkled up he jumped on Indy's back and with his front paws clasped her firmly around her chest. We realized that his puppy days were over.

Sex is sex in any language! Evo was a bit of a late developer because he lives with spayed females and had not yet had the pleasure of being involved with an unspayed female before.

We handled Evo by going up to him, putting his lead on, and taking him away from Indy. He wanted to go back to her and tried several times, but we occupied his mind with training and he soon forgot all about her.

When Buddy experiences a surge of hormones during training, do some heeling or some retrieving to get his mind back into the proper frame of mind.

When hormones kick in, it's not always about sex

During this period, from 4 months to a year, the male puppy's hormones surge to four times their normal level, and this surge can have important effects on his behavior. Buddy may decide the time has come to buck for a promotion to pack leader. His attempted coup can take the form of an outright challenge, or it can be more subtle, as in "I'm not going to listen to you anymore." He may also try to lord it over other dogs in the household or ones he meets outside. Fortunately, after this enormous surge, his hormones ultimately return to normal.

Many pet owners discover at this stage that their dog is becoming difficult to handle, and so they seek professional help or enroll Buddy in an obedience class (see Chapter 21). This stage is also a good time to consider neutering the dog (see the following section).

Some puppies become aggressive in protecting their toys, their food, or their owners. It's also a time when puppies are not looking their best. With puppy fur falling out and adult fur coming in, they can appear quite moth-eaten. They get tall and gangly. It's just as well we loved them as pups, because right now, they are not looking or behaving in a very lovable way.

A sad fact of life

The majority of dogs in animal shelters are delivered at around eight months of age, when they are "no longer cute" and have "stopped listening." Millions of dogs are destroyed annually because their owners did not want to spend 10 to 15 minutes a day working with them while they were young.

Hormones drive behavior, which means that the intensity of behaviors is increased in direct proportion to the amount of hormones coursing through his system. So if you want your male puppy to become calmer, and not to assert himself quite so much, neutering him is a good idea.

Although female puppies going through puberty may show similar traits, they more often show greater dependency upon their owners. They follow their owners around, looking at them constantly, as if to say, "Something is happening to my body, but I don't know what. Tell me what to do." Females are just as apt to show mounting behavior as males, and you may consider spaying.

If you don't want to neuter your pet, the necessity for training increases. The freedom that the male puppy had before now becomes limited. The better trained he is, the easier this transition is, but it requires a real commitment on your part. The female, in turn, needs to be protected during her heat cycle, which usually occurs every six months and lasts around 21 days. Her attraction is so potent that you may discover unwanted suitors around your house, some of whom may have come from miles away.

Our first experience with a female in season involved our Landseer, Heidi. When we came home from work, we found a good-sized Basset Hound on our front stoop, patiently waiting for Heidi. As we approached, he made it perfectly clear that he was taking a proprietary attitude toward Heidi, as well as the house.

We had to enter the house via the back door. We then managed to subdue the little fellow with a few dog biscuits just long enough to check his collar. We were surprised to learn that the horny hound had traveled close to 3 miles to visit.

Spaying or Neutering

Unless you intend to exhibit your dog in dog shows to get a championship, or to breed the dog, you should seriously consider neutering your dog.

The advantages of neutering your pet generally outweigh the disadvantages. For the male, these advantages include the following:

- Keeps him calm.
- Reduces the tendency to roam.
- Diminishes mounting behavior.
- Makes training easier.
- Improves overall disposition, especially toward other dogs.
- Reduces risk of prostate problems developing in the older male.

In short, he will be easier to live with and easier to train. It also curbs the urge to roam or run away. So if the front door is left open by accident, he will not, like our friend the Basset we introduced in the preceding section, go miles to find a female in season.

It is not true that dogs who have been neutered lose their protective instincts — it depends on the age when the dog was neutered. Generally, dogs neutered after one year of age retain their protective instincts.

If you spay your female, she, too, will stay closer to home. Perhaps even more important are these benefits:

- You won't have to deal with the mess that goes with having her in season.
- You won't have to worry about unwanted visitors camping on your property and lifting a leg against any vertical surface.
- You won't have to worry about accidental puppies, which are next to impossible to place in good homes.
- You may have a healthier dog, with less chance of getting tumors of the mammary glands and infections of the uterus.

Knowing when to spay or neuter

When you have your pet altered, make sure that the operation occurs at least one month apart from his or her rabies shot, which should not be given before 6 months of age. Until 6 months of age, the puppy is protected against rabies through the antibodies passed along in the mother's milk. Vaccines should also not be given to a dog that is undergoing surgery because this can have long-term adverse effects. So if you decide to alter your dog, think about having the surgery after 7 months of age, for both sexes.

Depending on the breed and size of the female, she will go into her first season any time after 7 months of age. For a Yorkshire Terrier, it is apt to be sooner, and for a giant breeds, it is likely to be later, sometimes as late as 18 months of age.

If you want a dog to show more adult behaviors and take more responsibility, like being a protector or guard dog, training for competitive events, or working for a living, think about altering later.

A dog that has not been neutered until after one year of age, or a female that has gone through two seasons, is generally easier to train for competitive events such as obedience or agility trials. They have become fully grown by that time, are emotionally mature, have learned more adult behaviors, and can accept more responsibility.

Disadvantages to spaying and neutering

Altering changes the hormones in the body. Some dogs that are altered develop hypothyroidism as they mature. Hypothyroidism can cause these problems:

- Increased shedding
- Dull, oily, smelly coats
- Separation anxiety
- Skin problems
- A tendency to gain weight

Regardless of these disadvantages, we recommend neutering a dog that is not going to be bred simply because neutered dogs are so much easier to live with. For the males, neutering eliminates the stress they experience when they become aware of a female in season, makes training that much easier, and minimizes the unwanted roaming. For the females, it eliminates the violent mood swings they can experience during their cycle, followed by a false pregnancy, and followed in turn by imaginary puppies.

Finally He Grows Up

No matter how much you wish that cute little puppy to remain as is, your pup is going to grow up. It happens anywhere from 1 to 4 years. Over the course of those years, your dog will undergo physical and emotional changes. For you, the owner, the most important one is your dog's sense of identity — the process of becoming an individual in his own right. If you provide leadership through training, he will reward you with many years of loyal devotion.

Should you breed your dog?

Generally, you should not even contemplate breeding your dog unless:

✔ Your dog is purebred and registered.

✔ You did not find your dog, or get him from an animal shelter or pet store.

✔ You have at least a three-generation pedigree for your dog.

✔ Your dog has at least four titled dogs, such as conformation or working titles, in the last three generations.

✔ Your dog is certified free of genetic disorders applicable to the breed.

✔ Your dog confroms to the standard for its breed.

✔ Your dog has a stable temperament.

Breeding dogs for the purpose of exposing your children to the miracle of birth is *not* a good idea. Rent a video!

Part III

Getting Down to Training Your Dog

The 5th Wave   By Rich Tennant

Andy has doubts about the canine-osmosis training he's signed up for.

In this part . . .

This part presents the nuts and bolts of training. Of critical importance to every dog owner is that the dog be housetrained, and we cover that process in detail here. We also tell you how to train your dog to walk politely on a leash so that both of you enjoy the exercise and both of you stay safe. Retrieving is fun, too, so we explain how to teach your dog to retrieve (only the things you want him to retrieve, that is). Finally, we explain the process of becoming a Canine Good Citizen — a dog who has mastered the respectable behaviors that you expect of him at home and in public.

Chapter 10

Housetraining

*T*he well-trained dog's education begins with housetraining. As with any training, some dogs catch on more readily than others. Some of the toy breeds are notoriously dense in this regard and vigorously resist all efforts requiring their cooperation.

As a general rule, however, the majority of dogs do not present a problem, provided you do your part. To speed along the process, we strongly recommend that you use a crate or similar means of confinement.

Initially, you may recoil from this concept as cruel and inhumane. Nothing could be further from the truth. You will discover that your puppy likes his crate and that you can enjoy your peace of mind. (Take a look at Chapter 9 for tips on crating Buddy during a particular puppy stage, as well as for helpful advice on surviving the puppy period altogether.)

Using a Crate: A Playpen for Your Puppy

When Jim and Laura went to pick up their puppy, the breeder asked them what they thought was a peculiar question. "When you were raising your children, did you use a playpen?" "Of course," said Laura, "I don't know what I would have done without it." "Fine," said the breeder, "a crate for a puppy is like a playpen for a child."

Whatever your views on playpens, dogs like crates. It reminds them of a den, a place of comfort, safety, security, and warmth. Puppies, and many adult dogs, sleep most of the day, and they prefer the comfort of their den. For your mental health, as well as that of your puppy, get a crate.

Here are just a few of the many advantages to crate-training your dog:

- It's a baby-sitter — when you are busy and can't keep an eye on your dog, but want to make sure he won't get into trouble, put him in his crate. You can relax, and so can he.

- It's ideal for getting him on a schedule for housetraining.

- Few dogs are fortunate enough to go through life without ever having to be hospitalized. Your dog's private room at the veterinary hospital will consist of a crate. His first experience with a crate should not come at a time when he is sick — the added stress from being crated for the first time will retard his recovery. There may also be times when you have to keep your dog quiet, such as after being altered or after an injury.

- Driving any distance, even around the block, with your dog loose in the car is tempting fate. An emergency stop and who knows what could happen. Having the dog in a crate protects you and your dog.

- When we go on vacation we like to take our dog. His crate is his home away from home, and we can leave him in a hotel room knowing he won't be unhappy, stressed, or tear up the room.

- It is a place where he can get away from the hustle-and-bustle of family life and hide out when the kids become too much for him.

A crate provides a dog with his own special place. It is cozy, secure, and his place to go to get away from it all. Make sure that your dog's crate is available to him when he wants to nap or take some time out. He will use it on his own, so he should always have access to it. Depending on where it is, your dog will spend much of his sleeping time in his crate.

Finding the right crate

Select a crate that is large enough for your dog to turn around, stand up, or lie down comfortably. If he is a puppy, get a crate for the adult size dog so that he can grow into it.

Some crates are better than others in strength and ease of assembly. You can get crates in wire mesh type material, cloth mesh, or in plastic, called *airline crates*. Most are designed for portability and are easy to assemble. Our own preference for durability and versatility is a wire mesh crate. Wire mesh crates are easy to collapse, although they are heavier than crates made out of mesh or plastic.

We recommend a good-quality crate that collapses easily and is portable so that you can take it with you when traveling with your dog. If you frequently take your dog with you in the car, consider getting two crates, one for the house and one for the car. Doing so saves you having to lug one back and forth.

Coaxing Buddy into the crate

Set up the crate and let your dog investigate it. Put a crate pad or blanket in the crate. Choose a command, such as "crate" or "go to bed." Physically place Buddy in the crate using the command you have chosen. Close the door, tell him what a great puppy he is, give him a bite-sized treat, and then let him out.

There's no rule against gentle persuasion to get your pup enthused about his crate. A treat placed inside can work wonders. If your puppy is not lured in, physically place him inside the crate and close the door. Next comes a little praise, a little treat, and the opportunity to exit.

Next, use a treat to coax him into the crate. If he does not follow the treat, physically place him into the crate and then give him the treat. Again, close the door, tell him what a great little puppy he is, and give him a bite-sized treat, then let him out.

Do this until Buddy goes into the crate with almost no help from you, each time using the command and giving him a treat after he is in the crate.

For the puppy that is afraid of the crate, use his meals to overcome his fear. First, let him eat his meal in front of the crate, then place his next meal just inside the crate. Put each successive meal a little further into the crate until he is completely inside and no longer reluctant to enter.

Helping Buddy get used to the crate

Tell your dog to go into the crate, give him a treat, close the door, and tell him what a good puppy he is, then let him out again. Each time you do this, leave him in the crate a little longer with the door closed, still giving him a treat and telling him how great he is.

Finally, put him in his crate, give him a treat, and then leave the room, first for 5 minutes, then 10 minutes, then 15 minutes, and so on. Each time you return to let him out, tell him how good he was before you open the door.

How long can you ultimately leave your dog in his crate unattended? That depends on your dog and your schedule, but for an adult dog, it should not be more than eight hours.

Never use your dog's crate as a form of punishment. If you do, he will begin to dislike the crate, and it will lose its usefulness to you. It is not in your interest for Buddy to develop negative feelings about his crate. You want him to like his private den.

The Fundamentals of Housetraining Your Puppy

The keys to successful housetraining are

- ✔ Crate-training your puppy first.
- ✔ Setting a schedule for feeding and exercising your dog.
- ✔ Sticking to that schedule, even on weekends, at least until your dog is housetrained and mature.
- ✔ Vigilance, vigilance, and vigilance until your dog is trained.

Using a crate to housetrain your puppy is the most humane and effective way to get the job done. It is also the easiest way because of the dog's natural desire to keep his den clean. The crate, combined with a strict schedule and vigilance on your part, ensures speedy success (see the preceding section for tips on crate-training your puppy).

Over the course of a 24-hour period, puppies have to eliminate two to three times more frequently than adult dogs. A puppy's ability to control elimination increases with age, from not being able to control at all to beginning to be able to control for up to eight hours and more. During the day, when active, the puppy can last for only short periods. Until he is six months of age, it is unrealistic to expect him to last for more than four hours during the day without having to eliminate. When sleeping, most puppies can last through the night. During the housetraining phase, take your puppy out immediately after he has had a meal.

Set up an elimination schedule

Dogs thrive on a regular routine. By feeding and exercising Buddy at about the same time every day, he will also relieve himself at about the same time every day.

Set a time to feed the puppy that is convenient for you. Always feed at the same time. Until he is four months of age, he needs four meals a day; from four to seven months, three daily meals are appropriate. From then on feed twice a day — it is healthier than feeding only once and helps with housetraining.

A sample feeding schedule follows:

- Seven weeks through 16 weeks — four times a day
- 17 weeks through 28 weeks — three times a day
- 29 weeks on — two times a day

Feed the right amount — loose stools are a sign of overfeeding, straining or dry stools a sign of underfeeding. After 10 minutes, pick up the dish and put it away. Do not have food available at other times. Keep the diet constant. Abrupt changes of food may cause digestive upsets that will not help your housetraining efforts. (For tips on how often and how much to feed, turn to Chapter 7.)

Fresh water must be available to your dog at all times during the day. You can pick up his water dish after 8:00 p.m. so he can last through the night.

A strict schedule for your dog is a great asset in housetraining. If you feed your dog at the same times every day, and take him out for exercise at the same times every day, he will tend to eliminate at the same times every day. After you and your dog have established a schedule, you can project when he'll need to relieve himself and help him to be in the right spot at the right time.

Establish a regular toilet area

Start by selecting a toilet area and always take Buddy to that spot when you want him to eliminate. If possible, pick a place in a straight line from the house. Carry your puppy or put him on leash. Stand still and let him concentrate on what he is doing. Be patient and let him sniff around. After he is done, tell him what a clever puppy he is and play with him for a few minutes. Don't take him directly back inside so that he won't get the idea that he only gets to go outside to do his business and learns to delay the process just to stay outside.

Witnessing the act of your puppy relieving himself outside, followed by play-time, is perhaps one of the most important facets of housetraining. The first sign of not spending enough time outside with your puppy is when he comes back inside and has an accident. Letting the puppy out by himself is not good enough — you have to go with him until his schedule has been developed.

Where you live will dictate your housetraining strategies. In a city, where dogs have to be curbed to relieve themselves, you need to keep Buddy on leash. You also need to pick up after him, *please!* If you walk your dog in a park or through a neighborhood, you also need to pick up after him (see Figure 10-1). Under no circumstances should you let him do his business in a neighbor's yard.

And even in your own yard, unless you have oodles of land, you need to pick up after him for sanitary reasons. If you have a fenced yard, and don't mind where he goes, you can let him off leash. If you want him kept to a particular spot, keep him on leash and then clean up.

Figure 10-1:
Use common courtesy, no matter where you walk your dog.

Photo courtesy Mary Bloom

You may also want to teach Buddy a command, such as "Hurry up" so that you can speed up the process when necessary. Time the command to just before he starts and then lavishly praise when he has finished. After several repetitions, Buddy will associate the command with having to eliminate.

Be vigilant

Take your puppy to his toilet area after eating or drinking, after waking up, and after he has played or chewed. A sign that he has to go out is sniffing the ground in a circling motion.

When you see your puppy sniffing and circling, take note! He is letting you know that he is looking for a place to go. Take him out to his toilet area so he doesn't make a mistake.

Setting up a housetraining schedule

First thing in the morning, Mary takes her 12-week-old poodle puppy, Colette, out of her crate and straight outside to her toilet area. Fifteen minutes after Colette's morning meal, she is let out again. Mary then crates Colette and leaves for work.

On her lunch break, Mary goes home to let Colette out to relieve herself, feeds her and then, just to make sure, takes her out once more. For the afternoon, Colette is crated again until Mary returns. Colette is then walked and fed, after which she spends the rest of the evening in the house where Mary can keep an eye on her. Before bedtime, Colette goes out to her toilet area one more time and is then crated for the night.

When Colette becomes seven months old, Mary will drop the noontime feeding and walk. From that age on, most dogs only need to go out immediately or soon after waking up in the morning, once during the late afternoon and once again before bedtime.

Special vigilance is required when it is raining because many dogs, particularly those with short hair, do not like to go out in the wet anymore than you do. Make sure the puppy actually eliminates before you bring him back into the house.

An accident is an accident is an accident

No matter how conscientious you are and no matter how vigilant, there are going to be times when your puppy will have an accident. Housetraining accidents may be simple mistakes, or they can be indicative of a physical problem. The key to remember is that, as a general rule, dogs want to be clean.

When Buddy has had an accident in the house, do not call him to you to punish him. It is too late. If you do punish your dog under these circumstances, it will not help your housetraining efforts and you will make him wary of wanting to come to you.

There is a popular misconception that the dog knows "what he did" because he looks "guilty." *Absolutely not so!* He has that look because from prior experience he knows that when you happen to come across a mess, you get mad at him. He has learned to associate a mess with your response. He has not and cannot make the connection between having made the mess in the first place and your anger. Discipline after the fact is the quickest way to undermine the relationship you are trying to build with your dog.

Dogs are smart, but they do not think in terms of cause and effect. When you come home from work and yell at your dog for having an accident in the living room, you are not encouraging your dog to use his toilet area. All you are doing is letting him know that sometimes you're really nice and sometimes you're really mean.

Swatting your dog with a rolled-up newspaper is cruel and only makes him afraid of you and rolled-up newspapers. Rubbing his nose in it is unsanitary and disgusting. Dogs may become housetrained in spite of such antics, but certainly not because of them.

When you come upon an accident, always keep calm. Put your dog out of sight so he cannot watch you clean up. Use white vinegar as a cleaner. Do not use any ammonia-based cleaners because the ammonia does not neutralize the odor and the puppy will be attracted to the same spot.

Accidents are just that — accidents. The worst thing you can do is call your dog to you to punish him. Your dog did not do it on purpose, and most dogs are just as horrified by what happened as you are.

Be ready for regressions

Regressions in housetraining will occur, especially during teething. Regressions after six months of age may be a sign that your dog is ill. If accidents persist, take him to your veterinarian for a checkup.

What to do if you catch Buddy in the act

If you catch your dog in the act, sharply call his name and clap your hands. If he stops, take him to his toilet area. If he doesn't, let him finish and don't get mad. Do not try to drag him out because that will make your clean-up job that much more difficult.

Until your puppy is reliable, letting him have the run of the house unsupervised is not a good idea.

Using an Exercise Pen for Housetraining

While a puppy can last in his crate for the night when he is asleep, you cannot leave a puppy for purposes of housetraining in his crate for longer than four hours at a time during the day. Your puppy will soil his crate, which is definitely not a habit you want to establish.

If your schedule is such that you cannot keep an eye on Buddy during the day or come home to let the puppy out in time, the alternative is an exercise pen. An X-pen is intelligent confinement and uses the same principle as a crate, except it is bigger and has no top (see Figure 10-2). An X-pen can also be used outdoors.

First, you need to acquire an X-pen commensurate to the size of your dog. For example, for a dog the size of a Labrador, the X-pen needs to be 10 square feet. Set up the X-pen where the puppy will be confined during your absence.

To get your dog comfortable in his X-pen, follow the same procedure as you would in introducing him to his crate. When Buddy is "at home" in the X-pen and you are ready to leave him for the day, cover one-third of the area with newspapers. Buddy will quickly understand what the paper is for. Cover one-third of the remaining area with a blanket, and leave one-third uncovered. The natural desire of your dog is to keep his sleeping area clean.

Buddy needs to have access to water during the day, so put his water dish on the uncovered area in the corner of the X-pen (some is bound to splash out and the uncovered floor is easy to clean). Before you leave, place a couple of toys on Buddy's blanket, put him into X-pen with a dog biscuit, and leave while he is occupied with the biscuit. Don't make a big deal out of leaving — simply leave.

Figure 10-2:
An exercise pen is an outdoor alternative to the crate.

Some people try to rig up confinement areas by blocking off parts of a room or basement or whatever. Theoretically this works, but it does permit Buddy to chew the baseboard, corners of cabinets, or anything else he can get his teeth on.

You will find that in the long run, your least expensive option, as is so often the case, is the right way from the start. Don't be penny-wise and pound-foolish by scrimping on the essentials at the risk of jeopardizing more expensive items. Splurging for an X-pen now will probably save you money later on your home improvement budget.

You may want to confine your dog to part of a room with baby gates. This option works well for some people and some dogs, but remember it's no holds barred for whatever items Buddy can access. Lots of chew toys are a must!

Leaving a dog on a concrete surface is not a good idea. There is something about concrete that impedes housetraining — many dogs don't seem to understand why it can't be used as a toilet area.

Managing Marking Behavior

Marking is a way for your dog to leave his calling card by depositing a small amount of urine in a particular spot, marking it as his territory. The frequency with which dogs can accomplish this never ceases to amaze us. Male dogs invariably prefer vertical surfaces, hence the fire hydrant. Males tend to engage in this behavior with more determination than females.

Behaviorists explain that marking is a dog's way of establishing his territory and provides a means to find his way back home. They also claim that dogs are able to tell the rank order, sex, and age — puppy or adult dog — by smelling the urine of another dog.

Those who take their dogs for regular walks through the neighborhood quickly discover that marking is a ritual, with favorite spots that have to be watered. It is a way for the dog to maintain his rank in the order of the pack, which consists of all the other dogs in the neighborhood or territory that come across his route.

Adult male dogs lift a leg, as do some females. For the male dog, the object is to leave his calling card higher than the previous calling card. This can lead to some comical results, as when a Dachshund or a Yorkshire Terrier tries to cover the calling card of an Irish Wolfhound or Great Dane. It is a contest.

Doing your doody

Being a good dog neighbor means not letting Buddy deface the property of others, and using only those areas specifically designed for that purpose. Even diehard dog lovers object to other dogs leaving their droppings on their lawn, the streets, and similar unsuitable areas. They also object to having their shrubbery or other vertical objects on their property doused by Buddy.

Part of responsible dog ownership is curbing and cleaning up after your dog. Don't let Buddy become the curse of your neighborhood. Do unto others as you would have them . . .

Be a responsible dog owner and clean up after your dog.

Annoying as this behavior can be, it is perfectly natural and normal. At times, it can also be embarrassing, such as when Buddy lifts his leg on a person's leg, a not-uncommon occurrence. What he is trying to communicate here we will leave to others to explain.

When this behavior is expressed inside the house, it becomes a problem. Fortunately, this is rare, but it does happen.

Here are the circumstances requiring special vigilance:

- Taking Buddy to a friend's or relative's house for a visit, especially if that individual also has a dog or a cat.
- When there is more than one animal in the house, another dog, or dogs, or a cat.
- When you have redecorated the house with new furniture and/or curtains.
- When you have moved to a new house.

Distract your dog if you see that he is about to mark in an inappropriate spot. Call his name, and take him to a place where he can eliminate.

When you take Buddy to someone else's home, keep an eye on him. At the slightest sign that he is even thinking about it, interrupt his thought by clapping your hands and calling him to you. Take him outside and wait until he has had a chance to relieve himself.

Should it happen in your house, and you catch Buddy in the act, you already know what to do. If it persists, you need to go back to basic housetraining principles, such as the crate or X-pen until you can trust him again.

Traveling by Car with Buddy

The same rules of housetraining apply when you're traveling with your dog. In the car, Buddy should be crated for his and your safety. If he is still a puppy, you should be prepared to stop about every two hours. An older dog can last much longer.

When we travel with one or more of our dogs, we make it a point to keep to their feeding schedule and exercising routine as closely as possible. Sticking to customary daily rhythm prevents digestive upsets that can lead to accidents.

Chapter 11

Walking and Heeling

I n grade school we learn the fundamentals. Tedious as the process may be, it is here that we acquire the skills we need to go through life. The lessons we learn now are never forgotten.

How important are they? How often do you hear coaches or mentors talk about execution of fundamentals? Master the basics and the rest will follow.

The same rules apply to the education of your dog. For the well-trained dog, the fundamentals are

✔ Walking on a loose leash

✔ Knowing how to heel with changes of direction and speed

✔ The sit-stay

✔ Down on command and stay

This chapter focuses on the first two fundamentals. For the other two, see Chapter 4.

Walking Your Dog

Taking your dog for a nice, long walk is balm for the soul and good exercise for both of you, provided he does not drag you down the street.

Learning to walk on leash calmly, at your side, will make both your strolls with Buddy and your trips to the veterinarian imminently more pleasant. Don't underestimate the importance of this basic aspect of training. (See Figure 11-1.)

Figure 11-1:
Appreciate
the
calmness of
walking
your dog.

Photo courtesy Mary Bloom

Even if you don't ordinarily take him for walks, the well-trained dog knows how to walk on a leash without pulling your arms out. For example, at least once a year you will have to take him to the veterinarian. If he has been trained to walk on leash, the visit will go much more smoothly than if he bounces off the end of the leash like a kangaroo.

Most of us want to be able to take our dog for a walk on leash and have him remain within the length of his leash without pulling. A leisurely stroll is an important daily routine, and for many dogs, the only opportunity to get some fresh air.

Although for most of us, the dog's pulling on the leash is our main concern, many dogs have to have a chance to become accustomed to the leash.

Leash training your dog

The majority of dogs readily accept the leash. Some, especially puppies, need a little time to get used to it.

Use his buckle collar and make sure it fits snugly so he can't slip out of it. Attach his six-foot leash to the collar and let him drag it around. You will need to supervise him so that he does not get tangled up. Once he ignores the leash, pick up the other end and follow him around. He will happily wander off wherever his fancy takes him.

You are now ready to show him where you want him to go. First use a treat to make him follow you and then gently guide him with the leash telling him what a good puppy he is. If you are teaching him outside, use the treat to coax him away from the house and the leash to guide him back towards the house. Before you know it, he will not only walk on the leash in your direction, but actually pull you along.

Teaching your dog not to pull

To teach Buddy not to pull, you need his training collar, his leash, and a few treats. Attach the leash to the live ring of the training collar.

Take him to an area without too many distractions, (you don't need other people and dogs, especially loose dogs, in the vicinity right now), and where you can walk in a straight line or a circle (about 30 feet in diameter).

Hold the leash in both hands and firmly plant them against your belt buckle, say "let's go," and start walking. Just before he gets to the end of the leash, say "easy," make an about-turn to your right and walk in the other direction. Be sure you keep your hands firmly planted.

This maneuver will produce a tug on his collar and turn him in the new direction. As he scampers to catch up with you, tell him what a clever boy he is and give him a treat.

Before you know it, he will be ahead of you again, and you will have to repeat the procedure. When you make your turn, do it with determination. Make your turn, and keep walking in the new direction. Don't look back and don't worry about Buddy; he will quickly catch up. Remember to praise and reward him when he does.

Make your turn deliberately and with determination. Be sure you keep your hands firmly planted against your belt buckle. When Buddy catches up — which he will — praise and reward him.

The first few times you try this, you will be a little late — Buddy is already leaning into his collar. Try it again. Concentrate on Buddy and learn to anticipate when you have to make the turn.

You will need to repeat this sequence several times over the course of a few training sessions until he understands that you don't want him to pull. Your goal is to teach him to walk within the perimeter of his leash without pulling.

Most dogs quickly learn to respect the leash, and, with an occasional reminder, they become a pleasure to take for a walk. Some, on the other hand, don't seem to get it. If your Buddy seems particularly dense about this simple concept, you may need a prong collar.

Remember, how readily your dog responds to his collar depends on

- How distracted he is by what is going on around him, including scents on the ground
- His size and weight in relation to your size and weight
- His touch sensitivity

The prong collar is an equalizer for these factors. It lets you enjoy training your dog without becoming frustrated or angry. Your dog, in turn, will thank you for maintaining a positive attitude and for praising him when he responds correctly.

Heeling On Leash

Heeling and walking on a loose leash are two different exercises. When Buddy is being walked for a bit of exercise, usually in order to do his business, he is on his own time. He can sniff, he can look around, or just aimlessly wander about, so long as he doesn't pull.

Heeling means walking close to the left side of the handler without swinging wide, lagging, forging, or crowding, either on a loose leash or off leash. Heeling means he has to walk at your left side, the traditional position, and pay strict attention to you. When your dog is heeling, he is now on your time. It is his responsibility to focus on you, and you have to teach him to accept that responsibility.

Here is what the previously listed "don'ts" mean:

- Swinging wide — leaving your left side
- Lagging — falling behind, not staying up with you
- Forging — getting ahead of you, not staying in heel position
- Crowding — so close to you as to interfere with your freedom of motion, bumping into you

Buddy has to learn to heel whether you make a right turn, left turn, do an about-face turn, run, or slow walk. The key to teaching heeling is to get Buddy to pay attention to you.

Heeling is used for walking your dog in traffic — when you need absolute control — and for competitive obedience events. The American Kennel Club definition of heeling is walking "close to the left side of the handler without swinging wide, lagging, forging or crowding," either on a loose leash or off leash.

Teaching your dog to sit at heel

Before teaching Buddy to heel with both of you walking, you are going to teach him what to do when you stop. This is called the automatic sit at heel.

Attach your leash to the live ring of your dog's training collar (see Chapter 3). Have him sit at your left side, both of you facing in the same direction, and put the leash over your left shoulder.

Say, "Buddy, heel." Take a step forward on your right foot, then a step with the left past the right, drop down your right knee, put your right hand against your dog's chest and fold him into a sit at heel position. Use the same technique described in Chapter 4, and avoid the temptation to push down on his rear end. Keep your hands in place as you tell him how clever he is.

Buddy already knows the sit command, but you are now showing him exactly where you want him to sit. Practice the sit at heel about five times or more until both of you feel comfortable with this maneuver.

Teaching heeling

Choose a location relatively free of distractions, preferably a confined area, such as your back yard.

Attach your leash to the live ring of your dog's training collar. Have him sit at your left side, both of you facing in the same direction, and put the leash over your shoulder. You need to allow about four inches of slack, so there is no tension on the leash when you start (see Figure 11-2).

Make a funnel with both hands around the leash. Keep both hands, about waist high, in front of your body. The object is not to touch the leash until necessary.

In a pleasant, upbeat tone of voice, say "Buddy, heel" and start to walk. Move out briskly, as though you are late for an appointment. Walk in a large clockwise circle, or in a straight line.

Figure 11-2:
Preparing
for heeling
on leash.

To teach your dog to heel, put the leash over your left shoulder and make a funnel with your hands around the leash. When your dog leaves your left side, close your hands around the leash and bring back to heel position.

As soon as both of you are in motion, you will notice that Buddy is forging, that is, he is getting ahead of you. Close your hands on the leash and firmly bring him back to your left side. Work on keeping his shoulder in line with your left hip. Anytime he gets out of position, bring him back and then tell him how clever he is.

When heeling your dog, walk briskly and with determination, as though you are trying to catch the next train home. The more energy you put into your pace, the easier it is to keep your dog's attention focused on you. If you dawdle, so will your dog.

After about ten steps, stop and place him into a sit at heel, and verbally praise him. It will take you a few tries to get the hang of it. At first, you will be a little slow on the uptake. Buddy will have joyfully bounded ahead of you, the leash has fallen off your shoulder, and you are scrambling to get it back. Just start over and work on anticipating what your dog is going to do.

By paying attention to your dog, you will learn when you need to bring him back to heel. If you can see his tail, you have waited too long.

Your initial goal is to be able to heel Buddy for ten paces without having to touch the leash. How long it will take you depends on

- ✔ Your dog
- ✔ What your dog was bred to do
- ✔ His response to the training collar
- ✔ Your attitude

Generally, if you have a Shetland Sheepdog, you will reach that goal in maybe five minutes; if you have a Wirehaired Fox Terrier, you will be out there considerably longer.

When Buddy will heel without you having to touch the leash for ten paces, gradually increase the number of steps before a halt. Bring him back to heel whenever necessary, then praise him. After about five training sessions, he should be getting the idea, at least in an area relatively free from distractions.

Changing direction

After you and your dog have pretty much gotten the hang of heeling, your next step is to introduce your dog to changes of direction while heeling. In this section, you find out about the three essential turns — a right turn, an about-turn to the right, and a left turn.

Turning right

To stay with you when you are making a right turn, Buddy needs to speed up. And, at this stage in your training, Buddy is not yet giving you 100 percent of his attention, and you are going to anticipate that he needs help with the right turn.

If you want your dog to pay attention to you, you have to pay attention to your dog. Learning to anticipate what he is going to do is the first step to successful heeling.

Just before you make the turn, enthusiastically say his name, make the turn, and keep moving. Using his name will cause him to look up at you and he will notice that you are changing direction, which will cause him to stay with you. Without giving him that cue, chances are that as you make the turn and go one way, he will keep going the other way.

About-turn

An about-turn is a right turn times two. When you make your turn, keep your feet together so Buddy can keep up. As you did for the right turn, use his name just before you make the turn to encourage him to stay with you.

In the event Buddy has a particularly difficult time remaining at your side for the right or about-turn, you can use a treat or other object of interest to him to help guide him around. The treat is held in your right hand as you are heeling. Before you make the turn, show it to your dog by bringing the treat directly in front of his nose and using it to guide him around the turn, then give him the treat.

This approach has a potential drawback. Some dogs become overly stimulated when they know you have a treat in your hand. Make no mistake about it, Buddy knows. If you see that your dog becomes difficult to control under such circumstances, you may want to eliminate use of the treat. The hassle is not worth the potential benefit.

Turning left

In order to make the left turn without crowding, Buddy needs to slow down as you make the turn and then resume normal speed after you made the turn. Just before you make the turn, slow down and with your left hand draw back on the leash, make the turn, and resume your normal brisk pace.

Practice heeling and the turns for a few minutes at a time as a regular part of your daily outings.

Changing pace

Next you are going to teach your dog to change pace with you while heeling. He has to learn that whether you walk slowly or quickly, he has to stay in heel position.

For the slow pace, cut the speed of your pace in half but maintain the same length of stride. As you go into the slow pace, draw back on the leash to keep your dog in heel position.

For the fast pace, double the speed of your pace, again keeping the length of your stride the same. Just before you go into a fast pace, use your dog's name in an excited tone of voice to encourage him to stay with you.

You are still working with the leash over your shoulder. By now you should also be able to tell whether Buddy is actually *heeling. Heeling* means that your dog stays with you as you change direction or pace. If heeling properly, Buddy does not swing wide on right and about-turns, crowd you on the left turn, lag behind you as you go into a fast pace, or forge ahead of you as you go into a slow pace.

Doing Down at Heel

The object of this exercise is to have Buddy lie down at heel on command. Command here means voice command, and pointing at the ground does not count. There are several sequences for accomplishing this goal, and you will be able to run through the first three quite quickly.

1. Down with pressure on the collar.

With Buddy sitting at heel position, attach the leash to the dead ring of the collar. Neatly fold the major portion of the leash into your left hand. Put two fingers of your left hand, palm facing you, through the collar, back to front. Say "down," and with a little downward pressure guide your dog into the down position. Verbally praise him, count to ten, and release with "OK." As he already knows the word, he should readily respond. Keep your elbow stiff and apply pressure straight down so that your dog lies down facing straight ahead, not curled in front of you.

Practice several times, each time with a little pressure.

2. Down with signal.

The down signal is given by bringing your right arm straight up, palm facing the dog. It is the same signal students use to get a teacher's attention (see Figure 11-3).

Figure 11-3:
The down
signal.

With Buddy sitting at heel position, attach the leash to the dead ring of the collar (see Chapter 3). Neatly fold the major portion of the leash into your left hand. Say and signal "stay," and step directly in front of your dog. Kneel down on your left knee or both knees, if your prefer. Put two fingers of the left hand, palm facing down, through your dog's collar, under his chin.

Say and signal "down" and at the same time push against his chest with your left hand and then apply downward pressure on the collar. Keep the signal up until he lies down. Then praise, count to ten, and release him.

Practice this three times in succession and over the period of several training sessions. Your goal is to have your dog respond to the command/signal without having to apply any downward pressure on the collar.

3. **With Buddy sitting at heel position, attach the leash to the live ring of the collar. Neatly fold the leash into your right hand, the part that goes to the dog coming out at the bottom of your hand, and take the end closest to your dog in your left hand, palm facing you.**

Say "down." If Buddy responds, praise, count to ten, and release. If he does not, slowly slide your left hand down the leash, all the way to the snap, and *check* straight down. Praise, wait, and release. Keep you body upright and resist the urge to point — remember, it is the down on command and not the down on point. This is the *review progression* for this exercise.

Repeat until your dog lies down on command without you having to check.

Once you have reached that point, you are ready to combine the command and signal as the dog is coming toward you.

4. **With Buddy sitting at heel position, attach the leash to the live ring of the collar. Say and signal "stay" and go to the end of the leash, turn and face your dog. Call with "Buddy, come" and just as he starts in motion, say "down," at the time you are giving the signal and stepping toward your dog on the right leg, keeping the left leg in place.**

As soon as he responds, lower your right arm and bring back the right leg. Praise, count to ten, go to your dog's right side, and release him straight-forward. If he does not respond, review the down at heel with *check*.

The purpose of the step toward your dog is to get him to stop his forward momentum so he can lie down.

When your dog responds to the down command reliably from 6 feet in front on leash, you can take the leash off. Start making a game of this exercise. Have a treat in your signal hand, show it to him and say/signal "down." Keep your hand up. You may have to wait a second or two before he responds. As soon as he does, give him the treat and then release him. Two or three repetitions of this exercise is enough for one training session.

Making a game of the down on command is a good way to maintain your dog's enthusiasm and motivation. If he is not terribly interested, use his favorite toy or a stick. Keep it fun and interesting by doing only two or three repetitions in a row.

Be sure he is in the down position when you give him the treat — you want to reward the lying down. Do not give him a treat if he gets up before that — you don't want to reward the getting up.

Your dog is still within 6 feet of you, and you are still using the step toward your dog together with the signal. Once he has made the association between the signal and the down, begin to reward him on a random basis.

You can also start to increase the distance between you and your dog, but keep using the step and the signal. Make sure he lies down in place, without coming toward you. If you see this happening, decrease the distance between you.

Chapter 12

Retrieving

Most of us are not too thrilled about having Buddy lug our possessions about. We would prefer he limited his retrieving instincts to his own things.

Many dogs like to retrieve, or at least chase, a variety of objects. For them, it is a self-rewarding activity. They do it because they enjoy it. Some of them actually bring back the ball, Frisbee, or stick so you can throw it again.

They will continue so long as it's fun. When it's no longer fun, they stop. They will also retrieve only articles they like. For example, your dog may happily retrieve a ball, but turn up his nose when you want him to pick up a glove.

The well-trained dog has been taught to retrieve and has learned to do it for you and not just himself. Of course, he can have fun in the process, so long as he understands that it's not a matter of choice.

Steps to Successful Retrieving

As a part of learning how to retrieve on command, your dog learns to take, as well as to give, an equally important lesson. If it hasn't happened to you already, it will. Buddy has picked up something he thinks is edible, but which you don't think is a suitable dietary supplement. Having taught him to retrieve, you will be able to convince him to give it up.

There is another practical side to teaching your dog to retrieve. One of our students wanted her Golden Retriever, Sunny, to bring in the morning paper, preferably in readable condition. So we first had her teach Sunny the formal retrieve. We then told her go out with Sunny, have him pick up the paper, bring it in the house and reward him with a dog biscuit.

It only took Sunny two repetitions until he figured it out and from then on, every morning he dutifully brought in the paper. After several days we got a frantic phone call. It seems that Sunny was somewhat of an entrepreneur. In an effort to garner more biscuits he started retrieving the neighbors' papers as well. Fortunately, that problem was easily fixed — a biscuit only for the first paper. When he realized that, he stopped bringing home other papers.

The retrieve sounds simple, but it consists of many separate behaviors, some or all of which have to be learned by the dog:

✔ Going to the object

✔ Picking it up

✔ Holding it

✔ Walking with and carrying the object

✔ Bringing it back

✔ Giving it up

For the dog that already retrieves on his own, teaching him to do it on command will be a cinch. For those who don't, you need to have a little more patience. Your dog's ability to learn to retrieve will depend on what your dog was bred to do and how many prey drive behaviors he has.

The object we use for the formal retrieve is a wooden dumbbell. These are available at your local pet store or through catalogs. You need to get one that is commensurate to the size of your dog and the shape of his mouth. The bells should be big enough so he can pick it up off the ground without scraping his chin, and the diameter of the bar thick enough so he can comfortably carry it. The length of the bar should be such that the bells just touch the side of his face.

Dumbbells can also be made of plastic, and these last a lot longer than wooden ones. They are terrific once the dog has learned how to retrieve. In the teaching process, however, we have found that dogs take more readily to wooden dumbbells than to plastic ones.

To get started, you need the following equipment:

✔ Enthusiastic handler

✔ Hungry dog

✔ Small can of cat food

  ✔ Metal spoon

  ✔ Wooden dumbbell

  ✔ Chair

 Cat food seems to be irresistible to dogs and works well as a reward. Because many dogs are not fond of retrieving metal objects, we use a metal spoon to get them used to the feel of metal. We also let Buddy lick out and play with the empty can.

Retrieving on command

Although many dogs retrieve a variety of objects on their own, they will not necessarily do so on command. To teach them to retrieve on command we begin by creating an association with the command and what we want the dog to do — take an object in his mouth. The one object few dogs can resist is food, so that is how we start.

The ideal time to start teaching Buddy to retrieve is when he is hungry, before he is fed. Place the food, spoon, and dumbbell on a chair. With Buddy sitting at your left side, face the chair. Put a small portion of food on the spoon and offer it to him with the command "Take it!" Give the command in an excited and enthusiastic tone of voice to elicit prey drive behavior. (Check out Chapter 2 for info on the basic drive behaviors.) Repeat this exercise ten times or until Buddy readily opens his mouth to get the food. Few dogs can resist this treat.

Introducing the object of retrieve

Once Buddy has an inkling of what the command "Take it" means, you're ready to introduce him to his dumbbell. But going from food to a dumbbell is quite a transition, so you need to be patient with him.

 When you're teaching Buddy any of the behaviors associated with retrieving, your body posture is important. You want to be at his right side without hovering or leaning over him because that posture would put him into defense drive when you want him in prey drive. (Chapter 2 has the details on the various drives.)

You now also need bite-sized treats, such as liver treats, hot dogs cut into ¼-inch squares, or some kibble. Our dogs like raisins, which are the ideal size for treats. You may need to experiment with different treats until you find one Buddy really likes. Put a dozen treats on the chair, and you're ready to start.

With Buddy sitting at your left side, again facing the chair, put your left palm lightly on top of his muzzle and place your left index finger behind his left canine tooth. Gently open his mouth and with your right hand place the dumbbell in his mouth with the command "Take it." Rest the thumb of your right hand on top of his muzzle, fingers under his chin, and cup his mouth shut. Praise enthusiastically, immediately say, "Give," and take the dumbbell out of his mouth. Reward with food. Repeat ten times each for five sessions.

When we teach one of our dogs to retrieve, we practice this exercise once a day on consecutive days. If you're the ambitious type, you can practice more frequently, as long as your dog remains interested.

What's not a good idea is to practice sporadically because your dog will forget what he has learned during the last session and you basically have to start all over.

Hold the dumbbell by the bell so you can easily put the bar in his mouth (see Figure 12-1). After one second, take it out with "Give."

The goal of this progression is for your dog to accept the dumbbell in his mouth without any resistance. It is only an introduction and you don't want to close his mouth over the dumbbell for longer than one second. When Buddy readily accepts the dumbbell consistently, you can go on to the next sequence.

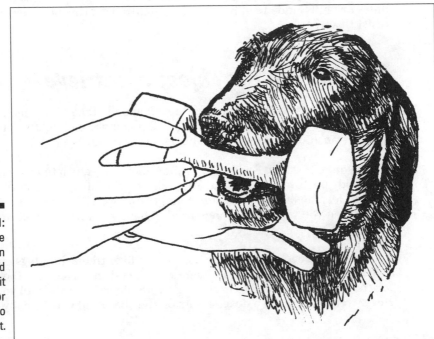

Figure 12-1:
Holding the dumbbell on its end makes it easier for your dog to take it.

Helping your dog retrieve

After Buddy has become accustomed to having the dumbbell in his mouth, you're ready to tackle the next step. The goal is for Buddy to take the dumbbell voluntarily in his mouth when you give the command.

Have Buddy sit at your left side, have the chair with treats in place, and put two fingers of your left hand through his collar, back to front, palm facing you, at the side of his neck. With your right hand, place the bar of the dumbbell directly in front of his mouth, touching the small whiskers. Say, "Take it," and when he takes it, briefly cup his mouth shut and tell him how clever he is. Say, "Give," take out the dumbbell, and reward with food.

At this point in the training, your dog may not yet take the dumbbell on his own but will open his mouth. In that case, just put the dumbbell in, cup his mouth shut, and so on (see Figure 12-2).

If he sits there like a bump on a log, watch for signs of intention behavior. Intention behaviors are those actions that tell you what the dog's intentions are. They range from the extremely subtle, such as bringing the whiskers forward as a play invitation to another dog, to the overt, such as sniffing the ground in a circular motion when the puppy is about to eliminate.

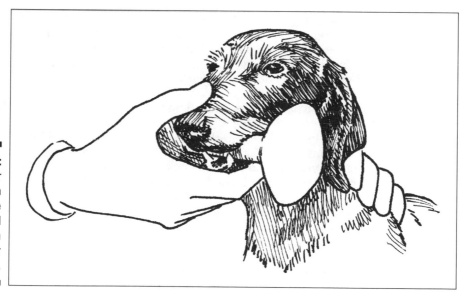

Figure 12-2: Closing your dog's mouth around the dumbbell will help him grasp your intent.

Intention behaviors indicating that he is thinking about taking the dumbbell in his mouth are

- ✔ Licking.
- ✔ Nosing the dumbbell.
- ✔ Intensely staring at it.

When you see intention behavior, take your hand out of the collar, open his mouth, put the dumbbell in, and briefly cup his mouth shut. Praise, remove the dumbbell from his mouth, and reward with food. Repeat until Buddy readily opens his mouth and accepts the dumbbell. It is important that you praise while he has the dumbbell in his mouth. (For more information about intention behavior, see Chapter 2.)

Be patient. Sometimes it can take several minutes before the dog makes a move. If absolutely nothing happens and the little wheels have come to a grinding halt, review the preceding step five times and then try again. Some dogs appear to be particularly dense about taking the dumbbell voluntarily on command, but with enough repetitions, they'll get it.

Learning to hold on

Before you can go any further with the retrieve part of this exercise, you need to teach Buddy what you want him to *do* with the dumbbell after he has it in his mouth. You want him to hold the dumbbell in his mouth and not spit it out before you give the "Give" command. You may think this concept is obvious, but it's not to Buddy until you've taught it to him.

Your goal is to have Buddy firmly hold the dumbbell until you say "Give."

Start in the usual position, with Buddy at your left side and the treats on the chair. Put the dumbbell into his mouth and say "Hold it." Keep the upper part of your body straight so you don't hover or lean over him. Make a fist with your right hand and hold it under his chin. Smile and count to five. Praise, remove the dumbbell, and reward him with food. Repeat 20 times, increasing gradually the time you have him hold the dumbbell in 5-second increments up to 30 seconds.

If Buddy starts rolling the dumbbell around in his mouth or looks as though he will open his mouth to spit out the dumbbell, give him a gentle chuck under the chin with "Hold it." Then remove the dumbbell with "Give," praise, and reward.

Learning to reach for the retrieve

Once Buddy understands that he has to hold the dumbbell, the next sequence is to teach him to reach for it. With two fingers of your left hand through his collar at the side of his neck, back to front, palm facing you, hold his dumbbell 2 inches in front of his mouth. Say, "Take it." If he does, cup his mouth shut with "Hold it," count to five, praise, remove dumbbell with "Give," and reward with food.

If he does not take the dumbbell, lightly twist his collar by rotating your left hand a quarter of a turn towards you, which will bring his head forward and toward the dumbbell, until he reaches for and takes it. Cup his mouth shut with "Hold it," count to five, praise, remove dumbbell with "Give," and reward with food.

Do not twist his collar for more than 30 seconds or try to increase pressure more than a quarter of a turn. Instead, put the dumbbell in his mouth, cup shut with "Hold it," praise, remove, and reward. Repeat until your dog voluntarily reaches for and takes the dumbbell.

If your dog shows signs of noticeable stress during this sequence, the following will happen:

- If he is a negative stresser, he will clamp his mouth shut and turn inward when you apply pressure on the collar. Pressure on the collar will not make him open his mouth. Stop, put the dumbbell in his mouth, praise, reward, and try again.
- If he stresses positively, he will try different behaviors, one of which will be to grab the dumbbell, at which point you praise and reward.

Increase the distance Buddy has to reach for the dumbbell in 2-inch increments to arm's length. After that, make a game of it by having him chase the dumbbell while you turn in place to your right. Remember to reward him every time he takes the dumbbell.

Walking after retrieving

The next step in the retrieve progressions is teaching Buddy to hold onto the dumbbell while walking with it in his mouth (see Figure 12-3). Okay, you're probably saying to yourself, "For Pete's sake, is all this really necessary?" The answer? It depends on the dog. At this point in the training, the majority of dogs understand the concept and are perfectly able to hold the dumbbell in their mouths and walk at the same time. If your dog will do it, you can skip this step. Still, we've seen dogs, including some of our own, that couldn't make this transition and had to be taught. So when we devised this approach to teaching retrieving, we included the walking-while-holding sequence just to make sure that all eventualities were covered.

Figure 12-3:
Retrieving
the
dumbbell.

With Buddy sitting at your left side, facing the chair with the treats on it from about 6 feet away, put the dumbbell in his mouth with "Take it," followed by "Hold it." Encourage him to walk toward the chair. To give Buddy confidence, put your right hand under his chin when he starts to move. When he gets to the chair, praise, remove the dumbbell, and reward him. Repeat until Buddy walks with the dumbbell without you holding your hand under his chin. Then gradually increase the distance to 20 steps in 5-step increments.

Teaching the pick-up

You and Buddy have arrived at the final progression of teaching him to retrieve — the pick-up. Resist the temptation to just throw the dumbbell and expect Buddy to pick it up and bring it back. He may actually do it, but he also may not. He may just chase it and then stand over it, not knowing what to do next. In the long run, it's better to make sure that he knows what you expect by teaching him.

Have Buddy sitting at your left side and place the chair with the treats on it behind you. With your fingers in his collar, hold the dumbbell about 2 inches from Buddy's mouth and say "Take it." When he does, praise enthusiastically, say "Give," remove the dumbbell from his mouth, and reward him with a treat. Your goal is to lower the dumbbell in 2-inch increments toward the ground and have Buddy retrieve it from your hand.

When you get to the ground, place the bell of the dumbbell on the ground and hold it at a 45-degree angle. Say, "Take it," and when Buddy takes the dumbbell, take your hand out of the collar, say, "Hold it," and back up two steps. He will quickly come to you to get his reward. Praise, remove, and reward. Repeat until he is comfortable picking up the dumbbell with you holding it at that angle.

Next, place the dumbbell on the ground but keep your hand on it. Have Buddy retrieve the dumbbell several times while you have your hand on it. Then hold your hand first 2 inches, then 6 inches, and then 12 inches away from the dumbbell until you can place it on the ground and stand up straight.

Each time he retrieves the dumbbell, back up several steps, praise, remove, and reward.

If your dog does not pick up the dumbbell from the ground, lightly twist the collar until he picks it up. Should this sequence become an issue and your dog continues to refuse to take the dumbbell, review the prior progressions. Make sure that you followed them religiously and that your dog has mastered each progression before you went on to the next.

Finally, say, "Stay," and place the dumbbell one foot in front of your dog. Say, "Take it," and when he brings it back, praise, remove and reward. Repeat by first placing it 3 feet and then 6 feet in front of your dog.

Your dog will tell you how many times in a row you can ask him to retrieve. If he has many prey drive behaviors, you can get in quite a few repetitions. If not, he will quickly lose enthusiasm and you are better off stopping after five repetitions and picking the game up again at the next session.

Remember also that for the dog, picking up a dumbbell that you have placed on the ground is not terribly exciting, and if it weren't for the reward, it would be an absolute bore. Still, it is a necessary sequence because you want your dog to learn he has to do it for you and not for himself.

Chasing to retrieve

Now comes the fun part, where you get to throw the dumbbell and Buddy gets to chase it. Throw the dumbbell a few feet and at the same time send your dog with "Take it." As soon as he picks up, tell him how terrific he is. When he gets back to you, take the dumbbell with "Give" and reward him with a treat.

Sometimes dogs get carried away by the fun of it all and don't come right back with the dumbbell. They might make a detour, or just run around for the joy of it. Should that happen, say, "Come," as soon as he picks up the dumbbell, and praise and reward him when he gets back to you.

Gradually increase the distance the dumbbell is thrown. As he gains confidence, introduce the sit in front with "Hold it." When he gets back to you say "Sit" and "Hold it." Since he has not done this before, you may have to hold your hand under his chin to prevent him from dropping the dumbbell. Praise, remove, and reward. From now on make him sit and hold the dumbbell every time he gets back to you.

Testing your dog's patience

Buddy also has to learn to stay while you throw the dumbbell and until he is permitted to get it. Making him wait will get him all the more excited about getting to his dumbbell.

Start with Buddy at your left side. Put two fingers of your left hand through his collar, say, "Stay," and throw the dumbbell about 15 feet. Very, very gingerly let go of his collar, count to five and say, "Take it." When he returns, praise, remove, and reward. Repeat until your dog holds the stay without having to hold him by the collar.

Remember to give the command in an excited and enthusiastic tone of voice to put the dog into prey drive. Never use a harsh or threatening tone of voice as that will put the dog in the wrong drive and make it more difficult for him to learn.

If at anytime your dog needs motivation, throw the dumbbell at the same time saying, "Take it," letting him chase after it.

Congratulations. You now have a dog that retrieves on command — at least a dumbbell. To play the game of fetch, however, most of us probably use a Frisbee, a ball, or a stick. Few dogs have any difficulty making the transition from the dumbbell to one of these objects. Usually, it's the other way around. The dog will happily retrieve a ball but will turn his nose up at the dumbbell.

You can also use the Retrieve command to have Buddy bring in the newspaper, carry his leash, and — size permitting — carry your handbag. We taught one of our dogs to open the refrigerator door and retrieve a can of beer. Unfortunately, we were unable to teach the dog to close the fridge door and had to abandon that trick.

Retrieving with Distractions

Once Buddy knows how to retrieve, he is ready for distraction training. During distraction training, you see the following responses, or variations thereof:

✔ He starts going toward the dumbbell but then backs off and fails to retrieve, meaning, "I don't have the confidence to get close enough to the distracter to retrieve my dumbbell."

Remedy: Without saying anything, slowly approach him, put two fingers of your left hand through the collar, back to front, palm facing you, at the side of his neck and take him to the dumbbell. If he picks up the dumbbell, praise, remove dumbbell and reward; if he does not, put the dumbbell in his mouth, then praise, remove, and reward. The command is not repeated.

Try again. Remember your dog's learning style and how many repetitions it takes before he understands. You may find that you have to help him several times before he has the confidence that he can do it by himself. Once he has done it on his own, stop for that session!

✔ He leaves altogether and does not retrieve, saying, in effect, "I can't cope with this."

Remedy: Same.

✔ He does nothing, meaning, "If I don't do anything, maybe all of this will go away."

Remedy: Same.

✔ He permits himself to be distracted, meaning, "I would rather visit than retrieve my dumbbell."

Remedy: Same.

✔ He takes the dumbbell to the distracter.

Remedy: Slowly approach your dog without saying anything, put the leash on the dead ring of the training collar and, with a little tension on the collar, show him exactly what he was supposed to do by guiding him to you. No extra command is given.

✔ He anticipates the retrieve, meaning he is catching on and wants to show you how clever he is.

Remedy: Without saying anything, slowly approach him, take the dumbbell out of his mouth, put it down where he picked it up, go back to the starting point and then send him. Whatever you do, don't shout "no," or do anything else that would discourage him from retrieving after you have just worked so hard to get him to pick up the dumbbell.

✔ He does it correctly and that is when you stop for that session.

Introduce your dog to distractions as follows: the distracter stands about two feet from the dumbbell. He assumes a friendly posture, not threatening to the dog. Send him and as soon as he picks up the dumbbell, enthusiastically praise. Look at the exercise as having been completed as soon as your dog picked up his dumbbell.

As he gains confidence, the distracter stands a little closer, and then over the dumbbell.

The distracter also hides the dumbbell by standing directly in front of it with his back to the dog, and then lightly puts his foot on it. You can use a chair as a distraction by putting the dumbbell under the chair and then on the chair.

Continue to use food rewards for Buddy on a random basis, that is, not every time, and not in a predictable pattern but often enough to maintain his motivation.

When your dog confidently retrieves under these circumstances, introduce the next level of distractions. The distracter crouches close to the dumbbell and tries to distract him by saying "here puppy, come visit for some petting." The distracter does not use your dog's name.

Once he has successfully worked his way through that level, favorite object distractions are added, such as offering the dog food or a ball or toy. Of course, the distracter never lets the dog have the food.

Distractions add an extra dimension and take training to a higher level. Distraction training builds your dog's confidence and teaches him to concentrate on what he is doing. This type of training is especially important for the shy dog, providing the confidence he needs to respond correctly under different conditions.

During distraction training, keep in mind that anytime you change the complexity of the exercise, it becomes a new exercise for the dog. If Buddy goes for the food, you would treat his response the same way you did when you first introduced him to distraction training. No, your dog is not defiant, stubborn, or stupid, just confused as to what he should do and has to be helped again.

You are now ready to work with different objects. When you do, you may have to review the first few sequences. Just because Buddy retrieves one object does not necessarily mean he will retrieve others. He may need to get used to them first.

By challenging Buddy to use his head, you can increase the strength of his responses and increase his confidence in his ability to perform under almost all conditions.

When using distraction training, it is also important to give Buddy a chance to work it out for himself. Don't be too quick to try and help him. Be patient, and let him try to figure out on his own how to do it correctly. Once he does, you will be pleasantly surprised by the intensity and reliability with which he responds.

Chapter 13

Your Dog's Citizenship Test

To demonstrate that Buddy has achieved the training level that you want for him, you may want to consider taking the Canine Good Citizen test. Many dog organizations offer it, and your local kennel club should know the particulars. You should be able to locate the kennel club in the Yellow Pages of your telephone directory, or you can ask your veterinarian, a dog groomer, or any obedience school.

The Canine Good Citizen uses a series of exercises that test the dog's ability to behave in an acceptable manner in public. Its purpose is to demonstrate that the dog, as a companion for all people, can be a respected member of the community and can be trained and conditioned to always behave in the home, in public places, and in the presence of other dogs in a manner that reflects credit on the dog.

The test is unique in that it is the only American Kennel Club-sponsored activity that includes mixed-breed dogs. The concept of a Canine Good Citizen is based on the premise that all dogs should be trained. It was also designed as an outreach program — to motivate dog owners and encourage them to go further in training their dogs.

Becoming a Canine Good Citizen

You and your dog should consider joining the ranks of those who have obtained their Canine Good Citizen certificates. Ideally, every dog should be trained to become a Canine Good Citizen and the more that are, the better the chances of counteracting the growing anti-dog sentiment in many communities. Irresponsible dog ownership has been the cause for this sentiment and only responsible pet ownership can reverse it. Demonstrate that your dog is a well-trained personal companion and a member in good standing with the community by training him to become a Canine Good Citizen.

A Canine Good Citizen is a dog that is well behaved around people and other dogs, at home and in public. It is the kind of dog that is a pleasure to own, one that is safe with children and one that you would welcome as a neighbor. It is a dog that is a nuisance to no one. To become a Canine Good Citizen your dog must demonstrate, by means of a short test, that he or she meets these requirements.

Exercise requirements of the Canine Good Citizen test

The Canine Good Citizen uses a series of exercises that test the dog's ability to behave in an acceptable manner in public. The examination consists of the following ten tests, all of which are scored on a pass/fail system:

- ✔ Accepting a friendly stranger
- ✔ Sitting politely for petting
- ✔ Appearance and grooming
- ✔ Walking on a loose leash
- ✔ Walking through a crowd
- ✔ Sit, down, and staying in place
- ✔ Coming when called
- ✔ Reaction to another dog
- ✔ Reaction to distractions
- ✔ Supervised separation

These are practical tests that determine the amount of control you have over your dog and the dog's ability to behave appropriately in public. The evaluators, in addition to deciding the dog's ability to pass these exercises, are asked to consider whether this is the kind of dog that

- ✔ He or she would like to own.
- ✔ Would be safe with children.
- ✔ He or she would welcome as a neighbor.
- ✔ Makes its owner happy and isn't making someone else unhappy.

We discuss each test briefly in the following sections, including what to expect during the test.

Test 1: Accepting a friendly stranger

This test demonstrates that the dog will allow a friendly stranger to approach and speak to the handler in a natural, everyday situation (see Figure 13-1).

The evaluator approaches the dog and handler and greets the handler in a friendly manner, ignoring the dog. The evaluator and handler shake hands and exchange pleasantries. The dog must show no sign of resentment or shyness and must not break position or try to go to the evaluator.

Test 2: Sitting politely for petting

This test demonstrates that the dog will allow a friendly stranger to touch him while he is out with the owner/handler (see Figure 13-2). With the dog sitting at the handler's side (either side is permissible) throughout the exercise, the evaluator pets the dog on the head and body only.

The handler may talk to the dog throughout the exercise.

After petting, the evaluator then circles the dog and handler, completing the test. The dog must not show shyness or resentment.

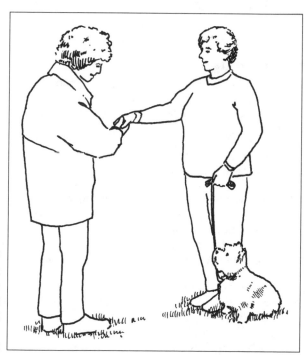

Figure 13-1: Your dog should let you meet and greet.

Figure 13-2:
Your dog should also accept those who want to meet and greet him.

Test 3: Appearance and grooming

This test demonstrates that the dog welcomes being groomed and examined and will permit a stranger, such as a veterinarian, groomer, or friend of the owner, to do so. It also demonstrates the owner's care, concern, and responsibility.

For the appearance and grooming test, make sure Buddy looks his best. If he needs a bath before the test, give him one.

The evaluator inspects the dog to determine if it is clean and groomed. The dog must appear to be in healthy condition (that is, proper weight, clean, healthy, and alert). The handler should supply the comb or brush commonly used on the dog. The evaluator then easily combs or brushes the dog and, in a natural manner, lightly examines the ears and gently picks up each front foot.

It is not necessary for the dog to hold a specific position during the examination, and the handler may talk to the dog, praise, and give encouragement throughout.

Test 4: Out for a walk — walking on a loose leash

Demonstrates that the handler is in control of the dog. The dog may be on either side of the handler, whichever the handler prefers. (*Note:* The left-side position is required in AKC obedience competition and all activities where the dog is in service to the handler, such as guiding the blind.)

The dog's position should leave no doubt that the dog is attentive to the handler and is responding to the handler's movements and changes of direction. The dog need not be perfectly aligned with the handler and need not sit when the handler stops.

For this test, the dog need not "march in formation" with the handler, but the dog should be attentive and clearly responding to the handler's movements.

The evaluator may use a pre-plotted course or may direct the handler/dog team by issuing instructions or commands. In either case, there must be a left turn, right turn, and about-turn, with at least one stop in between and another at the end. The handler may talk to the dog along the way to praise or command it in a normal tone of voice. The handler may also sit the dog at the halt, if desired.

Test 5: Walking through a crowd

This test demonstrates that the dog can move about politely in pedestrian traffic and is under control in public places. The test is a great incentive to train Buddy with distractions.

The dog and handler walk around and pass close to several people (at least three). The dog may show some interest in the strangers but should continue to walk with the handler, without evidence of over-exuberance, shyness, or resentment. The handler may talk to the dog and encourage or praise the dog throughout the test. The dog should not be straining at the leash.

Note: Children may act as members of the crowd in this test, as well as in the reaction to distractions test, discussed later in this chapter. However, whenever children participate in a test they must be instructed on their role and be supervised. It is also permissible to have one dog in a crowd but the dog must be on lead and well mannered.

Test 6: Sit and down on command — staying in place

This test demonstrates that the dog has training, will respond to the handler's commands to "sit" and "down," and will remain in the place commanded by the handler (sit or down position, whichever the handler prefers).

Prior to this test, the dog's leash is replaced with a 20-foot line. The handler may take a reasonable amount of time and use more than one command to make the dog sit and then down. The evaluator must determine if the dog has responded to the handler's commands. The handler may not force the dog into either position but may touch the dog to offer gentle guidance.

When instructed by the evaluator, the handler tells the dog to "stay" and, with the 20-foot line in hand, walks forward the length of the line, turns and returns to the dog at a natural pace (the 20-foot line is not removed or dropped). The dog must remain in the place in which he was left (the dog may change position), until the evaluator instructs the handler to release the dog. The dog may be released from the front or the side.

Test 7: Coming when called

This test demonstrates that the dog will come when called by the handler. For the test, the dog is on a 20-foot leash. If you have already trained Buddy to come when called off leash, he should not have any difficulty passing this test.

For this test, the dog remains on the 20-foot line that was used in the sit and down on command. The handler walks ten feet from the dog, turns to face the dog, and calls the dog. The handler may use body language and encouragement when calling the dog and may tell the dog to "stay" or "wait" or just walk away. The dog may be left in the sit, down, or standing position. If the dog attempts to follow the handler, the evaluator may distract the dog (for example, by petting) until the handler is 10 feet away.

The point of the test is to determine whether the dog comes when called and whether it stays, and the exercise is completed when the dog comes to the handler and the handler attaches the dog's own leash.

Test 8: Reaction to another dog

This test demonstrates that the dog can behave politely around other dogs.

Two handlers and their dogs approach each other from a distance of about 10 yards, stop, shake hands and exchange pleasantries, and continue on for about 5 yards.

The dogs should show no more than casual interest in each other. Neither dog should go to the other dog or its handler.

Test 9: Reaction to distractions

This test demonstrates that the dog is confident at all times when faced with common distracting situations.

The evaluator selects only two from the following list. (***Note:*** Because some dogs are sensitive to sound and others to visual distractions, most tests involve one sound and one visual distraction.)

- A person using crutches, a wheelchair, or a walker. This distraction simulates a disabled person who requires the use of service equipment.
- A sudden closing or opening of a door.
- Dropping a large book, pan, folded chair, or the like, no closer than 5 feet behind the dog.
- A jogger running in front of the dog.
- A person pushing a shopping cart or pulling a crate dolly passing 5 to 10 feet away.
- A person on a bicycle passing at least 10 feet away.

The handler may talk to the dog and praise him during the reaction to distractions test. In a similar situation in real life, you probably would talk in an encouraging way to your dog.

During the reaction to distractions test, the dog may express a natural interest and curiosity and may appear slightly startled but should not panic, try to run away, show aggressiveness, or bark. The handler may talk to the dog and encourage or praise it throughout the exercise.

Test 10: Supervised separation

This test demonstrates that the dog can be left with another person and maintain its training and good manners while the owner goes out of sight. Evaluators will say something like, "Would you like me to watch your dog?"

The handler fastens the dog to a 6-foot line, such as the dog's leash, gives the end of the leash to the evaluator, and goes to a place out of sight of the dog for three minutes. The dog should not continually bark, whine, howl, pace unnecessarily, or show anything other than mild agitation or nervousness. This is not a stay exercise; dogs may stand, sit, lie down, and change positions during this test.

Dogs are tested individually, not as a group, and more than one dog can be tested at a time.

Getting ready to take the exam

If you have done the basic training, you're already halfway to being ready for the Canine Good Citizen. The new exercises you need to teach your dog are the following:

- Accepting a friendly stranger
- Sitting politely for petting
- Appearance and grooming
- Reaction to another dog
- Reaction to distractions
- Supervised separation

Because Buddy's ability to sit-stay is so critical to success on many of the tests, make sure that he has this exercise down pat.

Four of the tests require a solid sit-stay in the face of a distraction, such as a person, another dog, or an auditory distraction. You have already trained for these except for the distraction of another dog. Even so, you need to practice these tests to make sure Buddy can do them, and to reassure yourself.

Training for accepting a friendly stranger and sitting politely for petting

We suggest that you start by teaching your dog the sit for examination and build from there. You will need a helper for these exercises.

If you have scored your dog for fight or flight, you remember that this score determines his response to the helper. For example, if the helper is a stranger and your dog is high in fight, he may show signs of aggression. On the other hand, if he is low in fight and high in flight behaviors, Buddy may try to hide behind you or show signs of shyness when the helper approaches. Because the sit for examination is the cornerstone for all the distraction tests, you need to condition your dog to perform this exercise correctly before you continue.

With Buddy in heel position, begin as you do for the sit-stay. Say and signal "stay" and have your helper approach your dog from 6 feet at a 45-degree angle to your left. Have the helper approach in a friendly and non-threatening manner, without hovering over the dog. Have the helper show your dog the palm of a hand and continue to walk by. If Buddy stays, praise, and release. If your dog wants to get up, check straight up with your left hand with "stay" and try again.

Buddy's response determines how close the distracter gets in the beginning. If he becomes apprehensive about the helper's approach, we suggest that he or she walk past the dog at a distance of 2 feet without making eye contact with or looking at the dog. As the dog gets used to that maneuver, have the helper offer a treat to the dog, placed on the open palm, as he or she walks by, still without making eye contact with the dog. It does not matter whether the dog takes the treat or not — it's the gesture that counts.

When your dog accepts that, have the helper first offer a treat and then pet the dog on the head, still without making eye contact, as he or she continues past the dog. After that, the helper can attempt to look at the dog as he or she touches the dog and goes past. For this particular test, it is the eye contact in connection with the examination that is the hard part of the exercise, and it may require several sessions before the dog is steady.

The aim of this exercise is for the dog to allow the approach of a stranger who also then pets the dog. For the majority of dogs, this exercise is not particularly difficult, but it does require a little practice.

Training for appearance and grooming

Appearance and grooming is a similar test that you can introduce as soon as your dog accepts petting by a stranger. Have your helper lightly comb or brush Buddy with you at his side or directly in front. The helper examines the ears and picks up each front foot. If your dog finds this difficult, have the helper give the dog a treat as he or she touches a foot. Condition the dog with praise and treats to accept having the feet handled.

The appearance and grooming test is one of the most frequently failed tests, and mainly because the dog will not permit the evaluator to handle his feet. If you make a point of handling your dog's feet when he is a puppy (and have your friends do it too), he will not be upset by this as an adult.

Because your dog's profile determines how he reacts to a particular distraction, you need to expose him to different distractions to see how he deals with them. Some dogs take it all in stride and others require several exposures to become accustomed to the distraction. The best foundation is a solid sit-stay.

Training for reaction to another dog

Again, this is a sit-stay exercise, but you should practice this exercise with someone else who also has a well-trained dog. With your dogs at heel position, approach each other from a distance of about 20 feet and stop close enough to each other so you can just shake hands. As you stop, tell Buddy to sit and stay.

Should he want to say hello to the other dog, reinforce the stay command. Be sure you instruct your training partner not to let his or her dog come to say hello to Buddy.

Training for reaction to distractions

Take another look at the list of distractions in the section, "Reaction to distractions," earlier in this chapter. If you think that your dog may be unduly startled by any one of them, you need to practice and condition him to ignore that distraction.

The evaluator will pick two distractions, one sound and one visual distraction. During the test, the dog may attempt to walk forward slightly to investigate the distracter but should not pull on the leash. A solid sit-stay is often the answer to an unforeseen reaction.

A dog that growls, lunges, or continuously barks at the distracter will not pass. One bark is acceptable.

Training for supervised separation

Although this test does not directly deal with distractions, it does evaluate a dog's response to the unforeseen, and so resembles the other tests. It shows that the dog can be left with someone else, which demonstrates training and good manners. You hand your leash to the evaluator who watches your dog, and in some cases, other dogs may be in the vicinity who are also doing this test or just being walked. The dog should not bark, whine, howl, or pace unnecessarily, or register anything other than mild agitation or nervousness.

You can leave your dog in either the sit or the down position; it is not necessary that he hold that position until you return, only that he does not vocalize or pace unnecessarily. Still, by having Buddy focus on staying in place, you reduce the likelihood that he will bark or howl, or become overly agitated. It can be done as a simple down-stay exercise with the owner out of sight, which is what we recommend.

How the Test Is Won

Organizations offering the Canine Good Citizen test have considerable leeway in making up the order in which to give the tests. The most common order is the one in which they are listed earlier in this chapter. The supervised separation test may take place in the presence of other dogs that are also doing this test.

Usually three evaluators conduct the test. The first evaluator conducts tests one through three, the second one tests four through nine, and the third one test ten. The test is scored on a pass/fail basis and in order to qualify for a Canine Good Citizen certificate the dog must pass each of the ten tests.

An automatic failure results when a dog eliminates during testing, except during test ten, provided it is held outdoors. Handlers are also not permitted to give their dogs food while the dog is being tested.

Any dog that growls, snaps, bites, attacks or attempts to attack a person or another dog is not a good citizen and must be dismissed from the test.

To participate in a Canine Good Citizen test you need to present, at the time of the test, a current rabies certificate and any other state or locally required inoculations and licenses.

All tests are done on leash and dogs need to wear a well-fitting buckle or slip collar made of leather, fabric, or chain. Snap-around collars, prong collars or head halters are not permitted. The leash can be either fabric of leather.

Do's and Don'ts of Taking the Test

The following few hints will help you prepare for and participate in the Canine Good Citizen test.

Your attitude and state of mind are the most important influence on the outcome of the test. If you are excessively nervous, your dog will become nervous, too. Handlers under stress sometimes do things they would never dream of doing any other time. If this happens, it will confuse your dog to the point where the dog might fail. Maintain a positive outlook and rely on your training.

Do:

- Practice the entire test with a helper and friends before you actually enter a test. This is more for your benefit than Buddy's. As you become familiar with the test, you will lose some of your nervousness. It will also identify Buddy's weak areas and give you additional time to work on them.

- Give your dog a bath and thoroughly groom him before the test.

- Use the correct equipment for the test — a well-fitting buckle or slip collar of either leather, fabric, or chain, and a leather or fabric leash.

- Exercise Buddy before you take the test. Should your dog eliminate at any time during testing, he must be marked failed.

- Warm up your dog before taking the test so that both of you are as relaxed as possible under the circumstances.

- Use a second command for any exercise, if necessary.

- Talk to your dog during an exercise to keep attention on you, if necessary.

- Ask the evaluator for an explanation if you don't understand a procedure or an instruction.

- Maintain a loose leash throughout the entire test, even between exercises, to the extent possible. While an occasional tightening of the leash is generally not considered a failure, it does become a judgment call for the evaluator in assessing your control over your dog. It is best not to put yourself or the evaluator in that position.

- Understand that your attitude and state of mind are the most important influence on the outcome of the test. If you are excessively nervous, your dog will become nervous, too. Maintain a positive outlook and rely on your training.

- Conduct yourself in a sportsmanlike manner at all times.

- Keep in mind the purpose of the Canine Good Citizen and become an ambassador of good will and good manners for all dogs.

Of course, if you take the time to participate in the Canine Good Citizen test, you obviously want Buddy to pass. Even if he doesn't, you should feel good about yourself and Buddy anyway. You're making an effort to train your dog to be a model member of the community. In that small way, you're doing a service to all dogs and their owners.

Don't:

- Lose your temper or attitude should your dog fail an exercise. If you berate your dog, you sour him on the entire experience. You may feel a certain amount of disappointment and frustration, but those feelings, too, you need to control. The more you work with your dog, the more attuned he is to your feelings. He will associate them with the circumstances and not the failure of an exercise.

✔ Change your attitude toward your dog after he has failed an exercise so that the dog is completely unaware that something went wrong. Your remedy is not to make the dog feel stupid or anxious, but to review your training, work on the difficult exercise, and try again. If you undermine your dog's confidence, training will take longer and become a less rewarding experience than if you realize that your job is to support and encourage your dog at every step of the way.

Part IV
Training for Competition

The 5th Wave   By Rich Tennant

"We had no trouble training him to sit, stay, and wear a business suit, but his people skills are still lacking."

In this part . . .

Harmony at home isn't the only benefit you get from training a dog. You and Buddy may enjoy entering competitions together in hopes that he will win awards for his good behavior. This part tells you all about two titles that you and Buddy can strive for — Companion Dog and Companion Dog Excellent — and what Buddy needs to know to enter into competition. If Buddy had passed those two tests with flying colors and you're interested in teaching him some skills that he can put to use, such as scenting, retrieving, and jumping, you can train him for competition in the Utility Class. This part shows you how to train Buddy for the Utility exercises as well.

Chapter 14

Getting Ready to Compete

In This Chapter

▶ Introducing your dog to competition

▶ Preparing for the Pre-Novice, Rally, and Novice classes

▶ Getting the attention of your dog

▶ Heeling and doing the Figure 8 for competition

▶ Reinforcing your dog's training

*I*f you and Buddy enjoy working together, the sky is the limit. You can participate in obedience competitions and earn obedience titles. Doing so is a lot of fun, and you meet lots of nice people. We must warn you, though, that once you get started, you can become addicted. And your life will never be the same.

Almost every weekend of the year, you can go to a dog show and show off what the two of you have accomplished. Dog shows are either conformation shows, where your dog is judged on his appearance, or obedience trials, where you and he are judged on his and your ability. The shows can be held together or separately.

If you have already been to a dog show and watched the obedience trial, you were probably amazed at the training and maybe thought to yourself, "My dog could never do that." Well, not necessarily. It all depends on his Personality Profile and whether the two of you enjoy spending quality time with each other.

Training for Competitive Dog Titles

Different organizations have licensed shows, including those that designer dogs can participate in. In this book, we concentrate on the shows held under the auspices of the American Kennel Club (AKC), the oldest and largest organization to license such events.

More information on dog organizations

Check out these Web sites for more information on the AKC and UKC:

✔ www.akc.org: The official Web page of the American Kennel Club offers information on almost everything to do with dogs. You can get the profiles of different breeds, how to register your dog or get answers to questions about registration. You can find out about dogs in competition and what titles dogs can earn. This Web page tells you about pedigrees and, if you have a purebred dog, how you to get a three-generation pedigree from the AKC. It offers reproductions from the Dog Museum where many famous pieces of art and old books are housed, and it has archives of articles that have appeared recently, together with information about how the AKC works.

✔ www.ukcdogs.com: The United Kennel Club is the second oldest and second largest all-breed dog registry in the United States. Founded in 1898 by Chauncey Z. Bennett, the registry has always supported the idea of the "total dog," meaning a dog that looks and performs equally well. With 250,000 registrations annually, the performance programs of UKC include conformation shows, obedience trials, agility trials, coonhound field trials, water races, night hunts and bench shows, hunting tests for the retrieving breeds, beagle events, including hunts and bench shows, cur, feist, squirrel and coon events, plus bench shows. The UKC world of dogs is a working world. That's the way founder Chauncey Bennett designed it, and that's the way it remains today.

The AKC awards three basic obedience titles:

✔ Companion Dog, or C.D., from the Novice class
✔ Companion Dog Excellent, or C.D.X., from the Open class
✔ Utility Dog, or U.D., from the Utility class

The level of difficulty increases with each class, from no more than basic control, to retrieving and jumping, to responding to signals and direction. The classes are designed so that any dog can compete successfully for titles. Once your dog has earned a Utility Dog title, you are then eligible to compete for the special obedience titles of Obedience Trial Champion and Utility Dog Excellent. All three classes and all levels of competition have one exercise in common: heeling. Which means that you and Buddy need to have a firm foundation and need to practice, practice, practice.

Understanding the system

The first class you and Buddy can enter is appropriately called either the Pre-Novice or the Novice class. The required exercises for both classes are designed to demonstrate the usefulness of the purebred dog as companion. You can also enter the Rally class.

The Pre-Novice and Rally classes are non-regular classes that do not lead to a title. There is no minimum point score required for a "qualifying" score, and whoever has the highest score wins the class. Pre-Novice is an ideal class for those who have never participated in a dog show before.

The cornerstones of the Pre-Novice and Rally classes, as of all the other obedience classes, are having a dog that does the following:

- ✔ Pays attention to yous
- ✔ Knows how to heel

Later in this chapter, we concentrate on these two concepts.

Requirements for Pre-Novice

The Pre-Novice class consists of six exercises, each with a specific point value. Your dog is expected to respond to the first command, and additional commands are penalized. All the exercises are done on leash. Before each exercise the judge asks, "Are you ready?" You say that you are, and the judge then gives the command, such as "Forward" for the Heel on Leash and Figure 8 exercises, or "Stand your dog and leave when ready" for the Stand for Examination. These exercises are always done in the order in which they are listed in Table 14-1.

Table 14-1	The Pre-Novice Class
Required Exercises	**Available Points**
Heel on Leash	45
Figure 8	25
Stand for Examination	30
Recall	40
Long Sit (1 minute)	30
Long Down (3 minutes)	30
Maximum Total Score	**200**

These exercises are an extension of those required for the Canine Good Citizen and a preview of those required for the Novice class.

The Rally class

The name *Rally* comes from the use of directional signs, similar to a Road Rally for cars.

After the judge has given the first "Forward," the handler and dog team move continuously from one sign to the next on their own, instead of waiting for the Judge's command for each exercise. Unlimited communication from handler to dog is encouraged, but physical guidance is penalized.

Obviously, this class is a lot more fun than the Novice class because you can give all the extra help to your dog he may need in the form of commands, encouragement, and praise. It is also much more fast-paced than Pre-Novice as you move from one sign to the next without any interruption, which makes it very exciting for the dog.

The starting score is 200, and deductions are made for any errors on the part of the dog performing the designated exercise at the sign, or for not completing an exercise indicated by the sign. There are about 40 different signs, representing all the basic obedience exercises and maneuvers. For example, a sign may say "Forward — normal pace," "Halt — sit and forward," "Halt — down your dog and forward," and so on.

Specific obedience exercises your dog needs to know in order to participate are heeling, sit, down, stand, stay, and come. In Level 1 Rally, all the exercises are done on leash with 18–20 signs. In Level 2 Rally, the exercises are done off leash with 18–22 sign exercises and one or more low jumps.

Dog show tidbits

To participate in a dog show, you need to enter about three weeks ahead of time. To participate in an AKC licensed event, your dog must be a purebred and registered with the AKC.

If you have a dog that appears to be a purebred but you don't have papers for him, you may be able to get an Indefinite Listing Privilege (ILP) number from the AKC that permits you to participate in obedience trials.

At a dog show, the dogs are exhibited in a clearly defined enclosure, often made of baby gates, called a *ring,* which is a rectangular area no less than 30 feet by 40 feet.

Prelude to Exercise 1: Teaching the Ready! Command

The first exercise in the Novice class is the Heel on Leash, and we like to teach our dogs a command that tells them that the two of us are going to heel together. The command we've chosen is *Ready!* Notice that the command includes an exclamation mark and not a question mark. It's said in a quiet and yet excited tone of voice — almost a whisper. The reason we've chosen this command is simple: In an obedience trial, the judge asks "Are you ready?" before he or she gives the order "Forward," at which point you give Buddy the command, "Buddy, heel!" and start to move.

When the judge asks you the question, naturally, you're expected to give some indication that the two of you are ready to go. We use the answer "Ready!" and Buddy snaps to attention and is all set to go.

No doubt you're wondering why all this is necessary when Buddy is supposed to respond to the Heel command and move with you when you do. The reason is that when you give the Heel command, you want to make sure that Buddy's attention is on you and not something else that may have attracted his attention. Otherwise, he may just sit there like a bump on a log, totally engrossed in what's going on in the next ring, and while you start to walk, he has to play catch-up.

To avoid this scenario, teach Buddy the Ready! command. In addition, you need to decide on your lead-off leg — the one that tells the dog when he is expected to go with you. If you're right-handed, you'll be more comfortable making your lead-off leg your right, but you can start on either leg as long as you're consistent.

Using control position

You are also going to graduate from leash over the shoulder to *Control Position,* which makes it easier for you to remind Buddy of his responsibility to pay attention to you and stay in heel position when he permits himself to become distracted. Control Position is used whenever you want to practice attention and precision heeling.

Following are the steps for holding the leash in Control Position:

1. **Put the loop of the leash over the thumb of your right hand.**

2. **Neatly fold the leash, accordion-style, into your right hand, with the part going to the dog coming out from under your little finger.**

3. **Place your right hand against the front of your leg, palm facing your leg.**

4. **With your left hand, grasp the leash in front of your left leg, palm facing your leg.**

   Keep both hands below your waist at all times, and your elbows relaxed and close to your body.

5. **Attach the leash to the live ring of your dog's training collar.**

6. **Position both rings of the collar under his chin.**

   Take up enough slack in the leash so that the leash snap is parallel with the ground.

Focusing Buddy's attention on you

Your Sequence 1 goal? To focus your dog's attention on you:

1. **Put the leash on the live, or stationary, ring of the training collar.**

   Training collars are used for training your dog but aren't permitted at obedience trials. To show your dog in a trial, you must have him wear a well-fitted plain buckle collar or a slip collar made of leather, fabric, or chain. (A *slip collar* has only two rings and slips over your dog's head.)

2. **Sit your dog at heel position.**

3. **Hold the leash in Control Position.**

4. **Look at your dog, keeping your left shoulder absolutely straight, and smile.**

5. **Say your dog's name, release with an enthusiastic "OK," and take five steps straight forward at a trot, keeping your hands in Control Position.**

6. **Repeat these steps ten times.**

Introducing Buddy to the Ready! command

Now for your Sequence 2 goal: to introduce your dog to the Ready! command.

When teaching Ready!, hold your hands in Control Position and keep your shoulders absolutely straight. You want to use body language to communicate forward motion to your dog. Dropping your left shoulder or pointing it back communicates just the opposite to your dog.

1. **Follow Steps 1 through 4 in Sequence 1.**

2. **Quietly and in an excited tone of voice, say "Ready!"**

3. **Say "Buddy, heel," move out smartly for five paces, and release.**

   Wait until you finish giving the command before you move. Otherwise, you're teaching your dog to move on his name or your motion — not a good idea.

4. **Repeat these steps ten times.**

Don't worry about what Buddy is doing. Concentrate on your part, which is making it exciting and fun for your dog, keeping your hands in position, and starting and releasing on the lead-off leg.

Getting Buddy to respond to Ready!

OK, your Sequence 3 goal is to teach your dog to *respond* to the Ready! command:

1. **Follow Steps 1 through 4 in Sequence 1.**

2. **Quietly and in an excited tone of voice, say "Ready!"**

3. **Say "Buddy, heel," start at a fast pace as quickly as you can for ten paces, and release.**

4. **Repeat these steps ten times.**

Here are a couple of helpful hints for you as you do this sequence the first few times:

- ✔ You may feel a little tension on the leash before Buddy understands that you want him to move with you. Wait until you've finished the command before you start to run. It would hardly be fair to your dog to take off without having told him what you want.

- ✔ Resist the temptation to let your left hand trail out behind you as you feel a little tension on the leash and resist the urge to let your left shoulder drop. Hook the thumb of your left hand under your waistband and lock it in place. And concentrate on keeping that left shoulder straight.

After four to five tries, you'll notice that Buddy is actually responding when you say "Ready!" and is outrunning you.

Rewarding Buddy's response

Ready for Sequence 4's goal? Reward your dog's response. Not all dogs pick up on the Ready! exercise at the same rate. For those that are a little slow or just to reward those that are doing it, this is a good remedial sequence:

1. **With your dog sitting at a heel position, neatly fold the leash into your left hand, placed at your belt buckle.**

2. **Hold a treat in your right hand and put it at your right side.**

3. **Look at your dog, smile, and say "Ready!"**

4. **Do one of the following:**

    If he looks at you, tell him how clever he is, give him the treat, and release.

    If he doesn't look at you, put the treat in front of his nose and move it in the direction of your face. When he follows the treat, tell him how clever he is, give him the treat, and release.

5. **Repeat these steps until your dog responds without hesitation to the Ready! command.**

Reinforcing the Ready! command

Now for Sequence 5's goal: to reinforce the Ready! command. There are going to be times when your dog is distracted to such an extent that he won't respond to the treat, much less the command. For those occasions, you need to be able to reinforce the command so that he'll learn that when you say the magic word, he *has* to pay attention no matter what's out there.

1. **Follow Steps 1 through 4 in Sequence 1.**

2. **Give the Ready! command.**

3. **Do one of the following:**

    If Buddy looks up at you expectantly, praise and then release.

    If he doesn't look up at you, check in the direction you want him to focus — usually, your face. When he looks up, praise and release.

Nagging your dog with ineffective checks is not a good training technique. Get a response the first time so you can praise and release him. If you repeatedly don't get a response, you are being too feeble or are using the wrong equipment.

4. **Repeat these steps until your dog is rock solid on responding to the Ready! command.**

Getting Buddy to ignore distractions

This next one is the last one. Sequence 6's goal is to ignore distractions. This sequence is the review progression for this whole Ready! exercise.

You can now start working with a helper who will try to distract your dog. Your helper can be a friend or family member. The three main distractions are

- ✔ **Visual, or 1st degree.** Helper approaches and just stands there.

- ✔ **Auditory, or 2nd degree.** Helper approaches and tries to distract Buddy with "Hello, puppy! Want to come and visit?" Or whatever else comes to mind. Note that the name of the dog is *not* used.

- ✔ **Object of attraction, or 3rd degree.** Helper approaches and offers Buddy a toy or a treat.

When doing the following steps, practice with 1st degree until your dog ignores the distracter. Then move on to 2nd degree and 3rd degree, respectively.

When you're working on distraction training, have the helper approach your dog at a 45-degree angle and not straight on from the front or the side. The helper starts to approach the dog from 10 feet away and stops 2 feet from the dog.

1. **Follow Steps 1 through 4 in Sequence 1.**

2. **Give the Ready! command.**

3. **Have the helper approach in a nonthreatening manner.**

4. **Do one of the following:**

   If your dog keeps his attention focused on you, praise and release.

   If he permits himself to become distracted, reinforce, praise, and release.

You will to review this exercise with Buddy on a regular basis.

Heeling with Distractions

Now that you have taught Buddy to pay attention to you on command and while he is sitting at heel, you now have to teach him to pay attention during heeling. Up to now, most of your heeling has probably been done in areas relatively free of distractions, perhaps even in the same location (see Chapter 11). The time has come to expand your and Buddy's horizons. You need to get him out to new places.

For Buddy, every new location is a form of distraction training. Brand new sights and, more important, brand new smells. When you do take him to a new place, let him acclimate himself first — take in the sights and smells. Give him a chance to exercise himself.

Heeling in new places

In a location new to your dog, and after he has had a chance to look around a bit, do some heeling with particular emphasis on having your dog paying attention to you. Anytime his attention wanders — he may want to sniff or just look around — remind him with a little check that he has to pay attention to you. When he does, tell him what a good boy he is, then release him.

Check in the direction you want your dog to focus — somewhere on you. Depending on his size, this can be your ankle, lower leg, upper leg, torso, or face. Focusing on your face would be ideal, and some dogs pick up on that quickly. Others are structurally not able to do that.

When you release him with "OK," take five steps straight forward at a trot. Keep both hands on the leash. You want to get him excited about heeling with you. If he gets too excited, release him with somewhat less enthusiasm. After a check to re-focus the dog's attention on you, release him. Make it as much fun as you can for your dog.

The goal of heeling with distractions is for your dog not to permit himself to become distracted. In the process he learns to pay attention to you. It is not so important how he does it, so long as he does.

Our Shepherd, Katharina (as did our Labrador, Bean), usually heeled with her head facing straight forward, seemingly without looking at any part of the handler. Both dogs were very attentive, it just didn't look that way.

Heeling with a distracter

You now need a helper to assist you. The next progression in teaching Buddy to heel is to go through the same sequences you did with the sit-stay (see Chapter 4), only this time with your helper trying to distract him. Distraction training is important because Buddy has to learn to pay attention to you even in the face something else that might be more interesting.

Heel your dog past your helper who can be standing, sitting, or squatting while smiling invitingly at your dog. If your dog permits himself to become is distracted, check and then praise. Repeat until your dog ignores your helper and instead looks at you as you pass the distracter.

Next, have your helper talk to your dog (the helper does *not* use the dog's name), then have your helper offer your dog a treat. You want your dog to ignore your helper and focus on you. When he does, be sure to praise him.

Transitioning to Heeling Off Leash

To make the transition from heeling on leash to heeling off leash we use a technique called "umbilical cord." Here is how it works.

- ✔ With your dog sitting at heel and the leash attached to the collar, take the loop end of the leash in your right hand and pass it around behind you into your left hand.

- ✔ With your right hand unsnap the leash from the collar, pass the snap through the loop of the leash and reattach it to the collar.

- ✔ Pull on the leash to tighten the loop end around your waist at your left side.

- ✔ Put your left hand against your belt buckle and let your right hand swing naturally at your side (see Figure 14-1).

Say "Buddy, heel" and start to walk your normal brisk pace. If your dog deviates from heel position, slowly reach for the collar, put two fingers of your left hand through the collar, back to front, palm facing you, at the side of his neck, and bring him back to heel position. Keep walking, let go of the collar and tell him what a good dog he is.

This maneuver lets you and your dog experience the feeling of heeling off leash while he is still attached.

When you reach for your dog, be sure you do it slowly so as not to frighten him. Remember, he is still on leash and can't go anywhere. If you start snatching at him, he will become apprehensive and try to bolt.

Slow, deliberate movements should be used when training. Just as you should not run toward your dog when he moves out of position, don't grab at his collar when you reach for him when practicing heeling.

For Buddy, there is another important lesson. He learns to accept the reinforcement of you reaching for the collar so that you can do it when he actually is off leash. That is why it is so important that you do it slowly so you don't inadvertently teach him to bolt from your side.

If you have difficulty getting two fingers through the collar — your dog may be small or have lots of hair around his neck — use the leash snap to bring him back.

This technique teaches your dog that it is his responsibility to remain in heel position. Unless he learns to accept that responsibility, he will not be reliable off leash. You can help the process by being consistent in reminding him of that responsibility. For example, Buddy deviates, you reach for the collar, but he corrects himself and you do nothing. Unfortunately, Buddy has not learned anything.

Figure 14-1:
The
umbilical
cord leash
technique.

Anytime you make a move to bring him back, you must follow through. This principle applies to other situations as well.

If there is a trick to this exercise, it is to keep it short and sweet. Take ten steps, then halt, put your right hand against his chest, place him into a sit and stand up. Praise, release, and start over.

Keep the time and distance short and you have a better chance of maintaining your dog's interest and attention.

This time, go ten steps, make a right turn, take another ten steps and halt, praise, and release. Remember to say your dog's name before you make the turn. Start over and incorporate an about-turn, using his name before the turn. Also incorporate changes of pace. You get the picture. By keeping the time and distance short, you have a better chance of maintaining your dog's interest and attention.

As you and your dog's proficiency increases, add distractions in the order you did before. You also need to gradually increase the time and distance that you heel your dog before a halt. How much total time should you spend on this exercise? After a two-minute warm-up of heeling in Control Position in a large circle or straight line with plenty of releases, no more than one to two minutes per training session.

Heeling Off Leash

You are now ready for heeling off leash (see Figure 14-2). If you have any doubt about what the little fellow will do, practice in a safe area, such as your back yard.

- ✔ Start with a two-minute warm-up in Control Position. Walk in a large circle or a straight line. Forget about turns and concentrate on keeping his attention on you. Now is the time to remind him to pay attention to you. Check, if you have to, then praise and release.

- ✔ Set up for umbilical cord. Heel for 10 to 15 steps and release. Set up again and heel for about the same distance and halt. Just as before, put your right hand against his chest, place him into a sit, and stand up.

- ✔ Unclip the leash from his collar and put the snap into your left pocket so that a loop dangles on your side.

- ✔ Say "Buddy, heel" and start at a brisk pace.

- ✔ Halt after 10 steps and sit your dog.

- ✔ Put the leash back on your dog and release.

- ✔ Go on to another exercise, or end your session.

Unclip the leash from the dog's collar and put the leash snap into your pocket.

If you need to reinforce, very slowly reach for his collar, bring him back, let go, and praise.

Proficiency comes in small increments and not all at once. Each session adds something new to your off-leash heeling, such as a turn — use his name — or a change of pace. Keep it short and snappy. Make it exciting and fun. Over the course of several sessions, both you and Buddy will become increasingly confident and begin to work as a team. Resist the temptation to go beyond his ability to be successful.

Heeling off leash with distractions

When both of you are comfortable doing this exercise in an area relatively free of distractions, you can go on to heeling off leash with distractions. Use the same order as you did before, that is, making it incrementally more difficult as you progress. Use the same reinforcement as you did for "umbilical cord." When you come to halt, put your right hand against his chest.

Figure 14-2:
Heeling off
leash.

Responsibilities during heeling

Both you and your dog have specific responsibilities for heeling (see Table 14-2). Notably, yours are far more numerous than your dog's.

Table 14-2	Responsibilities for Heeling
Yours	*Your Dog's*
Leash handling	Paying attention to you
Body posture	Staying in position
Pace and rhythm	
Concentrating on dog	
Use of the leash	
Anticipating when to check	
Direction of check	
When and how to reward	

The Novice Class: What's Expected from You and Buddy

The Novice class consists of six exercises, each with a specific point value (see Table 14-3). For a qualifying score, you and Buddy have to earn more than 50 percent of the available points for each exercise and a final score of 170 out of a possible 200.

A qualifying score at an obedience trial is called a *leg*. Your dog needs three *legs* under three different judges to earn the AKC title Companion Dog.

Table 14-3	The Novice Class
Required Exercises	**Available Points**
Exercise 1: Heel on Leash and Figure 8	40
Exercise 2: Stand for Examination	30
Exercise 3: Heel Free	40
Exercise 4: Recall	30
Exercise 5: Long Sit	30
Exercise 6: Long Down	30
Maximum Total Score	**200**

The six exercises are always done in the order listed in Table 14-1, and they're all pack behavior exercises.

"So where do I get those Obedience Regulations thingies?"

Piece o' cake: You can get your own copy of the Obedience Regulations free of charge by contacting the American Kennel Club at 5580 Centerview Drive, Suite 200, Raleigh, NC 27606-3390 (919-233-9767 or www.akc.org).

Go ahead and get them: It's a good idea to know the rules so you know what's expected from you and your dog.

The Novice class exercises are an extension of those required for the Canine Good Citizen test (discussed in Chapter 13). The Stand for Examination exercise, for example, is a form of temperament test similar to Accepting a Friendly Stranger and Sitting Politely for Petting in the Canine Good Citizen test.

But there are some important differences and additions:

✔ Buddy has to respond to the first command.

✔ Walking on a Loose Leash is now called Heeling and consists of both heeling on leash and off leash, and includes a Figure 8 on leash. It's also more exacting.

✔ The temperament test requires the dog to stand, and it's done off leash.

✔ The Heel Free is done off leash.

✔ The Come When Called is now called the Recall. It's done off leash and requires Buddy to come on command, sit in front of you, and then go to a heel on command.

✔ The Sit and Down-Stay are done off leash for one and three minutes, respectively.

The Novice class is tailor-made for the dog that is highest in pack drive behaviors. For the dog that is highest in prey drive behaviors, this class is a little more difficult because of his distractibility. To help your dog overcome this difficulty, you need to teach him a command, such as "Ready!" that lets him know he has to pay attention to you.

When you look at the Novice class exercises, you see that 120 points depend on your dog being able to *stay* — for the Stand for Examination, the Recall, the Sit, and the Down-Stay. So you can see how important that exercise is.

Exercise 1's Heel on Leash: "Let's Dance, Buddy"

Heeling is like dancing with your dog. And *you* have to be the leader. If you know anything about dancing, then you know that you have the tougher job. The dog will follow only your lead, and you need to give him the necessary cues to change direction or pace.

Heeling is a pack drive exercise. Before giving the command to heel, put your dog into pack drive by smiling at him and gently touching him on the side of his face.

Earlier in this chapter, you teach Buddy to heel around distractions, and you need to review that exercise on a frequent basis. In addition, you need to work on perfecting those turns and changes of pace.

Under the AKC Obedience Regulations (see the nearby sidebar for more info about that), the judge will call a heeling pattern for you. The pattern has to include — in addition to normal pace — a fast pace, a slow pace, and a right, left, and about turn. That's the bare minimum. A simple heeling pattern may look something like this: forward, fast, normal, left turn, about turn, halt, forward, right turn, slow, normal, about turn, halt.

If you have your dog's attention, and if you don't accidentally confuse him with incorrect cues, everything should go reasonably well. Still, you need to look at each of the maneuvers as a separate exercise that you and Buddy have to practice. Sort of like the steps of a particular dance.

Table 14-4 sets up how to practice the different component parts of heeling. (The following two sections get into the specifics.) The column Responses You May See alerts you about what to watch for so you can work on it in your training. If you need to check your dog, release after the check. When your dog is doing something correctly, or is trying, be sure to reward him with a treat or praise.

Table 14-4	Practicing the Components of Heeling		
Component	*Dog's Responsibility*	*What You Need to Practice*	*Responses You May See*
Start	Accelerate	Fast starts	Slow start, lags behind
Normal pace	Normal pace	Straight line or large circle. If the dog is distracted, check and release.	Lags or forges, crowds or goes wide, sniffs or becomes distracted (prey drive)
Halt	Decelerate	Check into sit and then release	Forges ahead, sits crooked
Normal to slow Fast to normal	Decelerate	Draw back on the leash as you slow down	Crowds, forges ahead as you slow down
Slow to normal Normal to fast Right turn About turn	Accelerate	Alternate between release, treat, and check	Lags, goes wide
Left turn	Decelerate	Draw back on the leash	Forges or crowds, then lags, goes wide
Left turn	Accelerate	Alternate between release, treat, and check	Forges or crowds, then lags, goes wide

The halt

For the halt, called the Automatic Sit at Heel, put the rings of the training collar on top of your dog's neck. As you come to a halt, check with your left hand straight up. Be careful that you don't inadvertently check toward or across your body because doing so will cause your dog to sit with his rear end away from you and not in a straight line. This maneuver is called the Automatic Sit because the cue for the dog to sit is that you stop. Under the Obedience Regulations, you aren't permitted to use a command or signal the dog to sit. The dog has to do it on his own.

Practice two or three Automatic Sits with a check and then try one without a check. Your dog will immediately tell you where you stand with that exercise.

Changes of pace and turns

For the changes of pace and turns, we train dogs to take their cue from the lead-off leg. We use three techniques to teach this concept:

- The release
- An object of attraction, which can be a treat or favorite toy
- A check

Changing pace

Here's a changing pace example: Suppose that you want to teach the dog to stay with you as you change pace from slow to normal. Do this:

1. **Release your dog from a slow walk on your lead-off leg.**

   The idea is to get your dog all excited about accelerating with you from slow to normal.

2. **As you go from slow to normal, use a treat to draw the dog forward as the lead-off leg makes the transition.**

   Hold the leash in your left hand and the treat in your right. Show the dog the treat just as you're about to make the change and draw him forward with your right hand as the lead-off leg accelerates into normal.

3. **Hold the leash in Control Position and give a little check straight forward at the same time that the lead-off leg makes the transition.**

   The check teaches your dog that ultimately it's his responsibility, on or off leash, to accelerate when you change pace.

Assume that over the course of two or three training sessions, you're going to practice this component of heeling ten times. Out of those ten repetitions, four should be done with a release, four with a treat, and only two with a check. This is the general rule for any exercise you use these techniques with, although your dog's Personality Profile may call for a slightly different mix.

A minimum of one-third of your repetitions of any of the heeling components should include the release. Another one-third should include a treat.

Making turns

When making turns, try to keep your feet close together so your dog can keep up with you.

For the right and about turn, Buddy needs to learn to accelerate and to stay close to your side as you make the turn. You can teach him by using

- The release as you come out of the turn
- A treat to guide him around the turn
- A little check coming out of the turn

When you use a treat:

- Neatly fold the leash into your left hand and place it against your right hip. Doing so keeps your shoulder facing in the right direction.
- Hold the treat in your right hand at your side.
- Just before you make the turn, show your dog the treat and use it to guide him around the turn.
- Hold the treat as close to your left leg as you can so that your dog learns to make nice, tight turns.

For the left turn, Buddy first needs to slow down so you don't trip over him and then accelerate again. Draw back on the leash just before you make the turn and then use the same techniques as you use for the right and about turns.

Once a week, test your dog's understanding of heeling by doing a little pattern with him that's similar to what you'd perform in the ring. In the ring, you're not allowed to check your dog, and you can't have any tension on the leash. The only true test is when your dog is off leash, but using umbilical cord or show position also gives you a good idea of what you need to practice. For show position, neatly fold the leash into your left hand and place it at your belt buckle, allowing anywhere from 3 to eight 8 of slack, depending on the size of the dog. (See earlier in this chapter for the umbilical cord position.)

The purpose of testing your dog's understanding of heeling is to see what you need to practice. Most of your time should be spent practicing. Test every fourth or fifth session.

Exercise 1's Figure 8: "Buddy, Do the Twist"

The Figure 8 is a fun exercise. In the ring, it's done around two people, called *stewards,* who stand 8 feet apart and act as posts. You and your dog start equidistant from the two posts and walk twice completely around and between them. In practice, you can use chairs as posts. In order to stay in heel position, your dog has to speed up on the outside turn and slow down on the inside turn, while you maintain an even brisk pace throughout.

One lament we frequently hear is "He does fine at home, but take him any-where and forget it!" Make it a point to seek out new locations, at first without distractions and then with distractions to see how Buddy does. Use your review progressions in new locations before you expect him to do the Figure 8 correctly.

Until your dog has learned this exercise, he'll have a tendency to forge or crowd on the inside turn and to lag or go wide on the outside turn. In teach-ing this exercise, use your body as your main communication tool. By rotat-ing the upper part of your body back toward your dog, or forward away from your dog, you'll cause him to slow down or speed up, respectively. Your left shoulder will be the cue for your dog, indicating what you want him to do. When the left shoulder points back, your dog will slow down; when it points forward, he'll speed up. Just as dogs communicate with each other through body language, so can you.

Go ahead and try it. It's almost the same motion as the twist, only from the waist up. Rotate the upper part of your body first to the left and then the right. This is the motion you'll use to control your dog's momentum.

Teaching Buddy when to go slow or fast

Sequence 1's goal is to teach your dog to slow down on the inside turn and to speed up on the outside turn.

For the inside turn:

1. **Start with your dog sitting at the heel position, with your leash in Control Position.**

2. **Say "Buddy, heel" and walk a circle to the left, about 4 feet in diame-ter, at a slow pace.**

3. **Twist to the left as you walk.**

4. **Release your dog after you have completed the circle.**

After two or three tries, you'll notice how your dog responds to your body cues. If nothing happens, exaggerate your body motion.

For the outside turn:

1. **Start with your dog sitting at the heel position, with the leash neatly folded into your left hand.**

2. **Put your left hand against your right hip.**

    Doing so keeps your left shoulder facing forward.

3. **Have a treat in your right hand.**

4. **Say "Buddy, heel" and walk in a circle to the right, about 4 feet in diameter, at your normal brisk pace.**

5. **Use the treat, which is held just in front of his nose, to guide your dog around and give him the treat after you have completed the circle.**

The Obedience Regulations are quite specific about the position of your hands. For the Heel on Leash, you can hold the leash in either hand or in both, provided that they are in a natural position. For the Heel Free, your hands can hang naturally at your side, or you can move your right hand and arm naturally at your side and place your left hand against your belt buckle, which is the position we use.

You're looking for a visible effort on the part of your dog to accelerate. Repeat these steps several times so you become comfortable with the maneuver. Then try going at a trot.

Teaching Buddy the actual Figure 8

The Sequence 2 goal is to teach your dog the Figure 8. This is the review progression for this exercise:

1. **Place two chairs about 12 feet apart.**

2. **Start with your dog sitting at the heel position, 2 feet from the center line, equidistant between the chairs.**

3. **Neatly fold the leash into your left hand and place it against your belt buckle; hold a treat in your right hand.**

4. **Say "Buddy, heel" and start to walk at a slow pace around the chair on your left, rotating the upper part of your body to the left.**

5. **When you get to the center between the two chairs, show your dog the treat and guide him around the chair on your right at a trot, keeping your left shoulder facing forward.**

6. **Stop at the center and sit your dog; then praise and release.**

Hold the treat at your right side and out of Buddy's sight until you get to the center and want him to speed up. Then hold it as close as you can to your left leg so he learns to stay close to your side. Don't show the treat to him on the inside turn, or he'll try to get to the treat instead of slowing down.

Your success in keeping Buddy at heel position without crowding or lagging depends on how well you use your shoulders to communicate with him.

Doing the perfect Figure 8

Sequence 3's goal is the perfect Figure 8:

1. **Practice the review progression (see the preceding section), making two complete Figure 8s.**

2. **Start from the center and complete one Figure 8 at normal pace, using your shoulders to cue your dog.**

   Stop and sit your dog. Repeat the review progression often to maintain your dog's enthusiasm.

3. **Over the course of several sessions, put the chairs closer together in 1-foot increments until they are 8 feet apart.**

4. **Do a Figure 8 with umbilical cord, concentrating on the direction of your shoulders.**

   Keep your left hand on your belt buckle.

5. **Do a Figure 8 off leash.**

   Although in the Novice class the Figure 8 is done on leash, practicing it off leash is a good test. You'll quickly see where your dog needs more practice.

At one point or another, you may have to use a little check going into the outside turn to impress on Buddy how important it is to you that he speed up.

Your Dog Is Not an Elephant

True or false? Once my dog is trained, I will never have to practice his lessons again.

Answer: False.

Your dog does not have the memory of an elephant, so you will need to review his lessons on a regular basis.

For example, if you have used the Recall Game to teach Buddy to come when called, you need to reward him with a treat on a random schedule when he responds to your call and comes to you. If you get lax, the association between the command and the reward will weaken. You can tell when this begins to happen.

- ✔ It starts with Buddy not coming immediately.
- ✔ He may take a detour or lift his leg just one more time.
- ✔ Then, you have to call him again.
- ✔ Finally, he ignores you while you implore him to come.

We call this the principle of successive non-reinforced repetitions. It sounds more complicated than it is. Think of it terms of payday, which is your reward for slaving in the pits from nine to five. *Successive non-reinforced repetitions* are responses to a command without any reinforcement, such as not giving your dog a treat when he comes to you after you have called him.

Every time your dog responds to a command without reinforcement, it is a non-reinforced repetition. The number of these repetitions is finite and depends on the extent to which the behavior is in harmony with the dog's instincts or drives. A Labrador Retriever, once he has been trained to retrieve, will happily fetch almost indefinitely without any reinforcement. An Afghan Hound will probably retrieve only a few times without reinforcement. The Labrador was bred to retrieve; the Afghan was not.

Every command you have taught your dog needs to be reinforced on a random basis or the association between the command and the reinforcement will weaken.

Just recently we had a wonderful demonstration of this principle. Before tackling this book, we decided we needed a week off. For this vacation, we visited friends in Newfoundland, who have two delightful Whippets. Every morning, our friends take a short ride to the local park for their own daily walk and to let the dogs run. Naturally, we joined them.

The park covers about 100 acres, with wonderful walking trails, plenty of wildlife, and a large pond inhabited by a variety of fowl. Once inside the park, much to our surprise, our friends let the dogs loose. When we say surprised, it is because Whippets are sight hounds, extremely high in prey drive, who love to chase anything that moves. They are also incredibly fast and can cover great distances in seconds. We were wondering how our friends would get these dogs back.

To make a long story short, when the dogs ranged a little too far or started chasing something, our friends called them back. To our amazement, the dogs came instantly every time, and every time they got a treat. The response was reinforced!

Any taught response needs to be reinforced. You needn't worry about the exact number of non-reinforced repetitions your dog will retain of a given behavior. All you need to know is that they are not infinite. To keep him sharp, randomly reinforce — whether you think he needs it or not.

This principle applies to everything you have taught your dog, from the simplest responses to the most complex. The reinforcement can be a treat or a little check on the leash, depending on the exercise, and how you taught him. It is usually the review progression for the particular exercise.

It's easy to make excuses and blame the dog. But your dog is not an elephant and needs occasional reminders.

Chapter 15

The Companion Dog Title

Chapter 14 introduces the AKC's Novice class and its main goal — the Companion Dog title. That chapter gives an overview of the six required exercises for the title and the points needed to earn that title, and it also provides the nitty-gritty details for completing the first exercise. This chapter covers the remainder of the exercises for the Companion Dog title:

✔ Stand for Examination

✔ Heel Free

✔ Recall

✔ Long Sit

✔ Long Down

Note: The last two exercises are collectively known as the *group exercises*.

During a training session, practice different exercises and vary the order. Start with some brisk heeling as a warmup, including fast starts and changes of pace. Keep training interesting and fun for both of you.

The Stand for Examination

The Stand for Examination is a requirement for the Novice class, but it's also a practical and useful command to teach your dog in general. Brushing, grooming, and wiping feet, as well as visiting the vet, is certainly a lot easier with a dog that's been trained to stand still than with one that's in perpetual motion.

In the ring, Stand for Examination looks something like this: You give your leash to the steward. Then the judge says, "Stand your dog and leave when you are ready." You stand your dog in heel position, say "Stay," walk 6 feet straight forward in front of your dog, turn around, and stand facing the dog. The judge approaches your dog from in front and, with one hand, touches your dog's head, body, and hindquarters. The judge then says, "Back to your dog." You walk around behind your dog and return to the heel position.

When you put Buddy into a stand, watch his front feet. They should remain in place and not move forward. You can lock them in place by applying a little downward pressure with two fingers in his collar underneath his chin as you stand him.

When you begin teaching this exercise to your dog, you can either stand, kneel on your right knee or both knees, or have the dog on a table, depending on his size. What you want to avoid is leaning over him because if you do, he'll want to move away from you — especially if he is low in defense fight behaviors.

Teaching Buddy the Stand command

Your Sequence 1 goal is to teach your dog the command:

1. **Start with Buddy sitting at your left side, off leash, both of you facing in the same direction.**

   Make sure that your shoulders are square and not turned toward him.

2. **Put the thumb of your right hand in the collar under his chin, fingers pointing to the floor, palm open and flat against his chest.**

3. **Apply a little downward pressure on the collar, say "Stand," and at the same time, apply backward pressure on his *stifles* (the joint of the hind leg between the thigh and the second thigh — the dog's knees) with the back of your left hand.**

4. **Keep both hands still and in place, the right through the collar and the left against his stifles, and count to 10.**

5. **Praise and release.**

Repeat this exercise three to five times per session, over the course of several sessions.

Teaching Buddy to stand still: The hands-on method

Sequence 2's goal is to teach Buddy to stand still. This one's short and sweet:

1. **Place your dog into a stand (see the preceding section).**

2. **With both hands on your dog, keep him standing still to the count of 30.**

3. **Over the course of several sessions, increase the time you keep him standing still to one minute.**

Teaching Buddy to stand still: The hands-off method

Your Sequence 3 goal is to get your dog to stand still without you holding him in position:

1. **Place Buddy into a stand (see "Teaching Buddy the Stand command").**

2. **Take away your left hand.**

3. **Count to 30.**

   If he moves, reposition him.

4. **Praise and then release.**

5. **When he's steady without you holding onto him with your left hand, take your right hand out of the collar.**

   It will take Buddy several sessions to learn this sequence.

Praise is a verbal thing — not a petting thing. When you praise Buddy, be sure that he remains in position. Praise tells him he's doing something correctly. It's not an invitation to move. Don't confuse verbal praise with the release.

Teaching Buddy the Stand-Stay command

Sequence 4's goal? Teach Buddy to stand and stay:

1. **Stand your dog as described in "Teaching Buddy the Stand command."**

2. **Take both hands off of your dog and stand up, keeping your shoulders square.**

3. **Signal and say "Stay."**

4. **Count to 30, then praise, and then release.**

5. **Practice until you can stand next to him for one minute without him moving.**

Learning the Stand command (or Sit or Down-Stay) is not exciting for your dog, so follow the exercise with something he enjoys. After the release, play ball or throw a stick. Give him something to look forward to.

Leaving Buddy in a Stand-Stay

Ready for Sequence 5? You're going to leave Buddy in a stand-stay position:

1. **Stand next to your sitting dog.**

2. **Put the thumb of your right hand through the collar as in Sequence 1 (see "Teaching Buddy the Stand command").**

   Depending on the size of your dog, you may have to bend at the knees to avoid leaning over him.

3. **With a little downward pressure on the collar, say "Stand."**

   He should now stand without you having to touch his stifles.

4. **Take your right hand out of the collar and stand up straight.**

5. **Say "Stay" and step directly in front of him.**

6. **Count to 30, step back to a heel position, praise, and release.**

   If he moves, reposition him.

7. **Gradually increase the distance you leave him to 6 feet in front.**

   From now on when you leave him, go 6 feet straight forward, turn and face him (do *not* back away from him), count to 30, go back, praise, and release.

Teaching Buddy the return

Your Sequence 6 goal is to teach the return behind your dog:

1. **Stand your dog and go 6 feet in front (see the preceding section).**

2. **Go back to your dog, put two fingers of your left hand on his *withers* (the highest part of the back at the base of the neck) to steady him, and walk around behind him to the heel position.**

3. **Pause, making sure that he doesn't move, praise, and release.**

4. **When he understands that you're going to come around behind him, eliminate touching him as you return to the heel position.**

Dog shows are held indoors and outdoors and in all kinds of weather conditions. If the dog show you're attending is outdoors and it's raining, the judge will have on rain gear — something your dog may not have experienced before. Don't be caught unprepared: Practice under those unpleasant conditions.

Teaching Buddy the actual examination

Yep, Sequence 7's goal is to teach Buddy the examination part of the exercise. For this sequence, you need a helper. At this time, the helper can be a member of the family. Eventually, however, Buddy will have to be examined by a stranger, and because the judge can be either male or female, you need to practice with both men and women.

To introduce your dog to this exercise, start with the Sit for Examination, which is almost identical to Sitting Politely for Petting in the Canine Good Citizen test (see Chapter 13). Do the following:

1. **Put the rings of the collar on top of the dog's neck.**

2. **Attach your leash to the live ring of the collar.**

3. **Sit your dog at the heel position.**

4. **Neatly fold the leash into your left hand, hold it above his head, and say "Stay."**

5. **Have your helper approach and offer your dog the palm of his or her hand.**

   If Buddy tries to say hello to the helper, reinforce the Stay command with a check straight up.

6. **Have your helper lightly touch Buddy's head and back.**

7. **Praise and release.**

8. **Repeat Steps 1 through 7 until he readily permits the examination.**

   Practice the examination over the course of several sessions.

9. **Repeat the steps with your dog standing at heel, then with you standing directly in front, then 3 feet in front, and finally 6 feet in front.**

When Buddy has mastered this sequence, follow the same progressions off leash. Congratulations.

Before every exercise, the judge asks, "Are you ready?" We answer with "Ready!" for the heeling exercises and "Yes" for everything else. (Check out Chapter 14 for how to prepare your dog for the Ready! command.)

The Heel Free

Heeling off leash, although it is really only an extension of heeling on leash, is not quite the same. Buddy knows when he is on leash and when he is off leash. When he is on leash, he may give you the impression that he is perfect. Then you take the leash off and he acts as though he has no idea what the exercise is all about. The reason is simple — he knows he is off leash.

If this happens to you, review heeling on leash and reinforce the heel command with a treat or a check where he needs help. For normal pace, he usually will not need any reinforcement, but he probably will for changes of pace and turns. Follow the same techniques outlined for heel on leash in Chapter 12.

You can also remind your dog of his responsibility to remain in heel position by taking him by the collar as you do when heeling with umbilical cord. Remember that heeling off leash is the ultimate test of your training. With a little practice, he will get the hang of it. To make sure he understands, most of your practicing should be done on leash, so you can remind him what you expect from him.

The Recall

The Recall exercise is different from the traditional Come command, where all you're concerned about is the dog coming to you. The Recall consists of four components:

- ✔ Stay
- ✔ Come
- ✔ Front
- ✔ Finish

The Recall is performed from one end of the ring to the other. The judge tells you to leave your dog in a Sit-Stay and to go to the other side of the ring. He or she then tells you to call your dog. You give the Come command, Buddy comes, and he's expected to sit directly in front of you. The judge then says "Finish," and you say "Buddy, heel," and Buddy goes to the heel position.

Stay

Chapter 4 covers the basics of the stay command, and training your dog to stay with distraction is covered later in this chapter. For the Recall, or come-when-called exercise, the judge designates the starting point for the exercise, usually at the far end of the ring. He or she tells you to leave your dog. You say, "Stay," and leave your dog, going to the opposite end of the ring. The judge then tells you to call your dog. You call, Buddy comes, and he sits directly in front of you. The judge then says, "Finish," and you give the heel command and Buddy goes to heel.

Come with distractions

Even though Buddy already knows the Come command, you still need to work on distraction training — for which you need a helper. Leave Buddy in a Sit-Stay and go 20 feet in front. Have your helper position him- or herself equidistant between you and Buddy — about 2 feet from Buddy's anticipated line of travel. Facing Buddy, the helper crouches and smiles.

Call your dog and, as he passes the distracter, release backward with an enthusiastic "OK!" Then give him a treat when he gets to you. If he goes to the distracter, smile and very slowly approach Buddy; then put the leash on the dead ring of the training collar and, with a little tension on the leash, show him exactly what he should have done by trotting backward to the spot where you called him. Praise and release backward. You may have to show him a few times until he catches on. Once he's successful, stop for that session.

Release backward any time you want to encourage the dog when he is coming toward you. Lean backward, throw up your hands invitingly, and take a few steps back with an enthusiastic "OK!"

If your dog veers from the distracter, use two distracters, separated by about 10 feet, and teach your dog to come between them. As Buddy progresses in his training, work your way through 2nd and 3rd degree distractions (see Chapter 14 for info about 1st, 2nd, and 3rd degree distractions).

The purpose of distraction training is to build your and your dog's confidence that he can do it. It also teaches him to concentrate on what he's supposed to do. If at any time you feel the exercise is too much for him, stop. Come back to it at another session.

Front

The object of both the Front and the Finish is to teach the dog a position, and both exercises can be practiced inside in the form of a game. The front is similar to the Automatic Sit at Heel in that the dog is supposed to come to you and sit in front without a command to sit. We like to use a chute to teach the dog exactly where we want him to sit when he comes to us. For a chute, we use plastic rain gutters, commensurate to the size of the dog. They should be about as long as your dog. Place them on the ground, just far enough apart so your dog can sit comfortably in between.

When practicing the Front, keep the upper part of your body erect. If you lean over or toward your dog, he won't come in close enough. If you need to get down to his level, bend at the knees.

Getting Buddy used to the chute

Sequence 1's goal is to get Buddy used to the chute:

1. **Place the chute on the ground.**

2. **Walk your dog through the chute a few times.**

3. **Heel your dog into the chute and have him sit in it.**

4. **Repeat Steps 1 through 3 until he readily sits in the chute.**

Teaching Buddy to come into the chute

Yep, Sequence 2's goal is indeed to teach your dog to come into the chute:

1. **Heel your dog up to the chute and tell him to stay.**

2. **Walk through the chute and face your dog.**

3. **Hold a treat in both hands below your waist.**

4. **Call your dog and, as he comes, bring your hands to your waist — using the treat to make him sit.**

5. **Give him the treat, praise, and release backward.**

    (The section "Come with distractions" has info on the release backward.)

6. **Practice Steps 1 through 5 about five times.**

7. **When your dog understands this part, leave him on a stay 3 feet from the entrance of the chute and call him.**

8. **Increase in 2-foot increments the distance that you leave him facing the entrance of the chute, until he is 35 feet from the entrance.**

You want to teach Buddy to sit as close as possible in front of you without touching you. Using treats, you can practice this sequence inside without the chute. Call him to you and use your treat to make him sit. Only give him the treat when he sits straight. If he doesn't, try again.

In the ring, you're not allowed to carry food or give second commands. You can give either a command or a signal but not both. The exception is the Stay command, which can be accompanied by the Stay signal.

Ultimately, Buddy has to sit in front of you with your hands hanging naturally at your side, so you need to wean him from seeing you with your hands in front of you. You can still reward him in practice when he does the exercise correctly.

Finish

After your dog comes to you and sits in front, the judge says "Finish." You say "Buddy, heel," and your dog goes to the heel position. He can go either to the left or to the right. We like to teach both, just to keep the dog guessing. For the Finish to the left, we use the command Heel, and for the Finish to the right, we use the command Place. Actually, we prefer giving a signal because a signal is more readily understood by the dog than a command — and it more clearly indicates to the dog the way we want him to go.

Teaching a Finish to the left

Your Sequence 1 goal is to introduce Buddy to the Finish to the left:

1. **Sit your dog at heel, say "Stay," and step directly in front of him.**

2. **Say "Buddy, heel" and then take a step back on your left leg, keeping the right leg firmly planted in place, as you guide him with a treat held in your left hand in a semicircle into heel position.**

   Make the semicircle large enough so that he winds up in the correct position. His head has to pass your knee so he can make the turn.

3. **Give him the treat, praise, and release.**

4. **Repeat Steps 1 through 3 until he enthusiastically and briskly goes to heel.**

You'll quickly see that the guidance of your left hand becomes his signal to go to heel.

Any time we want a dog to move, we use his name before the command — for example, "Buddy, come." Any time we don't want him to move, we eliminate the name — for example, "Stay." Using a dog's name makes him excited and ready to move, while not using his name on the stationary exercises helps him to focus on the exercise and stay still.

Teaching a Finish on command or signal

Your Sequence 2 goal is to teach Buddy to finish on command or signal:

1. **Put the leash on the live ring of the training collar.**

2. **Neatly fold the leash into your left hand.**

3. **Step in front, say "Buddy, heel," and step back on your left leg, using the leash to guide him into heel position.**

4. **Reward him with a treat, praise, and release.**

5. **Practice Steps 1 through 4 until he goes to heel without any tension on the leash.**

6. **Now eliminate the step back on the left leg and experiment using either the command or signal.**

   The signal is the same guiding motion you used in Sequence 1 (see the section "Teaching a Finish to the left").

Teaching a Finish to the right

The Finish to the right uses the same progressions as the finish to the left, except that you step back on the right leg and guide Buddy around behind you into heel position. When you're using a treat, you have to switch it behind your back from the right hand into the left. The same applies to the leash.

Your dog's response to this, to the finish to the right or left, will tell you which direction is better for him. As a general rule, a long-bodied dog does better going to the right.

The Group Exercises

The group exercises are the last part of the Novice Class test. They consist of a Long Sit and a Long Down for 1 and 3 minutes, respectively, and they're done off leash in a group not to exceed 12 dogs. The judge tells you where to line up the dogs in the ring, then tells you to leave, and then tells you to return when the requisite amount of time has expired. When you return, you have to walk around behind your dog to heel position.

When you're training your dog, change only one variable at a time. When teaching a stay, for example, change the distance or the time but not both together. Increase one and, when Buddy is steady, then the other.

Look at the stay exercises from the perspective of time and distance. Teach Buddy to stay in place for a specific period of time with you about 3 feet in front. Then the first time you increase the distance from your dog, decrease the time you're away from him.

Although you can give a command and/or signal for any stay exercise, your dog's Personality Profile will influence whether you want to use a signal. Any stay is a pack drive exercise, so you want your dog in pack drive. For dogs low in defense fight behaviors, a stay signal puts them into defense drive, where they're uncomfortable. Using a stay signal may cause the dog to break the stay and come to you — or to whine and fidget.

Since he's competing for the Companion Dog title, Buddy already knows the basics of the Sit and Down-Stay. You just need to fill in the missing pieces, meaning you need to practice

- With distractions
- Off leash
- At the right distance
- The requisite length of time plus 1 minute
- At different locations and on different surfaces

The review progression for any stay is the sit-stay test.

Introducing self-generated distractions

Put the leash on the live ring of the collar, with the rings under his chin. Then say and signal "Stay" and step 3 feet in front. Place your left hand against your belt buckle and hold your right hand ready to reinforce. Jump to the right, the middle, the left, the middle, forward, and backward. Any time Buddy wants to move, reinforce the stay. How vigorously you do these distractions depends on Buddy's Personality Profile and your physical condition.

As he learns, add clapping and cheering. And periodically review the distraction training you've done previously.

Increasing the level of difficulty

Practice with self-generated distractions off leash from about 3 feet and then 6 feet in front of Buddy. When Buddy is off leash and you need to reinforce the stay, slowly approach him and put him back by placing two fingers of each hand through the collar at the side of his neck. If he's coming to you, put him back from in front — that is, guide him back to the spot where you left him in such a way that you're facing him when you reinforce the stay. The command is not repeated.

You also need to practice the Down-Stay using the same distractions, both on and off leash.

Whenever you approach your dog, do so in a non-threatening manner so he doesn't become anxious. Your dog should never become frightened when you approach him.

Gradually increase the time to 2 minutes for the Sit-Stay and 4 minutes for the Down-Stay. Although practical, these are boring exercises for both you and your dog. There's usually no need to practice them every session. Once or twice a week will do. Afterward, reward your dog with something he enjoys, like throwing a frisbee or a stick.

When Buddy stays for the requisite length of time, gradually increase the distance you're away from him to 35 feet. Increasing the distance should go quickly since this isn't a new exercise for him. Finally, you need to practice in different locations and on different surfaces.

Oops: Playing the yo-yo game

Some handlers have unintentionally taught their dogs, or vice versa, what we call the yo-yo game. The scenario goes something like this:

1. **Buddy is on a sit-stay with his handler standing 30 feet away.**

2. **Buddy lies down, and the handler approaches to reinforce the stay.**

3. **Buddy sits up by himself, and the handler retreats.**

This scenario can, and often does, deteriorate into the yo-yo game. Buddy lies down, the handler approaches, Buddy sits up, and the handler retreats, with Buddy not having learned a blessed thing — except, perhaps, the rules of the game and that he definitely wants to figure out how many times he can play it.

Moral of the story? When you make a move — any move — to reinforce a command — any command — you *must* follow through, even if Buddy corrects himself before you've had a chance to reinforce the command. But always do it with a smile.

Chapter 16

The Companion Dog Excellent Title

*A*fter you obtain your Companion Dog title from the AKC's Novice class, you're eligible to enter the AKC's Open class and compete for the Companion Dog Excellent title. The Novice class is tailor-made for the dog highest in pack behaviors, but the Open class is for the dog that also has many prey behaviors.

This chapter gets you up to speed on what's required in the Open class and what the point system is, and it provides the details for how to achieve your goal.

The Open Class: What's Expected from You and Buddy

The Open class consists of seven exercises, each with a specific point value (see Table 16-1). For a qualifying score, you and Buddy have to earn more than 50 percent of the available points for each exercise and a final score of at least 170 out of a possible 200. This class is ideal for the dog high in pack and prey behaviors.

Some Open class exercise trivia

The first obedience trials held under the auspices of the American Kennel Club took place in 1936. The classes were the same as today, but the requirements varied somewhat. For example, the Open class included a Speak on Command exercise. But contrary to popular belief, not all dogs are instinctive barkers, and the exercise was subsequently eliminated.

The first obedience test was held in 1933 and consisted of what are now the Open class exercises. For the Retrieve on Flat, the dumbbell weighed 2 pounds. The Retrieve Over High Jump was a 3-foot-6-inch obstacle, and the dumbbell weighed 8 to 10 ounces. The Broad Jump was 6 feet wide.

Table 16-1	The Open Class	
Required Exercises	**Available Points**	**Behavior/Drive**
Exercise 1: Heel Free and Figure 8	40	Pack
Exercise 2: Drop on Recall	30	Pack
Exercise 3: Retrieve on Flat	20	Prey
Exercise 4: Retrieve Over High Jump	30	Prey
Exercise 5: Broad Jump	20	Prey
Exercise 6: Long Sit	30	Pack
Exercise 7: Long Down	30	Pack
Maximum Total Score	**200**	

All the exercises for the Open class are done off leash, and the group exercises (the Long Sit and Long Down) are performed with the owners out of sight of the dogs for three and five minutes, respectively. For your dog, the Open class is the most exciting of the classes.

Note that some of the exercises require equipment. You can either buy the equipment or make it yourself. The specifications are contained in the AKC's Obedience Regulations, which you can get by contacting the AKC at 5580 Centerview Drive, Suite 200, Raleigh, NC 27606-3390 (919-233-9767; www.akc.org).

The Heel Free and Figure 8

You've no doubt discovered that heeling is not as simple as it looks. You certainly need to keep practicing on a regular basis. Here's some food for thought: Heeling is the only exercise that's done as a team; all the other exercises the dog does on his own. But it's with heeling that many handlers have a hard time: Makes you wonder, doesn't it?

The Heel Free is done in exactly the same way as it is done in the Novice class and the only difference is the Figure 8, which is now done off leash (see Chapter 14).

The Drop on Recall

The Drop on Recall uses a combination of the Come and Down commands. As your dog is coming to you, you tell him to lie down, and then you call him again. The exercise starts as a recall, but after you've called your dog, the judge indicates for you to give the Down command or signal and then for you to call again. The command sequence goes like this: "Buddy, come," "Down," "Buddy, come." The dog has to remain in the down position until called. The Front and Finish are also part of the exercise.

Being that Buddy's competing in the Open class, by now he certainly knows the Down and Come commands. The only really new concept he has to learn is to stop immediately when the command is given.

Getting Buddy to obey Down on command

Your Sequence 1 goal is to teach Buddy to obey Down on command.

You need to test Buddy's understanding of the command. With Buddy sitting at heel and without giving him any visual cues, like pointing to the ground, bobbing your head, leaning over, or bending your knees, quietly say "Down." If he lies down, praise, count to five, and release.

If Buddy doesn't respond to the command, or his response is unacceptable (not prompt enough, for example), slowly slide your left hand down the leash all the way to the snap and check straight down. Keep your elbow locked and your arm at your side. Avoid checking across your body because that teaches Buddy to curl in front of you. Stand up, count to five, praise, and release. Repeat until your dog lies down on command at your side. This is the review progression for this exercise.

Some tidbits and tips for you here:

✔ Many of us are blissfully unaware of our own body motions, and you may not be aware of the visual cues you're giving your dog. Always make sure that you aren't inadvertently moving some part of your body — even as much as a finger — and that you're facing straight forward. Note that because visual cues are so important to success in training, it helps to have someone else watch you and then tell you what you're doing. Better yet, occasionally videotape each other. Or stand in front of a mirror and watch yourself.

✔ The purpose of counting to five after a given response is so the dog focuses on what it is you want and doesn't immediately start doing something else.

✔ When you're trying to decide what's an unacceptable response, keep in mind that your dog's size and structure determine how he performs the Down exercise. Some dogs are structurally unable to lie down without first going into the sitting position. Others can only lie on one side or the other but not square, which is the ideal.

Getting Buddy to down while he's walking

Sequence 2's goal? Get Buddy to respond to the Down command while he's in motion. Buddy has to learn to respond promptly to the Down command even when he's moving.

With Buddy sitting at heel, say "Let's go" and start to walk. Don't use the Heel command because this isn't a heeling exercise. After several steps, say "Down" as you come to a halt and not after you have stopped. If you aren't careful about the timing of the command, Buddy may confuse the down command with the automatic sit.

Praise if he does it, count to five, and then release straight forward. The release here is the beginning of teaching Buddy to move briskly forward from the down position.

If he doesn't drop, slowly slide your left hand down the leash to the snap and check straight down. Then praise, count to five, and release.

Getting Buddy to down while you're still walking

Sequence 3's goal is to get Buddy to go down at your side from motion, while both of you are in motion and while you continue walking. *Note:* Before you try Sequence 3, review Sequences 1 and 2 in the preceding two sections.

Say "Let's go" and start walking. After walking several steps, say "Down" and continue walking to the end of the leash. Turn to face Buddy, praise, count to five, and release backward (see Chapter 15 for info about releasing backward). When you release him, remember that you're teaching him to come briskly to you after you've dropped him.

If Buddy doesn't drop, start again. As you give the command, slowly slide your left hand down the leash to the snap and check straight down. Then go to the end of the leash, turn, praise, pause, and release. When he responds reliably, go on to the next progression.

Getting Buddy to down while he's running

Sequence 4's goal is to get Buddy to obey Down while he's moving fast — *and* while you continue moving.

Before you try Sequence 4, review Sequences 1 and 3. Then visualize how your dog comes to you on a recall. It's at *that* speed that he has to drop on command and without any unnecessary steps. Although you may not be able to run as quickly as he can, teach him to drop from a fast pace as you continue to the end of the leash.

Getting Buddy to stop and drop when coming toward you: The on-leash method

Sequence 5's goal is to teach Buddy to stop and drop from in front. The leash is on for this exercise.

When Buddy has mastered the drop from a fast pace, you're ready to try the exercise with him coming toward you. Leave him in a sit-stay position and go to the end of the leash — facing him. Call with "Buddy, come." As he comes to you, take a step toward him on your right foot, keeping the left foot in place, then signal by bringing your right arm straight up, and then say "Down." Keep the upper part of your body straight. Stepping toward Buddy will cause him to stop his forward progress.

After he has dropped, bring your right foot back, lower your arm, praise, count to five, and release. Use the release backward (see Chapter 15) to teach him to come again quickly and enthusiastically after you've dropped him. If Buddy doesn't drop, review Sequence 1 with a check and Sequence 4; then try it again.

Once Buddy is coming toward you, don't check him into a down or do anything else that he may perceive as unpleasant. The reason is that doing will slow down his recall. What's important here is your dog's view of what is unpleasant — not your view. If he doesn't drop, or the drop is unacceptable, review Sequences 1–3.

Getting Buddy to stop and drop when coming toward you: The off-leash method

Sequence 6's goal is to teach Buddy to stop and drop from in front — off leash.

Go through Sequence 5, only do it off leash. You may want to review Sequence 1 with a little check before you try this exercise. As Buddy responds, gradually increase the distance between you and him.

Maintain the step-command-signal sequence until he's reliable. After that, first eliminate the step and then decide whether you prefer voice or signal. You'll probably want him to respond to either.

Getting Buddy to ignore distractions

Sequence 7's goal is to teach Buddy to ignore distractions.

Begin by having a distracter crouch about two feet from Buddy's line of travel and where you intend to drop him. Call and give him the command or signal to drop.

He may do one of several things:

- ✔ Anticipate the drop — that is, slow down or drop before you have given the command or signal.
- ✔ Drop after he's gone past the distracter.
- ✔ Not drop at all.
- ✔ Avoid the distracter by arcing away from him or her.
- ✔ Not respond to the Come command.
- ✔ Actually do it correctly (not likely the first time you try this exercise).

Avoid having Buddy anticipate the drop by randomly alternating between straight recalls and drop on recalls.

Here's what you do if Buddy does one of those preceding things:

✔ **If Buddy anticipates the drop:** You need to show him exactly what you wanted him to do, that is, keep coming to you until you tell him to down. You show him as follows: Slowly go to him without saying anything, put the leash on the dead ring of the collar, and with a little tension on the collar, guide him to the spot where you were when you called him. (You go backward, Buddy goes forward.) Have Buddy sit in front, then praise and release him backward. No extra command is given. Alternate on a random basis between straight recalls and drop on recalls to avoid anticipation.

✔ **If Buddy drops past the distracter or doesn't drop at all:** Slowly approach him without saying anything. Put two fingers of your left hand, palm facing you, through the collar, back to front, at the side of his neck. Take him to the spot where he should have dropped and reinforce the command from in front. The command is not repeated. Praise your dog, count to five, and enthusiastically release backward.

What Buddy is telling you is that he lacks the confidence to drop near the distracter. Your job is to show him that he can do it. His confidence will increase with each successive correct repetition.

✔ **If Buddy arcs away from the distracter or doesn't respond to the Come command:** Use two distracters, facing each other about 8 feet apart, and teach Buddy to drop between the distracters.

Note that Buddy may also start to anticipate the come from the down. If he does, you should slowly approach your dog without saying anything; then put two fingers of your left hand, palm facing you, through the collar, back to front, at the side of his neck; and then take him back to the spot where he should have stayed and reinforce the down from in front. Do not repeat the command. Praise, count to five, and enthusiastically release backward.

As Buddy gains confidence and responds correctly, work your way through the different levels of distractions. Being that you're competing in the Open Class, you've already trained him to ignore these distractions for the Novice recall, so it won't take him very long to figure out what you want.

At some point, you have to decide whether to use a signal or a command to drop your dog because you can't use both. Experiment with Buddy to decide whether you should use a signal or a command when in the ring. Buddy's Personality Profile should help you with your decision. If he's weak in defense (fight) behaviors, you'll be better off using the command rather than the signal. If he's high in prey behaviors, you'll be more successful with a signal.

The Retrieve on Flat

For this exercise, the judge tells you to throw the dumbbell and then send your dog, who's expected to retrieve the dumbbell, present to front, give up the dumbbell on command, and then finish on command. Your command sequence is "Stay," "Take it," "Give," and "Buddy, heel." Buddy must do all the other parts of this exercise on his own.

Anytime you change the content or the complexity of an exercise, it becomes a new exercise for the dog, and you have to go back to the teaching progressions. If your dog was bred to do it, he should learn quickly. If he was not bred to do it, it'll take longer.

The details of the Retrieve command are covered in Chapter 12. Note that many dogs retrieve without being formally taught, and this kind of retrieving is called a *play retrieve*. If you've done distraction training, your dog will have shown you whether you can rely on his cooperation. Ask yourself, "Is he retrieving for me or for himself?" For greater reliability, teach him to retrieve for you.

You also may need to review the teaching progressions for the Front while your dog is holding the dumbbell. For your dog, a Front with the dumbbell is not the same exercise as a Front without a dumbbell. It becomes a new exercise. You need to review the Front progressions in Chapter 15 with Buddy carrying the dumbbell in his mouth.

How quickly Buddy will generalize the Front while carrying the dumbbell depends on the extent to which the exercise is in harmony with his instincts. Retrievers, for example, do it almost automatically, but other breeds may need a few repetitions.

The Retrieve Over High Jump

The principal features of this exercise are that your dog jumps over the jump, picks up the dumbbell, and promptly returns with it over the jump. The judge's commands are "Throw the dumbbell," "Send your dog," "Take it," and "Finish." Your commands to Buddy are "Stay," "Jump," "Give," and "Buddy, heel."

For this exercise, we introduce the concept of *target training*. As the name implies, you teach the dog to go to a target. Once your dog has learned that, you can then place a jump or other obstacle between your dog and the target. In order to get to the target, the dog has to jump the obstacle.

Target training gives the appearance of being a game. Yet it is a highly effective way of teaching your dog a variety of complex exercises.

Target training

The principle is simple, and so is the execution. Place a target on the ground, three feet in front of you and Buddy. The target can be a paper plate, a wooden disk, a square piece of wood, or anything else suitable. Put a treat on the target and send Buddy to the target.

Make the exercise fun and exciting for your dog by using several targets, with the objective that he goes where you tell him to.

The progressions are as follows:

- **Progression 1:** Get your dog's attention on the treat, go to the target, say "Out," place the treat on the target, and let your dog pick up the treat. Repeat three times.

- **Progression 2:** Start three feet from the target, say "Stay," place the treat on the target, go back to your dog, and say "Out" as you motion with your left arm and hand in the direction of the target. Praise him when he gets there and call him back to you. Repeat three times.

- **Progression 3:** Over the course of several sessions, increase the distance from the target to 50 feet in increments of 2 feet.

- **Progression 4:** Have a helper place a treat and then you can send your dog.

This is an exciting exercise for your dog, especially if he is high in prey behaviors. How many repetitions your dog will perform depends on his Personality Profile and the number of prey behaviors he has.

Anytime you work with treats, make sure that your dog is hungry. Depending on the number of his prey behaviors, you may need to use something special, such as homemade liver treats. Experiment to find out what works best to keep your dog interested.

The sequences for teaching the Retrieve Over High Jump

Most dogs have to jump an obstacle equal in height to the height of the dog at the withers. A short definition of withers is the highest part of the dog behind the neck, where the shoulder blades meet. Some breeds have to jump only three-fourths of their height at the withers. The AKC Obedience Regulations specify which breeds jump three-fourths of their height and which ones jump once their height.

Not all dogs are natural jumpers and for all of them it is an athletic activity; as any other athletic activity, it requires conditioning. Just because Buddy jumps on the furniture does not mean he automatically will jump over the High Jump. You have to teach him and, for his safety, teach him correctly as explained in the following sequences.

Getting Buddy used to the jump

Your Sequence 1 goal is to get Buddy accustomed to the jump:

Put your leash on the dead ring of Buddy's training collar and walk him up to the jump, which is set at *teaching height* (the dog's height at the elbows). Touch the top board with your left hand and let him examine the jump. Step over the jump and encourage him to follow. You can use a treat to get him to go over. Repeat three times or until he goes over the jump without hesitation.

Teaching Buddy to jump on his own

Sequence 2's goal? To teach your dog to jump on his own:

Sit Buddy 3 feet from the center of the jump. Put his target 3 feet from the jump on the other side. Say "Stay," step over the jump, place a treat on the target, go back to your dog, and send him with "Out." (You can also stay with the target, tap it with your fingers, and call him over the jump.)

Repeat until Buddy is comfortable going over the jump — five to ten times per session. Jumping repetitions are necessary not only to teach Buddy the exercise but also to condition him physically.

You need to look at any jumping exercise as an athletic endeavor on the part of your dog, which requires the same kind of conditioning that applies to human athletic endeavors.

Getting Buddy to jump by himself — and from different angles

Your Sequence 3 goal is to get your dog to jump by himself and from different angles:

Leave Buddy 10 feet from the jump, go to the other side by stepping over the jump, focus his attention on the center of the top board, take three steps backward, pause, and say "Buddy, jump." It's not a good idea to tap the top board as you say "Jump" because it teaches your dog to jump on a visual cue instead of on the command. Once you see that he has committed himself to jump, back up to give him enough room to land. Praise as he lands and release backward, giving him a treat.

Few of us can throw the dumbbell so that it always lands in the right spot, and some of us never get it there. So you might as well teach your dog to jump from different angles. Leave Buddy facing the right upright of the jump, ten feet away. Go to the other side by stepping over the jump, focus his attention on the center of the top board, take three steps backward, pause, and say "Buddy, jump." Repeat the exercise by having Buddy face the left upright.

Getting Buddy to jump while holding the dumbbell

Yep. Sequence 4's goal is to get your dog to jump while holding the dumbbell:

Simply repeat Sequence 3 with Buddy holding his dumbbell as he jumps. Here, you're teaching the Return Over the Jump part of the exercise, which, like any other part of an exercise, has to be taught.

Teaching Buddy the Motivational Retrieve

Sequence 5's goal is indeed to teach your canine friend the Motivational Retrieve:

We've produced a videotape called "The Motivational Retrieve — Teaching, Practicing, Testing." For information on how to obtain this tape, check out the coupon in the back of this book.

With Buddy at heel, put two fingers of your left hand, palm facing you, through your dog's collar at the side of his neck, back to front. Hold the dumbbell in your right hand and get him excited about retrieving the dumbbell. From 10 feet, say "Buddy, jump" and briskly approach the jump. Two feet before you get to the jump, throw the dumbbell and let go of your dog. Continue to approach the jump and, as he picks up the dumbbell and turns around to look at you, focus his attention on the center of the jump. As he commits himself to jump, back up to give him enough room to land. Praise, take the dumbbell, and release. Repeat until your dog jumps, retrieves, and returns reliably.

Also practice this sequence with "bad" throws so your dog learns to come back over the jump from different angles. Picture a 45-degree line going away from you from each upright and condition Buddy to return over the jump from anywhere within that area.

Getting Buddy to wait

The Sequence 6 goal is to teach Buddy to wait:

From 10 feet, tell Buddy to stay. Put two fingers of your left hand through his collar and throw the dumbbell. Very, very gingerly let go of the collar, count to five, and say "Buddy, jump."

After he jumps, quietly follow him. And after he picks up and turns to face you, focus his attention on the center of the jump. As he commits himself to return, back up so he has enough room to land, take the dumbbell, and release. Repeat until he stays without two fingers in the collar and returns without any help from you. Position yourself facing the center of the jump, at least 8 feet away, and throw the dumbbell at least 8 feet beyond the jump.

For the Retrieve Over High Jump, you're required to stand at least 8 feet from the jump and throw the dumbbell at least 8 feet beyond the jump.

And be sure to practice some "bad" throws, too (see Sequence 5).

Raising the jump

Sequence 7's goal is to raise the jump:

Begin raising the jump in 2- or 4-inch increments, depending on the size of your dog. If the height of the jump becomes an issue, condition your dog at a lower height. Difficulties with jumping are never disciplinary in nature — your dog's trying to tell you something. Your dog's structure may be such that he's unable to do what you ask, or he may experience pain for any number of reasons.

Getting Buddy to ignore distractions

Your Sequence 8 goal? Teach Buddy to ignore distractions:

Follow the program outlined in Chapter 14. In addition, have a distracter stand close to an upright while the dog is jumping and, once he's successful, have the distracter try to get your dog to go around the jump on the return by talking to him or enticing him with food. Your helper does not, of course, use the dog's name.

Anytime your dog goes around the jump on the return, slowly approach him and put two fingers of your left hand (palm facing you) through the collar at the side of his neck, back to front. Take him back to where he picked up the dumbbell, tell him to stay (he can stand, sit, or lie down), go over the jump yourself to the other side, focus his attention on the top board, step back, and tell him "Jump." Praise as he lands and then release. Then try it again.

How high is high enough?

How high your dog has to jump depends on his breed. Some breeds jump once their height at the withers and some three-fourths their height. The AKC Obedience Regulations specify the height each breed has to jump. The jump height is set at the nearest multiple of two inches. For example, Landseer Newfoundlands have to jump three-fourths of their height at the withers. Or a 27½-inch-tall dog has to jump 20 inches.

Buddy may also try to go around the jump on the way out. If so, slowly approach him. If he has already picked up the dumbbell, take it out of his mouth and put it back where he picked it up. Now return with Buddy to the starting point and send him again.

Under no circumstances should you say "No" or do anything else that might discourage your dog. You want to put Buddy in a position where he can figure out for himself the desired response. Instead of doing anything that might discourage him, you're going to help him by literally showing him exactly what it is you want, which may include physical guidance. The hardest part for you will be to keep your mouth shut and remain patient.

You know how many repetitions it takes for your dog to figure something out, so there's no need to get impatient. You want him to keep on trying until he has figured it out, which is called the Aha response. Translated, it means "Aha! Now I know what you want." It's a powerful response because the dog has figured it out by himself, albeit with your help, instead of being told what to do. As a result, he responds with great reliability and enthusiasm.

The Broad Jump

For the Broad Jump, your dog is required to jump a distance equal to twice the height of the High Jump. Depending on the distance, that can be two, three, or four boards. It starts with you lining your dog up in front of and at least eight feet from the jump. The judge then says, "Leave your dog." You say "Stay" and go to a position facing the right side of the jump, with your toes about two feet from the jump, anywhere between the first and last board.

We've authored a training book on the Open class, as well as produced a video-tape. For information on where to obtain these resources, see the coupon in the back of this book.

The judge then says, "Send your dog." You say "Buddy, over." As your dog jumps, you execute a right-angle turn in place. The dog must sit and finish as in the Novice class's Recall (see Chapter 14).

Getting Buddy used to the jump

Sequence 1's goal is to get your dog used to the jump:

1. **Set up the jump at twice the height of your dog at the elbows.**

   With a small dog, this means only one board.

2. **Put a target 8 feet from the center of the jump.**

3. **Walk Buddy up to the jump and let him examine it.**

4. **Position yourself and your dog 8 feet from the center of the jump.**

5. **Show him a treat and use it to lure him over the jump with the command "Over."**

    At this point, it does not matter how he gets to the other side, just so he goes from one side to the other.

6. **Place the treat on the target and let him have it.**

7. **Praise and release.**

Repeat this sequence three times.

Getting Buddy to jump on command

Sequence 2's goal is to teach Buddy to jump on command:

1. **Put your dog in a sit-stay 8 feet from the center of the jump.**

2. **Walk over the jump and place a treat on the target.**

3. **Face your dog and attract his attention to the treat by tapping the target.**

4. **Call him over the jump with "Buddy, over."**

Repeat this sequence ten times.

To save time and steps, you can do this in either direction.

Getting Buddy to make the turn

Sequence 3's goal? To teach your dog to make the turn:

Start as in Sequence 2 but then take a step away from the target and send your dog over the jump. In increments of 8 inches, begin moving to the position you'll have to assume in the ring, calling Buddy to you after he picks up his treat. After you call him, make sure that he sits in front. Praise and release backward.

So that the dog doesn't always turn to the right, we also like to practice the making-the-turn exercise from the opposite side of the jump — so the dog has to turn to the left.

As Buddy becomes proficient with this exercise, eliminate the Come command and introduce the Finish. For most of your repetitions, you want him to sit in front. For the Finish, you want to keep him guessing, so do that one infrequently.

Dogs learn very quickly what the end product is supposed to look like, and they begin taking shortcuts. For example, instead of first sitting in front, Buddy goes directly to heel. You can forestall that scenario by varying your routine and making sure that no matter what, he has to sit in front before he gets to finish.

Getting Buddy to ignore distractions

Sequence 4's goal is to work on Buddy to ignore distractions:

Practice with a distracter about two feet from the target and work your way through 1st, 2nd, and 3rd degree distractions. Remember to stop for that session after the correct response. That's the one you want Buddy to remember. Resist the temptation to do the exercise just one more time. Your dog just may become creative, in which case you may be there for a *long* time until you get another correct response.

Out-of-Sight Stays

The last two exercises in the Open class are the three-minute sit-stay and the five-minute down-stay. Any of the stay exercises are boring to practice, but are nerve-wracking when you are in competition. So you do need to practice them and under various conditions, including in the rain, and in our part of the country, in the snow.

As an introduction to out-of-sight stays, leave Buddy in a sit-stay and go 6 feet in front of him. Pause for 10 seconds, walk past him, and stand 6 feet behind him with your back to him. Practice with distractions and have your helper tell you when Buddy moves and you have to reinforce the stay. At this stage, that scenario will be highly unlikely.

When you're ready to go out of sight, gradually increase the length of time you leave Buddy. Begin with 10 seconds and, over the course of several sessions, work up to the 3 minutes for the sit-stay and 5 minutes for the down-stay. If you experience difficulties, like if Buddy's breaking the stays, shorten your time and rebuild the exercise. Nine out of ten times, the problem is caused by lack of confidence on the part of the dog, and *that's* what you have to work on.

Chapter 17

The Utility Dog Title

*A*fter your dog obtains the AKC's Companion Dog Excellent title, you're eligible to enter the Utility Class, which is intended to be the most difficult and challenging class. Curiously, what makes this class difficult is not the exercises themselves but the order in which they're done. This chapter fills you in on what to expect.

Each year the American Kennel Club awards approximately 10,000 Companion Dog titles, 3,000 Companion Dog Excellent titles, and 600 Utility Dog titles.

The Utility Class: What's Expected from You and Buddy

The Utility Class consists of six exercises, each with a specific point value (see Table 17-1). For a qualifying score, you and Buddy have to earn more than 50 percent of the available points for each exercise and a final score of at least 170 out of a possible 200.

Table 17-1	The Utility Class
Required Exercises	*Available Points*
Exercise 1: Signal	40
Exercise 2: Scent Discrimination, Article No. 1	30
Exercise 3: Scent Discrimination, Article No. 2	30
Exercise 4: Directed Retrieve	30
Exercise 5: Moving Stand with Examination	30
Exercise 6: Directed Jumping	40
Maximum Total Score	**200**

Not All Exercises Are Created Equal

We characterize the exercises the dogs are required to do in two categories:

- Action
- Control

Action exercises tend to be motivational for the dog — something he enjoys. Examples of action exercises are heeling, retrieving, jumping, and coming. *Control exercises* are demotivational — not something that is fun and exciting. Examples of control exercises are the Sit and Down-Stay, the drop for the Drop on Recall, and the Stand for Examination. The Front and the Finish can be either, depending on the dog's perception.

With that in mind, take a look at Table 17-2, which lists which category the various exercises for the Utility Class fall into.

Table 17-2	Drives and Categories for the Utility Class Exercises	
Required Exercise	*Behavior/Drive*	*Category*
Signal:		
Dog heels	Pack	Action
Dog stands at heel	Pack	Control
Dog lies down on signal	Pack	Control

Required Exercise	Behavior/Drive	Category
Dog sits on signal	Pack	Control
Dog comes on signal	Pack	Action
Scent Discrimination:		
Dog selects by scent one article out of eight	Prey	Control (that is, more control than action because the article is placed rather than thrown, and the dog has to discriminate)
Dog retrieves and brings it back to handler	Pack	Action
Directed Retrieve:		
Dog is sent out	Prey	Action
Dog retrieves one of three articles	Pack	Action
Moving Stand with Examination:		
Dog heels	Pack	Action
Dog stands on command	Pack	Control
Dog is examined by judge	Pack	Control
Dog goes to heel	Pack	Action
Directed Jumping:		
Dog leaves handler	Prey	Action
Dog jumps	Prey	Action

You can see from Table 17-2 that the potentially most devastating impact on the dog's motivation comes from the Signal exercise, which is immediately followed by another control exercise. It's not until the Directed Retrieve that the dog starts to have any real fun.

To maintain your dog's enthusiasm in practice sessions, alternate as much as possible between action and control exercises.

Obviously, the dog can learn the Signal exercise and even do it with some degree of verve, provided that you don't turn him off in the teaching and practicing phases. When you see that an exercise has a dampening effect on your dog, immediately follow it with something he likes, such as a retrieve. You may have to split up the Signal exercise into its component parts to keep your dog motivated and only once or twice a week practice it the way it's supposed to be done.

Your dog doesn't look at all exercises in the same light. Some he considers more fun than others. By observing the impact an exercise has on the psyche of your dog, you can keep him enthusiastic and motivated.

We've authored a training book on the Utility Class, as well as produced a videotape. For information on where to obtain these materials, see the coupon at the back of this book.

The Signal Exercise

For the Signal exercise, you dog needs to give the correct responses to the signals to heel, stand, stay, drop, sit, and come. The exercise starts with a regular heeling pattern. Then the judge says, "Stand your dog." At that point, you come to a halt and signal your dog to stand at heel. The position is the same as the Automatic Sit at Heel except the dog has to stand at heel. The judge then tells you, "Leave your dog," and you give the stay signal and go to the other side of the ring and face your dog. The judge then signals you to drop, sit, call, and finish your dog. You're not allowed to use verbal commands. The entire sequence is done with signals.

Giving the hand signal to heel

You give the hand signal to heel with your left hand, which moves from left to right, palm down, in front of the dog's eyes (see Figure 17-1). First, give the signal together with the command. After several repetitions, eliminate the command.

Getting Buddy to stand at heel on signal

You give the signal with your left hand, from right to left. Your palm is down and parallel to the ground, above and ahead of the dog's eyes (see Figure 17-2).

The stand isn't a very exciting or motivating exercise for your dog, so we don't recommend practicing it more than five times during a session. And always follow it with something your dog likes.

Figure 17-1:
Signaling
your dog
to heel.

Figure 17-2:
Signaling
your dog
to stand
at heel.

Introducing Buddy to the stand signal

Your Sequence 1 goal is to introduce your dog to the stand signal:

1. **Review standing your dog at heel (see Chapter 15).**
2. **Put the thumb of your right hand through the collar under the dog's chin.**
3. **Stand your dog with the command and signal.**
4. **Make sure that his front feet remain in place.**
5. **Praise and release.**

Repeat this sequence ten times, not necessarily at one session.

Getting Buddy to stand at heel from motion

Your Sequence 2 goal is to teach your dog to stand at heel from motion:

1. **With Buddy in heel position, with the leash in Control Position, say "Let's go" and start walking.**
2. **As you come to a halt, and before you've brought your feet together, put the leash in your right hand, place it against your dog's chest, give the signal with your right hand, and say "Stand."**

   Concentrate on putting your right hand against his chest so that Buddy can't advance past heel position. If you bring your right hand forward, Buddy will follow it and stand wherever you hold it.

   Also, make sure that you stop him *standing* in heel position. If necessary, prevent him from sitting by placing your left hand against his right thigh.
3. **Praise and release with a treat.**

Repeat this sequence five times per session over the course of several sessions. After each stand, praise and release enthusiastically with a treat. The object is to have Buddy stand at heel without any tension on the leash.

Getting Buddy to stand out of turns

Sequence 3's goal? To teach the stand out of turns:

Repeat Sequence 2 after a right turn, an about turn, and a left turn. In the ring, you have to do a stand right after a turn, so that's the maneuver you want to practice most.

Getting Buddy to stand from a fast pace

Sequence 4's goal is to teach the stand from a fast pace:

Teach Buddy Sequence 2 from a fast pace. Although not absolutely necessary, standing him from a fast is a good indicator of how well he knows the stand at heel from motion. It's also a fun way to practice.

At some point, you may have to use a check to stop Buddy's forward momentum. If doing so becomes necessary, put the rings of his collar on top of his neck. Just before you give the command, check straight back. Be sure the check is straight back. If you check up, you're telling him to sit.

Getting Buddy to do the stand off leash

Yep. Sequence 5's goal is to practice the stand off leash:

Review Sequences 1, 2, 3, and 4 off leash. Then review Sequence 2 again — eliminating the verbal command.

Getting Buddy to drop from a stand and sit from a down

Use the same signal that you use for the Drop on Recall (see Chapter 16) by bringing your right arm straight up above your shoulder as though you're reaching for the ceiling.

Getting Buddy to drop from a stand

Sequence 1's goal is to teach your dog to drop from a stand:

1. **Stand your dog at heel.**

2. **Neatly fold the leash into your left hand.**

3. **Say "Stay" and step in front of your dog.**

4. **Kneel down and place two fingers of your left hand, palm facing down, through his collar, under his chin.**

5. **Signal with the right hand and say "Down," at the same time pushing against his chest with your left hand; then apply downward pressure on his collar.**

   The purpose of the pressure against his chest is to prevent Buddy from moving his feet forward as he drops — the natural tendency for most dogs. You want to teach him to collapse in place because that's what the Obedience Regulations require. Look at his feet as you drop him. With pressure against his chest, they don't move forward.

   The downward pressure on the collar reinforces the drop. Be careful that you don't inadvertently pull him toward you because that would make him move his feet forward. Practice until he lies down in place without any pressure on his collar — and with the signal only.

6. **Say "Stay," stand up, praise, and release with a treat.**

Getting Buddy to sit from a down

Sequence 2's goal? To teach your dog to sit from a down.

You give the signal with your right hand. With your right arm hanging naturally at your side, the back of the hand facing the dog, turn your hand so the palm faces your dog. Then bring your arm out and away from your body, no higher than your waist, keeping your elbow locked. The object is to train your dog to respond to the turning of your hand. In the teaching phase, the arm moves in front of your body so you can lure Buddy into a sit with a treat:

1. **Down your dog from a stand as in Sequence 1.**

2. **Say "Stay" and stand up.**

3. **Put your left hand, which holds the leash, against your right hip.**

4. **Have a treat in your right hand, held naturally at your side, and make sure that the back of your hand is toward the dog.**

5. **Say "Sit," turn your right hand so that the palm faces your dog, and lure your dog into a sit with the treat.**

   Bring the treat to a point directly above his head so that your dog sits straight up by bringing his front feet under him instead of moving forward. Practice this maneuver until the dog sits as soon as you turn your right hand. That's what you want, so be sure you reward that response with a treat.

6. **Praise and release backward.**

Play a game of sit from a down and down from a sit. Hold the treat in your signal hand and randomly reward correct responses. Be sure to count to 5 after every change in position so that your dog can focus on what you want. Play only as long as Buddy is an enthusiastic participant.

Reinforcing the sit

Yes, indeedy. Sequence 3's goal is to teach the reinforcement of the sit:

1. **Start as in Sequence 2 but without a treat in your hand.**

2. **Give the command and signal and — at the same time — give a little check with your right hand on the leash straight up, palm up, to a point directly above your dog's head.**

3. **Bring your hand back to your side.**

4. **Praise and release with a treat.**

This is the review progression for this exercise. Alternate on a random basis between using a treat and a little check. Then eliminate the command and practice until your dog responds reliably to the signal.

Increasing your distance

Sequence 4's goal? To increase the distance:

1. **Down and sit your dog from 3 feet in front — on leash.**

2. **As you give the signal, take a step toward Buddy with your right foot, keeping your left leg in place.**

   The step toward your dog reinforces the response by keeping your dog in place and stops him from moving forward. Note that as you increase the distance, you may need to reinforce the sit with a little check.

3. **Bring your leg and arm back to their original positions.**

4. **Praise and give him a treat for every correct response.**

After Buddy masters this exercise from 3 feet, increase the distance to 6 feet. As you increase the distance, continuing with the step is important. Remember, Buddy's natural tendency is to come to you, and you want him to drop and sit in place.

Introducing distractions

At this point in the training, introduce distractions, beginning with 1st degree (see Chapter 14 for info on the degrees). The distracter stands 10 feet from the dog at a 45-degree angle. After you leave Buddy in a stand, the distracter approaches in a non-threatening, benign manner to within 2 feet of him. Give the signal to drop, with the step toward your dog. If he does drop, praise and enthusiastically release. If he doesn't drop, slowly go to him and reinforce the down by putting two fingers of your *left* hand (not the one that gave the signal) through his collar, under his chin, and placing him down. When he does it correctly, praise, release with a treat, stop, and go on to something else.

Carefully work your way through the three levels of distractions from 6 feet in front, on leash. After that, take the leash off and gradually increase the distance until Buddy does the exercise with you standing 40 feet in front of him.

Giving the come and finish signals

Time to wrap up this whole Signal exercise:

1. **Leave your dog in a sit-stay and go to the end of the leash.**

2. **With your left hand holding the leash at your left side, say "Come" and give the signal by bringing your right arm shoulder-high and then to the center of your chest.**

3. **Praise and release.**

   Note that at this point — when you *release* your dog — there is no Front or Finish.

4. **Do five repetitions of Steps 1 through 3 — not necessarily in a row or during the same session.**

5. **Now go through it again but eliminate the command; then praise and release.**

   If Buddy doesn't respond to the signal, give him a little tug on the leash.

   Be sure to practice without the command until your dog responds reliably to the signal.

6. **Now try the exercise off leash from 6 feet in front; then praise and release (see Figure 17-3).**

   From 6 feet away you can't expect much speed. There's little motivation to come quickly for such a short distance. As soon as you increase the distance, though, Buddy will pick up speed. Keep making it exciting for him by using a treat and the release.

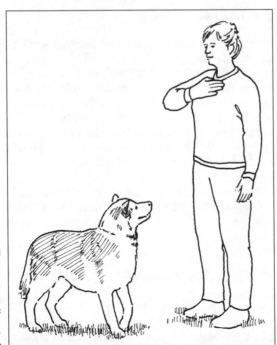

Figure 17-3:
The come and finish signal off leash.

7. **For the Finish, use the same signal that you use for the Novice Class and Open Class.**

   Remember, you don't want to front or finish the dog every time he comes to you. Use the release as an alternative.

The Scent Discrimination

Maybe you've already taught your dog the Find Mine trick with dollar bills (see Chapter 20). If so, this exercise should go quickly. The only difference between the two is that the Scent Discrimination exercise is done with metal and leather articles, usually dumbbells, five of each. Buddy is required to retrieve first one, either metal or leather, and then the other, which you have scented, from among the remaining four leather and four metal.

When teaching your dog the Scent Discrimination exercise, avoid the He Should Know Better pitfall if your dog brings back the wrong article. Under no circumstances should you second-guess your dog. He obviously thought he retrieved the right one.

Getting Buddy to retrieve leather and metal articles

Your Sequence 1 goal is to teach your dog to retrieve leather and metal articles:

You may have to review the teaching progressions for the Retrieve command (see Chapter 12), depending on how your dog responds. Leather items are rarely a problem, but metal items can be. Your dog must retrieve either kind reliably before you can go on.

Getting Buddy to use his nose

Sequence 2's goal is to teach Buddy to use his nose:

First, you need to introduce him to the game of Find. For example, when training outside, hide the article around a corner. Let him see you take the article and return. Send him with "Find it." When he brings it back, release backward with great enthusiasm and reward him with a treat. Note that the first time you try this game, you may have to show him where you put the article.

As Buddy catches on, increase the difficulty so that he has to use his nose to find the article.

Introducing Buddy to the articles

Your Sequence 3 goal is to introduce Buddy to the articles:

For this purpose, use a *scent board*, a piece of pegboard commensurate with the size of your dog and large enough to accommodate all eight articles placed 6 inches apart. Get Buddy accustomed to walking on the board by heeling him over it several times and having him sit on it. Then have him retrieve an article from the board — first by throwing it on the board and then by placing it. Release backward and reward. *Note:* It's important that your dog is comfortable retrieving from the board before you begin to add other articles.

Prepare the board for the next sequence by tying one of each article on the board, with the tie underneath. Give it anywhere from 0.5 to 6 inches of slack. Let the board air out for 24 hours, so it has little, if any, of your scent on it.

Tying an article to a board prevents the dog from picking up the incorrect article and encourages him to keep looking for the right one. You can also tie the articles to a piece of carpeting, although some of the larger dogs sometimes bring back the entire piece of carpeting. If that happens to you, use a board.

Teaching Buddy the concept of scent discrimination

Sequence 4's goal is to teach your dog the concept of scent discrimination:

1. **Make sure that your hands are clean and free from chemicals and perfumes.**

2. **With you and Buddy facing the board from 10 feet away, scent a metal article by slowly rubbing the bar of the dumbbell for 20 seconds.**

3. **Say "Find it" and let him briefly hold the article.**

4. **Take the article out of his mouth, say "Stay," and place the article on the board, letting him watch you place it on the board.**

5. **Go back to heel and send him with "Find it."**

6. **If Buddy tries to pick up an incorrect article, encourage him to keep looking by saying "You can do it!" in an excited tone of voice — or anything other than the original command.**

7. **When he picks up the correct one, quietly say "That's it" with a big smile on your face.**

8. **Release backward and reward.**

Repeat the sequence by placing the scented leather article in a different location on the board until you're sure that Buddy is using his nose to find the correct article. At the same time, gradually increase the distance you stand from the board to 20 feet. During this sequence, stop the praise for picking up the correct article but continue to smile. You don't want Buddy to become dependent on praise and wait for it before he returns, so eliminate it as soon as you can. Release and reward Buddy after he has returned. Stop after two successive successful responses — one metal and one leather.

Tie two more articles on the board, varying the length of slack for each article. After each successful round, tie two more articles on the board until all eight articles are tied on the board.

Getting Buddy to discriminate between your scent and someone else's

Sequence 5's goal is to teach your dog discrimination between your scent and another person's. Up until now, Buddy has learned only to find your article among unscented ones. The object of this exercise is to teach him to find your article among those that have been touched by someone else:

Before you send your dog, have a helper briefly touch the articles on the board. Then place yours. You and Buddy are still facing the board.

Some handlers make an effort to give the dog their scent by briefly holding their hand in front of the dog's nose. But we feel that by now our dogs should know our scent and consider the effort superfluous. It also loads up the dog's nose with scent just when you want his nose to be clear.

Some dogs catch on quickly, and others need to go back to the beginning with two articles tied down. You'll have to experiment with Buddy to see how he does. Try it with all eight articles tied down. If he gets hopelessly confused, start at the beginning.

When your dog is reliable at this step, introduce distractions the same way that you do for the retrieve.

Weaning Buddy off the board

Your Sequence 6 goal is to wean your dog off the board:

Reverse the procedure and untie two articles. After each successful round, stop. Over the course of several sessions, repeat until all the articles are loose on the board. If he comes back with the wrong article, don't take the article from him and send him again. Under no circumstances should you ever do anything that might discourage your dog.

Teaching your dog the Scent Discrimination exercise mainly involves building his confidence. You want to encourage him and not discourage him.

Doing this exercise on the board and doing it on any other surface is not the same. You can work with the board and place two articles on the ground and, as Buddy is successful, place the remainder, two at a time, on the ground in front of the board. You can also start again with just two articles on the ground and build from there. Once he's proficient at this part of the exercise, use the same procedure to move the articles from the board onto grass and rubber matting.

Right after it looks like Buddy has finally gotten the hang of it, he may go through one or more regressions, meaning that he may give the appearance of not having the foggiest idea of what this exercise is all about. You can recognize it by the number of successive incorrect responses: He brings back the wrong article, you send him again, and he brings back another incorrect article, and so on. This situation is *normal*, and you should expect it. The best advice we can give you is to put him back on the board for several days as a form of review.

Teaching Buddy the turn and send

Sequence 7's goal is to teach your dog the turn and send:

For the finished product, you and Buddy will have your backs turned to the eight articles as the article you scented is placed by the judge among the articles. The judge then says, "Send your dog." You can then make a right about-turn in place, at the same time sending your dog, or you can have him sit at heel and then send him.

With Buddy in heel position, show him the article, give the command "Find it," make an about turn in place, and throw the article, letting him chase it. Practice several times until Buddy catches on to the maneuver. Then put out your articles and repeat the procedure, only this time throwing the article into the pile. Following a few repetitions of that maneuver, line up with Buddy in heel position with your backs to the articles from about 20 feet away. Tell him to stay, place your scented article in the pile, return to Buddy, and send him with "Find it" as you make an about turn in place to the right.

Unless there's a compelling reason to have your dog sit at heel, we suggest that you send him as you make the turn. It's more motivational.

The Directed Retrieve

This particular exercise requires Buddy to retrieve one of three gloves, which are placed at the unobstructed end of the ring about 15 feet apart. You're required to give your dog the direction to the designated glove and the command.

The exercise starts with you and Buddy in the center of the ring with your backs to the gloves. The judge says something like "Glove number one," which designates the glove behind you on your right. Glove number two is the one directly behind you, and number three is the one to your left.

Other than teaching Buddy how to retrieve a glove, the only new maneuver you have to teach Buddy is the turns in place, with the emphasis on *place*. When working on the turns in place, keep in mind that the more accurate your dog is on heel position, the less likely he is to make a mistake.

The turns in place are the make-or-break maneuvers for the Directed Retrieve exercise.

All turns in place start with Buddy sitting at heel, leash in Control Position.

Teaching a right turn in place

You can teach this turn in three progressions — first placing your right leg, then taking a step on the right leg, and then making the turn in place by turning your right foot at a 90-degree angle to the left, heel to heel to the left:

- **Progression 1:** Place your right foot at a 90-degree angle one large step to the right. With "Buddy, heel," close with your left foot and guide your dog into heel position. Praise and release. Repeat 25 times.

- **Progression 2:** Say "Buddy, heel," take a step to the right, close with the left, and guide your dog into heel position. Praise and release. Repeat 25 times.

- **Progression 3:** Say "Buddy, heel" and turn in place to the right, closing with the left. Praise and release.

Teaching a right about-turn in place

Here's what you need to do:

- **Progression 1:** Say "Buddy, heel," take two steps forward, turn around to your right (keeping your feet together), take two steps forward, and guide your dog into heel position. Praise and release. Repeat 25 times.

> ✓ **Progression 2:** Say "Buddy, heel," take one step forward, turn around, take one step forward, and guide your dog into heel position. Praise and release. Repeat 25 times.
>
> ✓ **Progression 3:** Say "Buddy, heel," make two right turns in place, and guide your dog into heel position. Praise and release.

Teaching a left turn in place

Here are your progressions:

> ✓ **Progression 1:** Place your left foot directly in front of your dog's front feet. Say "Buddy, heel," take a large step with your right foot (past the left), and close with the left, guiding your dog into heel position with slight backward pressure on the leash. Praise and release. Repeat 25 times over the course of several sessions.
>
> ✓ **Progression 2:** Place your left foot directly in front of your dog's front feet. Say "Buddy, heel," take a small step with your right foot (past the left), and close with the left, guiding your dog into heel position with slight backward pressure on the leash. Praise and release. Repeat 25 times over the course of several sessions.
>
> ✓ **Progression 3:** Say "Buddy, heel," put your right foot at a 90-degree angle directly in front of your left (in a T position), and guide your dog into heel position with slight backward pressure on the leash. Praise and release. Repeat 25 times over the course of several sessions.
>
> ✓ **Progression 4:** Say "Buddy, heel" and make two left turns in place, guiding your dog into heel position with slight backward pressure on the leash. Praise and release.

Teaching how to retrieve the gloves

Give the direction by holding your left arm at the side of the dog's head, with your hand and fingers pointing straight toward the glove, held ahead of his nose, and your fingers pointing straight to the glove. Immediately following, say "Take it." What you may *not* do is give your dog the direction and then pump your left arm as you send him for the glove.

Although the Obedience Regulations permit you to send your dog as you give the direction, the regulations also permit you to first point in the direction of the glove, called *marking,* and then send your dog for the glove. This is the method that we teach.

For the center glove, your arm is stretched out so that your elbow is in line with the dog's nose, which gives him a better mark. You may bend your body and knees to the extent necessary in giving the direction to your dog. When giving the direction, make sure that your fingers are indeed pointing at the designated glove.

Before you start on this exercise, you may want to review the Retrieve command with a glove.

Here's what you do:

- **Progression 1:** With your dog sitting at heel and a glove in your left hand (held between your thumb and fingers), get your dog excited about the glove. Throw the glove, holding your arm as you would if you were to mark the glove, and say "Take it." After he picks it up, praise, and release. If he doesn't retrieve, review teaching him to retrieve the glove (see Chapter 12 for retrieving).

- **Progression 2:** Once your dog retrieves the glove and you've introduced him to the direction, place a glove 15 feet to your right, 15 feet to your left, and 15 feet in front of you. Say "Buddy, heel" and make a right turn in place. Buddy now faces the glove on your right. Mark the direction with your left arm. You may have to hold on to your dog by placing two fingers of your right hand through his collar. Send your dog with "Take it." Praise and release after he has picked up the glove.

  Repeat for the glove on the left and the center glove. After three successful repetitions, move the gloves on your right and left 2 feet straight ahead and start all over. After each set of three successful repetitions, move the gloves on your right and left 2 feet straight ahead until they're in line with the center glove. Send your dog to different gloves in a random pattern.

What if he goes to the wrong glove? Let him try to work it out for himself by maintaining the signal. For example, suppose that Buddy goes to number two instead of number one. Hold the signal facing number one. When Buddy returns to you, he immediately notices that something is wrong: You're not standing up straight but are still pointing to the glove. He may try to do one of several things, like

- Insist on giving you the glove, which you do *not* take.

- Give up and do nothing.

- Go for another glove, probably the correct one.

If he retrieves the correct glove, stand up, praise, and release. If he does nothing, approach the number one glove while still holding the signal and get him to pick it up — preferably just by pointing at it and without an extra command. When he does, praise and release. If he doesn't, reinforce the retrieve.

Every time you help your dog, you're assuming the responsibility for his behavior. You want him to learn that it's *his* responsibility to make the right decision. To do that, you have to give him a chance to work things out for himself.

Once Buddy has learned the direction portion of the exercise, you can introduce the turn and send. Remember that Buddy will not see the gloves being placed; he will have his back to them in the ring. The Obedience Regulations permit you to turn either to the left or to the right. You need to experiment to discover which is best for you and your dog.

The Moving Stand with Examination

For this exercise, you're required to heel your dog for about 10 feet when the judge tells you to "Stand your dog." Without pausing or breaking your stride, you give the command and/or signal to stand and continue walking 10 to 12 feet. Then you turn and face your dog. The judge examines your dog, a little more thoroughly than he does in the Novice Class, and then he says, "Call your dog to heel." You then give the command and/or signal for Buddy to go to heel.

Here are the progressions:

✔ **Progression 1:** With your dog on leash and at heel, say "Let's go" and start walking. After several steps, give the signal to stand, say "Stay," and continue walking. When you get to the end of the leash, turn and face your dog. Tell him what a clever fellow he is, count to five, and release. Practice ten times over the course of several sessions.

For the Moving Stand, the dog must stand and stay on command without taking any steps forward while you keep walking.

If Buddy needs help to stand and stay, use the same technique you use to teach a stand at heel.

Now try it off leash.

✔ **Progression 2:** Start again with your dog on leash. Take several steps, stand your dog, go to the end of the leash, and face him. Count to five, signal, and say "Buddy, heel," guiding him into heel position. Praise and release. The Obedience Regulations permit you to give both the signal to heel and the command for this exercise.

When Buddy correctly goes to heel on leash, try it off leash. Then gradually increase the distance you leave him in a stand until you can go about 10 to 12 feet, as required by the regulations, before you turn and face him.

✔ **Progression 3:** Finally, you do need to practice the examination part of the exercise with a helper.

The Directed Jumping

For this exercise, your dog has to go — on command — from one end of the ring to the other, between the bar and the high jump. The bar and the high jump are in the center of the ring about 18 feet apart. You then give your dog the command and/or signal for one of the jumps, after which he has to front and then finish. The entire procedure is then repeated for the other jump.

The Go-Out command takes a little time to teach because the dog can see absolutely no rhyme nor reason for this exercise.

We approach this exercise in three parts: the go-out, the jumps, and putting the two together. To start, teach the go-out without reference to the jumps. When Buddy has learned the go-out and the directed jumping parts, then put them together.

Teaching Buddy the Go-Out command

Here's Progression 1:

To teach Buddy to leave, use food or an object, like a stick or a toy. To teach him where to go, use a box, made from PVC pipe, that's commensurate to the size of the dog. Then put the box in front of a barrier, such as a section of fencing, a fence, or the side of a house.

1. **Get your dog used to the box by heeling him into the box and then calling him into it.**

2. **Put a target, commensurate with the size of your dog, inside the box.**

3. **With Buddy on leash, show him a treat and say "Out" as both of you go into the box.**

4. **Place the treat on the target and let him pick it up. Praise, encourage him to turn around in the box, and release backward.**

5. **Repeat until Buddy is comfortable with going into and turning in the box.**

6. **Leave Buddy in a sit-stay 10 feet in front of the target, let him see you place a treat on the target, go back to heel position, and send him with "Buddy, out."**

   You may signal him at the same time with your left hand in the direction you want him to go.

7. **When he gets to the target, let him take the treat, praise, and call him back.**

With each successive repetition, increase the distance to the target by 2 feet until you're 75 feet from the target. Repeat at that distance 50 times over the course of several sessions.

Teaching the go-out is pure target training with the addition of the box so that the dog knows where to sit.

Now you're ready for Progression 2:

1. **Remove the target.**

2. **Leave Buddy in a sit-stay 10 feet from the barrier, go into the box, face your dog, point to the ground, and go back to heel position.**

3. **Send your dog and, after he has left, quietly follow him so that when he gets to the spot you indicated, you're in front of the box.**

4. **Say "Buddy, sit," using the sit hand signal and a step forward to make him sit in place.**

5. **Reward him with a treat, held in the hand that gave the signal.**

   From now on, Buddy is only rewarded for going to the designated spot, and he has to learn that the reward comes from you.

With each successive repetition, increase the distance to the target by 2 feet until you're 75 feet from the target. Repeat at that distance 50 times over the course of several sessions.

The Obedience Regulations don't specify the commands you have to use, and the commands don't have to be in English. But excessively loud commands, as in yelling at the dog, aren't permitted.

During this progression, Buddy learns to turn and sit in the box. Continue to follow him and use the step and signal so he understands that you want him to turn and sit immediately. The step and signal prevent him from getting into the habit of taking several steps toward you, which you don't want.

So what do you do if Buddy doesn't leave or only goes part of the way? Without saying anything, slowly approach him, put two fingers of your left hand through the collar (back to front, palm facing you, at the side of his neck), and take him to the spot you indicated. Reinforce the sit with "Sit," let go, give him a treat, and release. Send him again.

Now for Progression 3:

1. **Send your dog two times in a row.**

2. **Leave Buddy in a sit-stay, go into the box, point to the spot, and go back to heel position.**

3. Send him and, when he gets to the spot, say "Buddy, sit."

4. Praise, count to five, release, and call him back to you.

5. Line him up at heel position and send him again.

6. When he gets there, have him sit; then go to him, praise, reward, and release.

Repeat this sequence 50 times.

If he doesn't leave you or doesn't go to the designated spot, show him where you want him to go.

Introduce distractions as you have for previous exercises by having the distracter first stand midway between you and the designated spot, 2 feet from Buddy's line of travel and then 2 feet from the designated spot. Work your way through 1st, 2nd, and 3rd degree distractions. If Buddy veers away from the distracter, use two distracters, starting at 8 feet apart, and teach him to go straight through.

Teaching Buddy directed jumping

Progression 1 is to introduce your dog to the bar jump:

1. Set the bar jump at *teaching height* (the height of your dog at the elbows).

2. Walk your dog up to the jump, on leash (dead ring), and touch the bar with your left hand.

3. Let him investigate the jump.

4. Start from 10 feet away, say "Bar," and briskly walk toward the jump.

5. Let him jump as you go over with him or around the jump.

Repeat until he jumps without any hesitation.

Progression 2 is to introduce your dog to direction:

1. Set up the high and the bar jumps at teaching height, 18 feet apart.

2. Place your target 10 feet from the center of the high jump.

3. Leave your dog in a sit-stay facing the high jump.

4. Go over the jump to the target and place a treat on the target.

5. Stand 2 feet behind the target facing your dog.

6. **Say "Jump" and give the signal by bringing your arm up from your side, shoulder height, pointed toward the jump.**

   Buddy should go over the jump to reach the target and his treat.

7. **Praise and release.**

Repeat the exercise for the bar jump, saying "Bar."

Gradually work your way to the center and increase the distance from the jumps to 20 feet. You should always be in the mirror position to Buddy. Always step over the jump and place your treat. Then test Buddy's understanding by eliminating the treat. This is the review progression for this exercise, so don't hesitate to use the treat on a random basis.

Begin raising the jumps in 2- or 4-inch increments, depending on the size of your dog. Difficulties with jumping are never disciplinary. If your dog is having a problem with a jump, he's trying to tell you something. Listen to him.

Putting it all together

You're ready to combine the go-out with directed jumping:

1. **Put your box in front of the fence.**

2. **Leave Buddy midway between the two jumps.**

3. **Go to the box and point to the spot where you want him to go.**

4. **Return to heel position, send him to the box, and tell him to sit and stay.**

   Buddy remains in the box for the sit-stay.

5. **Go back to the spot from which you are ultimately going to send him, that is, 20 feet from the center line between the jumps.**

6. **Give the command and signal to jump.**

7. **Praise as he lands and release.**

Repeat the exercise for the other jump.

Now start with Buddy at heel position, 2 feet back from the center line between the jumps, and follow the same procedure. Repeat in 2-foot increments until you stand at the appropriate spot for the exercise before sending your dog. This procedure is a precaution for the first few times you put the go-out together with the directed jumping. It should prevent Buddy from coming up with the idea (as he otherwise might) that he has to jump on the way out.

After every two go-outs, reinforce that exercise with five repetitions into the box. Reward the first, third, and fifth with a treat.

Give your dog a chance to work out on his own what it is you want. Before you jump in to help him, see what he does. He may surprise you. Be patient and keep your mouth shut.

What if Buddy makes a mistake and goes over the wrong jump? Try letting him work it out. Maintain your signal and wait. The response you want to see is Buddy going back into or near the box without any help or command from you. When he does, lower your arm, tell him to sit, and repeat the signal.

Suppose that Buddy does nothing and just sits in front of you not knowing what to do. Give him a chance until you're absolutely certain that he has stopped trying. Then take him back to where he started, leave him, return, and send him again.

Seeing a dog have the Aha! response — Buddy shows you that the penny has dropped and he's figured out what you want — is perhaps one of the most exciting aspects of training a dog. To get there, you must never discourage your dog from trying, even if the response is incorrect. Permit and encourage your dog to solve these training problems, and you'll have a motivated student.

Part V
Beyond Training

In this part . . .

Because Buddy's health is so important to his overall well-being, this part talks about two issues that can affect how he behaves: aggressive tendencies and health care. Even the best-trained dogs can exhibit aggression from time to time; if you understand its causes, you can redirect Buddy and coax him back to being his polite old self. And meeting your dog's physical needs — with both preventive care and care for acute conditions — will help ensure that the two of you have a long and fulfilling life together. Finally, this part is where to look for outside help to train your dog.

Chapter 18

Dealing with Aggression

· ·

· ·

he term *aggression* means different things to different people. For example, a dog that runs along the fence in his yard barking furiously at a passerby may well be considered aggressive by the passerby. But if he's your dog, you may consider the behavior to be a perfectly normal reaction: The dog is defending his territory, which is what you expect from him.

Many dog owners expect a certain amount of protectiveness, or aggression, from their companions — but only at the right time and under the right circumstances. For the dog, that can be a tough call. This chapter helps you sort out how to manage the aggression issue in a variety of situations.

What Is Aggressive Behavior?

The terms *aggression* and *vicious* are often used incorrectly for behaviors that are not true aggression. True aggression is defined as unpredictable biting — without warning — with the intent to draw blood. By far, the greatest majority of so-called aggressive incidents are either predictable, preceded by a warning, or both.

For example, you are walking your dog when a stranger approaches and your dog starts to growl, maybe because he is afraid (defense flight) or he wants to protect you (defense fight). In either case it is not true aggression because the dog is giving you ample warning of his intentions. It is now your job to manage the situation correctly.

You can cross the street; you can turn around and go the other way; or you can tell your dog to heel and pass the stranger, keeping yourself between the stranger and your dog. Under no circumstances should you make any effort to calm your dog down by reassuringly petting him and telling him in a soothing voice, "There, there, it's perfectly okay, blah, blah, blah." Buddy will interpret that as, "He wants me to growl." Well, perhaps you do, but if you don't, these kinds of reassurances reinforce the behavior.

Aggressive behavior can be directed toward any or all of the following:

- ✔ Owner
- ✔ Family
- ✔ Strangers and other dogs and animals

Signs of aggression include the following:

- ✔ Low-toned, deep growling
- ✔ Showing of teeth and staring
- ✔ Ears and whiskers pointing forward with the dog standing tall and with his hackles up from his shoulders forward
- ✔ Actual biting

When this behavior is directed toward you, ask yourself whether the question of who is Number One has been resolved. Usually it has not, and the dog is convinced that he's Number One or thinks that he can become Number One. It's not that he's a bad dog. It's just that he is a pack animal and is looking desperately for leadership. If that leadership is not forthcoming on your part, he'll fill the vacuum. Dogs are very happy and content when they know their rank order.

Looking at the Causes of Aggression

Aggressive behavior can be hereditary, caused by poor health, or the result of the dog's environment. Hereditary aggression is relatively rare as it would contradict the whole concept of domestication. Much more frequent is aggressive behavior caused by the dog feeling poorly or being in discomfort, even pain (see Chapter 19). In these cases, the dog's action is not a behavior problem, but a health problem. The most common cause for dog bites is environmental — the result of a misunderstanding or outright mismanagement.

A misunderstanding can occur during play, when the puppy nips at the owner's hand, or when playing retrieve and the puppy/dog tries to get the stick and accidentally bites the hand. Most dog owners can recognize when a bite occurred as a result of a misunderstanding — the dog will be as horrified as the owner.

Bites occurring as a result of mismanagement are an entirely different matter. For example, the kids are playing with Buddy, when Buddy has had enough and retreats under the bed. When one of the children crawls after Buddy and tries to drag him out, Buddy snaps at the child's hand and causes a scratch. Not an uncommon scenario and certainly not aggression, even though there was no warning. Or was there? The fact that Buddy retreated should have told the children he had had enough.

Aggression is a natural and even necessary phenomenon. In the case of unwanted aggression, human mistakes or misunderstandings are the usual cause. The owner may be unintentionally rewarding the undesired behavior, causing it to occur again and again, or the owner may not have socialized the dog properly. Only when you are unable to manage aggression, or don't understand its origin, does it become a problem.

A few years ago, it was brought to our attention that a number of Rottweilers, when taken for their six-month checkups, had bitten the veterinarian. Apparently, the situation had gotten so bad that many veterinarians didn't want these dogs as clients anymore. At that point, we were consulted by the Rottweiler Club of England. We found that the very veterinary community who didn't want these dogs as clients anymore had advised the dogs' owners *not* to let the dogs out in public before they had all their vaccines — that is, until they were 6 months of age. Those who followed this advice ended up with completely unsocialized dogs.

This is a classic case of aggression on a grand scale caused by a lack of understanding of behavior. Socialization is a continuing necessity throughout your dog's life. If you don't socialize Buddy, you *will* have problems as he grows up. Take this advice very seriously and get Buddy into a good puppy class as soon as you can. And continue to take him out so that he can mix with other dogs as he continues to mature.

Keeping your dog at home until he's had all his vaccinations at 6 months of age prevents proper socialization with people and other dogs, which can be a cause for aggression.

Managing Your Dog's Aggression — Prey, Pack, Fight, and Flight Drives

This section examines the triggers of aggression in the context of the three drives — prey, pack, and defense. The triggers are different in each drive, and so is the *management,* or cure. Your dog's Personality Profile will tell what the likely triggers are going to be so that you can predict what Buddy will do under certain circumstances.

Learning to anticipate your dog's reaction under certain situations is part of managing his behavior.

Other than ignoring or putting up with the behavior, you have three basic options:

- **Expending the energy.** Each behavior has a *time frame,* or energy, and it can be managed by expending that energy, which means exercise specifically focused on that energy. The exercise can be playing ball, jogging, playing tug-of-war games, or whatever. Training is always a good idea.

- **Suppressing the energy.** This option means that the dog is not given an outlet for the energy. Suppression can be an effective *temporary* solution, provided that the dog has periodic opportunities to expend the energy. Absolute or long-term suppression is not a good idea. The energy will only redirect itself into another undesirable behavior.

- **Switching the drive.** When Buddy growls at another dog, for example, he is in fight drive. To manage the situation, switch him into pack drive. Cheerfully say something like "You must be joking" and walk away in the opposite direction.

Depending on the circumstances, you're going to use a combination of the three options in your management program.

Aggression from dogs high in prey drive

It shouldn't come as a surprise to you that *prey behaviors,* those associated with chasing and killing prey, are one of the leading causes for aggression. In a sense, aggression coming from this drive is the most dangerous because it can be triggered by so many different stimuli. Dogs high in prey drive are stimulated by sounds, smells, and moving objects.

Triggers

Anything that moves triggers prey behaviors. Dogs high in prey drive chase cars, bicycles, joggers, cats, other dogs, squirrels, bunnies, you name it. And if they catch up with whatever they're chasing, that's when the problem starts.

Management

Play retrieve games on a regular basis and make sure that the dog gets plenty of exercise. When you take him for a walk and he spots a cat or a squirrel, give him a check on the leash to refocus his attention on you and then go in the opposite direction.

If he doesn't reliably respond to the Come command, don't let him loose in situations where he might take off. Better yet, train him to come reliably on command. Whatever you do, don't let Buddy chase cars, joggers, or cyclists.

Taxing your dog's mental faculties also expends this energy. For example, we use a very simple game to keep this drive under control with our Landseer Newfoundland, Evo. He loves to retrieve, and on our daily walks, he has ample time to play. But he's rarely satisfied, always wanting to do it one more time. So in the evenings, we play the Find It game. First we put Buddy on a stay, and then we hide his favorite toy in different parts of the house, and then we tell him to find it. He searches until he does. Doesn't sound like much of a game, but since he has to use the little gray cells, after four to five retrieves, he's mentally wiped out and peace reigns.

Aggression from dogs high in fight drive

Once they understand who's in charge, these dogs are terrific companions and protectors, great competition and show dogs, and a joy to own. As young dogs, they may start bucking for a promotion. You may see signs of aggression toward you when you want the dog to get off the furniture or in similar situations — when he doesn't want to do what you tell him.

If a puppy is allowed to grow up doing anything he likes and is not given parameters for what he can and can't do, he'll assume that you are not strong enough to be the pack leader.

If a puppy isn't given strong, consistent guidance as to what he may and may not do, he'll develop a sense that you're a pushover. He'll try to take over. Full-fledged signs of aggression don't just suddenly occur. There are many warnings, from growls to lip lifting to staring at you. If you condone these behaviors and don't deal with them, your dog is on his way to becoming aggressive.

Buddy may also be aggressive toward other dogs. When meeting another dog, he'll try to lord it over him. The classic sign is putting his head over the shoulder of the other dog. The dog of lesser rank lowers his body posture, signaling that he recognizes the other dog's rank.

But when two dogs perceive each other as equal in rank, a fight may ensue. Left to their own devices, though, most often both dogs decide that discretion is the better part of valor. Both know that there are no percentages to fighting. They slowly separate and go their own way.

A true dog fight is a harrowing and horrifying experience, and most of us would prefer not to take the chance that it'll occur. We learn to read the signs and take the necessary precautions by keeping the dogs apart. Dogs are no different from people: Not all of them get along.

Some owners inadvertently cause dog fights by maintaining a tight leash on the dog. A tight leash alters your dog's body posture, thereby giving an unintended aggression signal to the other dog. Maintain a loose leash when meeting another dog so you don't distort Buddy's body posture. And at the slightest sign of trouble, such as a hard stare from the other dog, a growl, or a snarl, happily call your dog to you and walk away. *Happily* calling is important because you want to defuse the situation and not aggravate it by getting excited. What you want to accomplish is to switch the dog from fight drive into pack drive.

When a female dog tells off a male dog who's making unwanted advances, she is entitled. This behavior is *not* aggression but perfectly normal dog behavior.

Triggers

There can be a variety of triggers. Some of the more common ones are

- Trying to take something out of his mouth (see the nearby sidebar for some specific tips)
- Telling him to get off the couch
- Hovering or looming over the dog
- Staring at the dog
- Approaching the dog in a threatening manner
- Teasing the dog

You can avoid some of these triggers altogether — things like teasing him, staring at him, or hovering over him. Just don't do it. Other triggers, though, you need to deal with.

Taking something out of Buddy's mouth

There will be times when you have to take something out of Buddy's mouth. It could be a chicken bone from the garbage or anything else inappropriate. Don't yell at him or chase him. He'll redouble his efforts to eat whatever it is. A great solution is to get Buddy to *trade*. Offer him a piece of cheese or raw meat. As he reaches for it, of course, the chicken bone will drop out. Then you can pick it up and throw it away.

The trade is an easy and simple way to work out the problem. We've always trained our dogs to accept treats off a spoon (see Chapter 13). This technique works really well because when they see us holding a spoon and coming toward them, they immediately think they're getting a special treat. No matter what they have in their mouths at the time, they spit it out in favor of getting what's on the spoon.

Remember: Never chase Buddy and corner him. Doing so will destroy the very relationship you've been working so hard to achieve.

Management

Four solid ways are available for managing this kind of aggression.

Provide exercise and training

One way is to provide lots of exercise and training. Exercise physically tires the body, and training tires the brain. In this situation, lack of mental stimulation gets the dog into trouble. Aim for two training sessions a day, each at least ten minutes long. If you keep to the same time schedule, you'll have a happy puppy.

Play tug-of-war

Another way is to expend the energy in this drive by a good game of tug-of-war. This game allows the dog to use up his time frame of wanting to growl and tug and bite.

Some dog trainers discourage playing tug-of-war with dogs because they believe that it causes aggressive behavior. At one point, we believed that tug-of-war games would cause aggression and that aggressive behaviors should be suppressed. But we no longer hold that view. Playing tug-of-war helps to dissipate aggressive behavior. Just as we expend the energy in prey drive through retrieve games, we can expend the energy in fight drive with tug-of-war games. It's the same principle at work. The absence of an outlet for that energy, or efforts to suppress it, will only make matters worse.

Put aside ten minutes a day to play tug-of-war. It should be the same time every day. Here's what you do:

1. **Get a pull toy, a piece of sacking, or a knotted sock to use for the game.**

2. **Allow your dog to growl and bite the object and shake it.**

3. **Let him bring the object back to you to play again.**

4. **Be sure to let him win each and every time.**

5. **When he's had enough, or the ten minutes are up, walk away from this session with the dog in possession of the toy.**

The game effectively discharges the energy and the time frame in that drive. The game should be removed from regular training sessions and done when you and your dog are alone with no distractions. It's his time and his only. You'll be amazed at how satisfying the game is to your dog and at the calming effect it has on him.

A tug-of-war case in point

When we came up with this *tug-of-war-is-good* concept, we were teaching a class of students who were very advanced in their training. Many of them were training their second or third dog, and all were experienced competitors. They had chosen dogs with a relatively high fight drive because they knew how well those dogs trained and how good the dogs looked in the show ring — bold and beautiful. But they had to live with the dogs' tendency toward aggressive behavior and always had to be careful in a class or dog show situation — when the dog was around other dogs.

For the entire eight-week session, they were told to put time aside daily to play tug-of-war with their dogs. By the third week, we already noticed a big difference in the dogs' temperaments. When together in class, the dogs became friendly toward each other, played more, and trained better, and they were perfectly well behaved when away from home.

Practice the Long Down

A third way to manage this type of aggression is with the Long Down. We can't emphasize enough the importance of this exercise. It's a benign exercise and establishes quite clearly who's in charge in a non-punitive way. For dogs that express any kind of aggressive behavior, go back to this exercise and do a ten-minute Down, last thing at night, for five out of seven days. It reinforces in your dog's mind that you're in charge. The Long Down and the tug-of-war game are simple solutions for the good dog that gets too pushy.

Use a muzzle

If your situation has reached the point where you're afraid of your dog, he tries to bite you, or you can't get him into the Down position, use a muzzle. You may also require outside help (see Chapter 21).

When you're nervous or anxious about what your dog might do if he encounters another dog or person, your emotions go straight down the leash, which can cause your dog to react in an aggressive manner. In a sense, your worries become a self-fulfilling prophecy. You can solve this dilemma with the use of a muzzle.

A muzzle allows you to go out in public with your dog without having to worry about him. A strange thing happens to a dog while wearing a muzzle. Once you've taken away his option to bite, he doesn't even try. It's almost as if he's relieved that the decision has been taken away from him. Even better, it allows you to relax.

Using a muzzle is a simple solution to a complex problem. It takes the decision about whether or not to bite away from your dog and gives you peace of mind.

Training to a muzzle should be done slowly and gently because, at first, many dogs panic having something around their faces. But with diligence, common sense, and some compassion for the dog, you can train him quite easily to accept it. Here's what you need to do:

1. **Put the muzzle on your dog for a few minutes and then take it off again.**

2. **Give him a treat and tell him what a good boy he is.**

3. **Repeat Steps 1 and 2 over the course of several days, gradually increasing the length of time your dog wears the muzzle.**

4. **When he's comfortable wearing the muzzle at home, you can use it when you take him out in public.**

Note: In some European cities, ordinances have been passed that require certain breeds to wear muzzles. We've seen many of these dogs happily accompanying their owners on walks. They were well behaved and seemed to be quite comfortable with their muzzles.

Many owners are reluctant to use a muzzle because of the perceived stigma attached to it. You have to make a choice — stigma or peace of mind. Something else to think about: Suppose that your dog actually bites someone. When you have such a simple solution, why take the chance?

Aggression from dogs high in pack drive

It's hard to believe that a dog high in pack behaviors could be aggressive. But this dog may

✔ Show signs of aggression toward people

✔ Attack other dogs with no reason

✔ Not stop biting when another dog submits

Triggers

The problem with this kind of aggression is that there don't seem to be many obvious triggers. It is frequently observed in dogs that are taken away from their litter and mother before 7 weeks of age. Between 5 and 7 weeks of age, a puppy learns to inhibit his biting (see Chapter 9). Also learned at this time is canine body language. In short, your puppy learns he is a dog. Puppies that haven't learned these lessons tend to be overly protective of their owners and may be aggressive to other people and dogs. They can't interpret body language and haven't learned bite inhibition. The result can be a fight.

In a household with more than one dog, while one dog is being petted and the other seeking your attention at the same time, the dog being petted may aggress toward the other dog. This over-possessiveness is not uncommon from adopted older dogs and rescue dogs.

Lack of adequate socialization with people and other dogs prior to 6 months of age can cause subsequent aggressive behaviors. We can think of several instances when a female owner has come to us because her dog was aggressive toward men. The cause in each case was lack of socialization or exposure to men. As long as the dog didn't come in close proximity with men, there was not a problem. A change of circumstances, such as a boyfriend, however, made it a problem.

Management

Lack of socialization with other people can be solved with a program of gradually getting the dog used to accepting another person. Take the case of a man-aggressive dog, for example. As always, the job is made easier when the dog has some basic training and knows simple commands like Sit and Stay. Here's what you need to do:

1. **Begin with Buddy sitting at Heel position, in control position (no tension on the leash and only ½ inch of slack).**

2. **Have the person walk past the dog from a distance of 6 feet, without looking at the dog.**

3. **Just before he passes the dog, have the person throw Buddy a small piece of a hot dog or another treat.**

4. **Repeat Steps 1 through 3 five times per session — but no more.**

5. **When Buddy shows no signs of aggression at 6 feet, decrease the distance.**

6. **Keep decreasing the distance until Buddy will take a treat, open palm, from the person.**

   The person should not look at the dog. He should pause just long enough to give the dog the treat and then pass.

7. **Once you've gotten to this point, follow the procedure outlined for submissive wetting (see Chapter 6).**

Aggression to other dogs, especially if the aggressor has had a few successes in his career, is not so simple. Prevention here is the best cure: Keep your dog on leash and don't give him a chance to bite another dog if you are away from home. If this occurs at home during the petting situation, make sure you enforce a down command to both dogs and stop petting the aggressor immediately. You may have to put one dog outside or in a crate, or even in a different room if this continues each time you pet your dog. Rotate your attention to both so that they both get petted but not together. Enforcing the down exercise for both dogs is a good way to manage this behavior.

To calm dogs with aggressive tendencies, get some essential oil of lavender from a health food store. Put just a couple of drops on a small cloth and wipe it onto your dog's muzzle and around his nose. Lavender has a calming effect, and we have had great success with it in class situations, where one dog aggresses at another dog. It enables the dog to concentrate on his work. We have also used it in a spray bottle (four drops of oil to eight ounces of water) and sprayed the room before the dogs come in. It really works wonders, and even calms the owners. Some of our students who have been in agility competition, and have dogs that couldn't concentrate because of the number of dogs and people around them, have found by wiping their dog's muzzles and nose with the oil, has made a dramatic improvement in their performances.

Feeding and Aggression

Your dog may growl when you get close to his food bowl. From his point of view, he's guarding his food — an instinctive and not uncommon reaction. The question is this: Should you try to do anything about it? And if so, what?

We have never been particularly concerned by food possessiveness in a dog, provided that it is the only time we see him act aggressively.

Sometimes owners unwittingly exacerbate the behavior by trying to take the dog's food bowl from him while he is eating. This is definitely not a good idea. Why create unnecessary problems? Don't attempt the practice of taking food away from him and then putting it back. Imagine how you'd feel if someone kept taking away your dinner plate and putting it back. In no time at all, you'd become paranoid at the dinner table. That sort of thing creates apprehension and makes the guarding and growling worse.

In order to change the behavior, you need to change the environment. Make sure that Buddy is fed in a place where the children or other dogs can't get his food. A good place to feed him is in his crate. Give him his bone in his crate and give him peace and quiet. And make sure that when he's in there, everyone leaves him alone.

Dealing with Fear-Biters — Dogs High in Flight Drive

The term *aggression* for these dogs is actually a misnomer. They don't aggress — only defend themselves. When they do bite, it's out of fear. And hence they're called fear-biters. Anytime this type of dog feels that he is cornered and unable to escape, he may bite. Biting to him is an act of last resort. He would much rather get away from the situation.

Avoid putting this dog in a position where he thinks he has to bite. Use a similar approach to the one described in Chapter 6 for submissive wetting.

Fear-biters are most comfortable when they know what is expected of them, as in training. Timid behavior can resurface when they're left to their own devices and not given clear instructions on how to behave.

Dogs high in flight drive can appear shy around strangers, other dogs, or new situations. They may hide behind their owners and need space. Keep them a good distance away from people and other dogs, and don't corner them for any reason. Use your body to reassure these dogs; bend down to their level, bending your knees and not hovering over them, and coax them to you with some food. Be patient to gain their confidence and never, ever grab for them.

What this dog needs is confidence building. Training with quiet insistence and encouragement is one way to achieve a more comfortable dog. To get the dog used to people and other dogs, enroll him in an obedience class. You need to be patient with this dog and learn to go slowly. If you try to force an issue, you may wipe out whatever advances you have made.

This dog needs a structured and predictable environment. Walk, feed, and play at certain times of the day so that the dog knows what's coming. Dogs have a phenomenal biological clock, and deviations from the time of walking and feeding can make undesirable behaviors resurface.

Rescue dogs — in particular, those that have gone from pillar to post — often have large numbers of flight behaviors. A tightly controlled schedule greatly helps in their rehabilitation.

Getting Attacked by Another Dog

What do you do when you're walking your dog down the street on leash and another dog comes out of nowhere and attacks your dog? You do this:

- No matter what, *don't* yell or scream. Remember, prey drive is stimulated by sound — especially high-pitched sounds.

- While you have hold of the leash, your dog is at the mercy of the other dog. Let go so he can either retreat or fend for himself.

- For your own safety, don't try to separate the dogs or you might get bitten. In the vast majority of incidents like this, one dog gives up and the other one walks away.

- Find out who the loose dog belongs to so you can take appropriate action.

Screaming just escalates the intensity of a dog fight. Try to keep calm at all times.

When we trained and exhibited our Yorkshire Terrier, Ty, we got into the habit of being ever vigilant about the intentions of other dogs. We learned to position ourselves between Ty and other dogs so that they could not make eye contact with each other. Fortunately, we never had any untoward incidents with him.

A Note about Electric Fences

The current fad in new housing developments is covenants against fences. That's a problem when you have a dog and you want to keep him confined. Tying a dog out on a line, except for brief periods, is not a humane option.

Never fear, technology is here, and the electric fence is the answer. A wire is buried around the perimeter of the property, where a fence would normally be. The dog wears a collar, which serves as a receiver. If he tries to cross the invisible fence, he receives an electric shock. The dog, being no dummy, figures this out very quickly and stays in the yard, well away from the fence.

Sounds too good to be true, and it is. In the heat of chasing a cat, some dogs — those high in prey with a high discomfort threshold — don't honor the fence. Plus, when the fence does work as it is intended to, it keeps your dog in the yard but it doesn't keep other dogs out. It is no protection against bullies coming into your yard and picking on your dog — or for a female in season. It may make your dog fearful of other dogs or aggressive toward them. Keep an eye on him when he's out there and don't leave him for prolonged periods without supervision.

Electric fences work fine to keep your dog in the yard, but they don't protect him from other dogs or children coming into the yard.

Chapter 19

Understanding Your Dog's Health

. . . .

In This Chapter

▶ Knowing when *more* doesn't equal *better* (the over-vaccinating problem)

▶ Knowing about the times when you'll have to vaccinate

▶ Looking at hypothyroidism

▶ Going to a doggy chiropractor

▶ Using a home remedy for anxiety

. . . .

A dog that is fed correctly, given enough exercise, and provided mental stimulation rarely exhibits behavior problems. He deals well with stress, hardly ever gets sick, and keeps his youthful characteristics into his teens.

In Chapter 7, we talk about the influence of nutrition on health and behavior. In this chapter, we cover some of the more common health concerns and how they can affect the behavior of your pet. It doesn't take a genius to figure out that when a dog doesn't feel quite right, he also doesn't act quite right.

Here Comes That Needle Again (The Over-Vaccinating Issue)

Over the past 20 years, we've seen a steady increase in the number of vaccinations that dogs receive. Sadly, instead of improving the dogs' health and longevity, the practice has had the opposite effect.

Over-vaccinating has created unintended and undesirable reactions to vaccinations, which result in *vaccinosis,* the term used to describe those undesirable reactions. The reactions can range from none or barely detectable to death. And they may occur as a result of one vaccine, several vaccines given at the same time, or repeated vaccinations given in a relatively short time frame.

Too many vaccinations too close together can cause a puppy's immune system to break down and can result in serious health problems (see the nearby sidebar for a pitiful case-in-point story about Caesar, a Great Dane puppy). We want to make it clear right here that we aren't against vaccinations. But what we are against is random, repetitive, routine, and completely unnecessary vaccinations.

And as for annual booster shots — where do they fit into this picture? Actually, they don't. According to Kirk's *Current Veterinary Therapy* XI-205 (W.B. Saunders Co., 1989) the textbook used in veterinary schools, there's no scientific basis or immunological reason that necessitates annual revaccinations. Immunity to viruses can last for many years — even for the life of the dog.

When your dog already carries the antibodies against a particular virus, a revaccination can cause havoc with his immune system. The many adverse reactions to unnecessary vaccinations have caused breeders, dog owners, and veterinarians to begin questioning the need for boosters and to become more cautious in the way vaccines are administered. By law, your dog only needs a rabies vaccination and the rabies booster only every three years. A rabies shot should never be given before the dog is 6 months of age.

Some breeds of dogs have extreme — even fatal — reactions to vaccines that are tolerated by other breeds of dogs. Some develop odd behaviors like these:

- Aggression
- Epilepsy and other seizure disorders
- Excessive licking
- Anxiety or fear
- Insomnia
- Snapping at imaginary flies

A rabies vaccine given in conjunction with other vaccines can be responsible for aggression, epilepsy, and other seizure disorders.

How do you know if your dog will have a reaction to a vaccine? You don't, and therein lies the problem. Fortunately, you don't have to take the chance. When you take Buddy in for his annual physical checkup, you can ask your veterinarian to do a *titer test*, which is a blood test that tells you whether Buddy has *antibodies* (or resistance) to the diseases that he's already been vaccinated for. If he has a high *titer*, or level of antibodies, to the disease, there's no point in revaccinating him. This process of titering is becoming more and more popular.

Immunologists are discovering a direct correlation between the increase in autoimmune and chronic disease states with the increased use of vaccines. Many holistically trained veterinarians now believe that the benefits of many vaccines are outweighed by the risks and that dogs are better off if you go with one of these options:

✔ Vaccinate lightly with vaccines spaced out by at least three to four weeks.

✔ Only vaccinate once for parvo and distemper when your dog is young with one booster four weeks later. Have your veterinarian draw some blood and send it off to a laboratory to establish the titer or level of anti-bodies your puppy carries. If the puppy is protected, there is no need for more vaccines. Titer again at one year and vaccinate only when the titers are low.

✔ Do not have your puppy vaccinated for rabies (which is mandatory) before 6 months of age. Make sure this vaccine is at least one month away from any other vaccines.

✔ Use a homeopathic alternative to vaccines.

If you're interested in the holistic approach, you can work out a vaccination schedule for your puppy by consulting *The Holistic Guide for a Healthy Dog,* 2nd Edition (IDG Books Worldwide, Inc., 2000).

The bottom line? Before vaccinating your dog, discuss the safety with your veterinarian if Buddy

✔ Is on any kind of medication

✔ Is not perfectly healthy

(***Note:*** In the literature that vaccine manufacturers supply to veterinarians, it specifically states that no dog should be vaccinated unless he in perfect health. Remember that.)

✔ Has any skin, eye, or ear infections

✔ Has recently been treated for fleas, ticks, or worms

✔ Has had prior reactions to vaccines

✔ Has not received supplemental vitamins and minerals

✔ Is scheduled for teeth cleaning, spaying or neutering, or any other surgical procedure

When You Absolutely Have to Vaccinate

Sometimes you have to vaccinate your dog. Many boarding kennels and obedience schools, for example, require proof of vaccination.

Our sad song about Caesar

We remember one consultation involving a 4-month old Great Dane puppy, Caesar. When he came to us, he was virtually paralyzed. The veterinarian had told the owners that Caesar probably had contracted some spinal disease, not uncommon in giant breeds, and that nothing could be done. The owners came to us as a last resort. By that time, Caesar didn't want to eat, had become urine incontinent, and was constipated. Our first step was to take Caesar to our own veterinarian. After a blood test and X-rays, a number of diagnoses were considered, but nothing definitive could be determined.

In the meantime, we examined Caesar's history with the owners, and here's what we learned:

✔ The breeder gave Caesar distemper and parvo vaccines at 6 weeks of age.

✔ Caesar was picked up by new owners at 7 weeks of age.

✔ Under the terms of the seller's guarantee, Caesar was taken to the owners' veterinarian within 48 hours of purchase for a health evaluation.

✔ On that visit, Caesar was wormed and given a 5 in 1 vaccination.

✔ These vaccinations were repeated at 9, 11, and 13 weeks.

✔ During that time span, Caesar was wormed two more times as a so-called precautionary matter, even though no fecal sample was taken to see whether he actually had worms.

✔ At 15 weeks of age, Caesar received another set of shots, to which the rabies vaccine had been added.

✔ Two days later, Caesar collapsed, having received 23 vaccines in 9 weeks.

This sad story does have a happy ending. Through acupuncture, chiropractic, dietary, and homeopathic remedies, we managed to piece Caesar back together into a normal dog.

So you need to know this: If you vaccinate Buddy and then immediately take him to a boarding kennel, you may be exposing him to the risk of the very diseases that the vaccine is supposed to protect him against. Immunity to disease develops about 21 days *after* your dog has been vaccinated against the disease, so make sure that Buddy's vaccine has been given a minimum of three weeks before you board him.

Before you vaccinate, call the facility. Some boarding kennels are now recognizing titer tests (see the preceding section for details about titer tests).

Since not everything's cut and dried in this world, suppose that your Buddy is one of those dogs who have adverse side effects from vaccinations, and as a result, you adamantly refuse to vaccinate him, and now you can't find a boarding kennel that will honor your wishes. What then? Well, you're going to have to find someone to come in and dog sit for you while you're away. And if the local obedience organization doesn't accept you either, then you may have to get a private trainer to come to your home (see Chapter 21).

Vaccinating even a healthy dog stresses his immune system, whether or not you see a reaction. And boarding a dog is stressful — even at the nicest boarding kennels. Under stress, Buddy is vulnerable to picking up disease.

The Rise in Doggy Hypothyroidism

Providing poor nutrition, over-vaccinating, and neutering or spaying a puppy too early can cause a disease called *hypothyroidism*. Hypothyroidism refers to an underactive thyroid gland, which causes physical as well as behavioral abnormalities. Rarely seen in the 1970s, this disease has become more prevalent as our way of managing dogs has changed in the last 30 years. Over 50 percent of all dogs today show some signs of this disease.

The thyroid gland is part of the endocrine gland system. This system not only controls many of the hormones in the body but also the brain's ability to deal with stress.

Hypothyroidism can be partially hereditary in nature. If your dog's parents had the disease, then the chances of him getting it are quite high.

The physical manifestations of hypothyroidism can be

- Lack of control over body temperature — the dog is either too cold or too hot under otherwise normal conditions
- Weight gain
- Oily, scaly skin and blackened skin on the belly
- Heart disorders
- Some kinds of paralysis
- Seizures

Behavioral manifestations may include

- Aggression to people or other dogs
- Over reaction to stressful situations
- Fear and anxiety, including separation anxiety and fear of thunderstorms
- Obsessive-compulsive behavior, such as spinning and extreme hyperactivity

- ✔ Lick granulomas, where the dogs licks constantly at one spot, usually on a leg, and goes down to the bone

- ✔ Self-mutilation

- ✔ Difficulty learning

Note: The preceding behaviors were reported in a 1997 English study, and nearly all the abnormal behaviors disappeared when thyroid medication was administered.

How can you tell if Buddy has a thyroid-related problem? If he's exhibiting any of the behaviors listed in this section, make an appointment with your veterinarian as soon as possible. If you want to reassure yourself that Buddy doesn't have hypothyroidism, have your veterinarian do a blood test and ask for a thyroid panel. The results will tell you whether Buddy needs medication. All laboratory reports indicate a low and high normal reading for each test done. Most veterinarians believe that when a dog shows a low normal reading, the dog should be on medication. High readings are uncommon in dogs.

The Bone Crusher: "Oh, My Aching Back"

Performance events, especially agility, are athletic activities for a dog. So it's not uncommon for various parts of performing dogs' bodies to go out of whack. Because the dogs' performances are affected, many competitors routinely take their dogs in for chiropractic adjustments.

To keep your dog in tiptop shape, have him examined by a chiropractor. Buddy may need an alignment.

Misalignments of your dog's musculoskeletal system can also affect his *behavior.* Our own introduction to a veterinary chiropractor came through our Briard, D.J. While he was growing up, D.J. was quite unpredictable when meeting new people or new dogs. His first reaction was to lunge and bark and show typical signs of aggression. We didn't take it too seriously, attributing it to his lack of maturity. We figured that with training and gaining confidence, he'd grow out of it.

Although the behavior diminished to a certain extent, it didn't disappear. At that point, we decided to have D.J. examined. We learned that one of the vertebrae in his neck was impinging on the optic nerve and that he had never been able to see properly. Once adjusted, he was a different dog.

After that experience, we had all our dogs examined. These examinations disclosed a number of weaknesses that we had been aware of but didn't know how to address. For example, our Dachshund's jaw was out, which caused him discomfort and affected his behavior and performance. With treatment, he became a much happier dog.

It's a good idea to have puppies looked at by a chiropractor to make sure that everything is in order. Vigorous play, especially with other dogs, can cause all manner of misalignments, which then may interfere with proper growth.

Sugar Pills: The Anxiety Eliminator

Many dogs experience anxiety under different conditions. For example, anxiety can occur

- ✔ When Buddy's taken on a trip away from home
- ✔ Before and during thunderstorms
- ✔ When Buddy's going to the vet
- ✔ When Buddy's encountering situations that he perceives as stressful

We've been quite successful in dealing with this sort of anxiety with homeopathic remedies. In fact, we carry a small homeopathic emergency kit with us wherever we go, just in case. You can find one at www.phdproducts.com.

Homeopathy is a different form of medicine relying on the energy of natural substances. These natural substances, which come from plants or minerals, are diluted to the extreme and then added to milk sugar pellets. This form of medicine, which was popular until the discovery of antibiotics, generally fell out of favor during the middle of the 20th century. Now these medicines are enjoying an enormous resurgence all over the world, and many veterinarians in Europe are trained both in traditional medicine and homeopathy.

Because the homeopathic remedies are so diluted, they are safe to use and do not cause side effects. They come in different strengths, called potencies. These potencies have numbers from 3X upwards. We use a diluted form at the 30C potency. These remedies are found in the health food section of many supermarkets, as well as in health food stores. Effective in dealing with many conditions, each dose will consist of three to five pellets that are put into the back of your dog's mouth.

Listed below are a few common homeopathic remedies we find useful and use frequently. All are in the emergency kit mentioned earlier in this section. There are many holistic veterinarians that are trained in homeopathy, and you should be able to find one in your area without difficulty.

- ✔ **Aconite:** fright, anxiety, and fear of thunderstorms

- ✔ **Apis:** bee stings

- ✔ **Arnica:** bruising from falls; recuperation from any operation

- ✔ **Belladonna:** heat stroke

- ✔ **Carbo Veg:** bloating or gas

- ✔ **Chamomilla:** vomiting of yellow bile; teething problems

- ✔ **Ferrum Phos:** stops bleeding

- ✔ **Hydrophobinum:** (sometimes called Lyssin) reaction to rabies vaccine

- ✔ **Hypericum:** stops pain after injury or operations

- ✔ **Ignatia:** grief, insecurity, stress, or sadness

- ✔ **Ledum:** insect or spider bites

- ✔ **Nux Vomica:** any kind of poisoning; recuperate after anesthesia

- ✔ **Phosphorus:** sound sensitivity

- ✔ **Rhus Tox:** poison ivy; rheumatism

- ✔ **Sulphur:** good skin and mange remedy

- ✔ **Thuja:** vaccine reaction

More Needles

Many veterinarians today use acupuncture for a variety of chronic conditions. We've found that among its many applications, acupuncture is particularly effective with allergies, skin disorders, incontinence in old dogs, and the aches and pains that come with age.

While it is beyond the scope of this book to delve into acupuncture in depth, the IVAS (International Veterinary Acupuncture Society) is one of the fastest growing veterinary organizations. Over 400 veterinarians are trained yearly by this group, and have been for the last ten years, so you should be able to find a trained veterinarian in your area without too much difficulty.

Acupuncture specializes in putting the body back into balance, and is ideal for conditions commonly found in dogs. Limps, incontinence, skin problems, and chronic diseases of major organs such as heart, kidney, liver, lungs, and stomach respond well to this modality. We advise seeking the help of an acupuncture veterinarian for middle-aged to older dogs. Treatments can make an older dog feel like a puppy again.

Where to go for other health-related concerns

Here are a few more resources available to you and your dog concerning his health:

✔ **Poison control:** As with your family, it's good to have a reliable poison control resource for your dog. We recommend the Animal Poison Control Center. You can call the center for 24-hour emergency information. The center has 20 full-time veterinary toxicologists on call to work with you on an emergency with your dog, for a $45 per case fee. The number is 888-426-4435. For more information, check out their Web site at www. napcc.aspca.org.

✔ **Holistic health:** The Pet Health and Nutrition Center is a phone consultation service that offers a holistic approach to your dog's health. Since 1995, this dedicated group of nutritionists has provided care for over 10,000 animals. They offer alternative therapies, modestly priced consultations, and supplemental support for the treatment of numerous diseases through metabolic therapies. While working with veterinarians, this group provides phone consultations and a support system by which pet owners are able to treat their dog or cat at home for most illnesses and diseases. If your dog needs help, these are the folks for you.

✔ **Nutritional and homeopathic products:** The secret is out about PHD Products. PHD (which stands for Perfect Health Diet) supplies one of the highest quality lines of dog foods and supplements on the market today. Used by professional dog trainers, behaviorists, holistic veterinarians in their practice, and discriminating pet owners to bring dogs back to health, we also use PHD for our own dogs. The products are all-natural, contain no preservatives, and the foods ship directly from the factory to you, getting to you within three weeks of manufacture. You will find the homeopathic emergency kit referred to earlier in this chapter, as well as the Natural Diet Foundation discussed in Chapter 7. PHD does no advertising, selling only by word of mouth and reputation, and was set up by professional dog people for dog people.

Chapter 20

Tricks for Fun and Gains

*F*or this chapter, we are indebted to Mary Ann Rombold Zeigenfuse, one of the lead instructors at our annual training camps and the trainer of Millie, the White House dog during the Bush administration. She wrote *Dog Tricks: Step by Step* (IDG Books Worldwide, Inc., 1997), thereby keeping alive the tradition of anyone who has ever had anything to do with the White House, no matter how remote, becoming an author.

Every well-trained dog knows a trick or two that will impress friends and family alike. Tricks you can teach your dog can be simple or complex, depending on your dog's drives and your interest.

One of the more astonishing tricks, at least until you know how it works, requires a solid retrieve on command. Others require no more than a simple "stay," but to the uninitiated, they are equally astonishing. This chapter offers just a few to get you started.

The Trick to Successful Tricks

The trick to teaching tricks is sequencing. *Sequencing* means breaking down what you want to teach your dog into components small enough for the dog to master, which lead up to the final product. For example, if you want to teach your dog to shake hands, also known as high five, you would start by taking Buddy's paw in your hand with the command you want to use and then praise and reward him. Next, you would offer your palm, and so on.

When you decide on the kind of tricks to teach Buddy, keep in mind his personality profile. Tricks like high five or roll over are easiest with dogs high in flight behaviors and not so easy with those high in fight behaviors. A dog high in fight behaviors wouldn't stoop so low — it's beneath his dignity.

Tricks learned quickly by dogs high in flight behaviors:

- ✔ High five
- ✔ Roll over
- ✔ Play dead

Tricks learned quickly by dogs high in prey behaviors:

- ✔ Find mine, such as keys, wallet, or whatever (dog must know how to retrieve)
- ✔ Jump through arms or hoop

Tricks learned quickly by dogs high in pack behaviors:

- ✔ Don't cross this line or wait until I tell
- ✔ You have food on your nose

When you see Buddy do something that could turn into a trick, such as sit up and beg, reward it and work on getting him to do it on command.

High Five

The object is to teach Buddy to raise one front paw as high as he can on command. This exercise has four Sequences.

Your goal for Sequence 1 is to introduce your dog to the concept of the exercise: let's shake hands.

1. **Sit your dog in front of you.**

2. **Reduce your body posture by kneeling or squatting in front of your dog so that you're not leaning or hovering over him.**

3. **Offer him at mid-chest level your palm and say "shake" or "gimme five," or whatever command you want to use.**

4. **Take the elbow of his dominant front leg and lift it off the ground about 2 inches.**

    (If you don't know your dog's dominant side, he will quickly tell you.)

5. **Slide your hand down to the paw and gently shake.**

6. **Praise enthusiastically as you are shaking his paw.**

7. **Reward and release him with "OK."**

Repeat this sequence five times over the course of three sessions to get your dog used to this exercise and to hearing the command.

When teaching your dog to shake and when you offer him your palm, reduce your body posture by either kneeling or squatting so that you don't lean or hover over him.

Your goal for Sequence 2 is for your dog to lift his paw.

1. **Sit your dog in front of you and reduce your body posture.**
2. **Offer your palm with the command "shake."**

   Pause. You are looking for some sort of response. If nothing happens, touch his elbow and offer your palm again. Give him the chance to lift his paw.
3. **When he lifts the paw on his own, take the paw, enthusiastically praise, reward, and release.**
4. **If *nothing* happens, take his paw, praise, reward, and release.**

You will find that as soon as you offer your palm, your dog will put his paw in it without waiting for the command. When this starts to happen, teach him to give you the other paw with the command "the other one."

Stay with this sequence until your dog is lifting his paw off the ground on command so that you can shake it.

Your goal for Sequence 3 is to put his paw into your palm.

1. **Sit your dog in front of you and reduce your body posture.**
2. **Offer your palm at mid-chest level and say "shake."**

   At this point, he should put his paw on your palm. Praise enthusiastically, reward, and release.
3. **If nothing happens, go back to Sequence 2.**

Stay with this sequence until your dog readily and without hesitation puts his paw on your palm.

Finally, your goal with Sequence 4 is to raise his paw as high as he can.

1. **Sit your dog in front of you and reduce your body posture.**
2. **Offer your palm at chin level and say "shake."**

   By now your dog should readily and without hesitation put his paw into your hand. When he does, praise, reward, and release. If not, go back to Sequence 3.

3. **Raise your palm, in 2-inch increments, until you have reached your dog's limit. (If you have a Yorkie, you're done.)**

   After several repetitions, your dog will stretch his paw as high as he can. Praise, reward, and release.

The Other One

This trick is an extension of "shake," which is part of the high five exercise in the preceding section. It follows the same sequences, except you want your dog to give you the other paw. What you will see happening is that as soon as you offer your palm, your dog will give you his paw without waiting for the command.

You are going to use the same sequences as in the high five exercise except that you will point directly at the leg you want the dog to lift, that is, the other one, and you will use a new command, such as "the other one," or whatever. It is not going to take Buddy long to figure out the difference, because he won't get the treat unless he gives you the correct paw.

You can now impress your friends and neighbors with how clever Buddy is.

Roll Over

Roll over is always a great favorite. It requires the dog to lay on the floor and completely roll over sideways. As a prerequisite, the dog must know how to lie down on command (see Chapter 4).

Roll over is always a crowd pleaser. It can easily be taught to most dogs that know the down command and respond to a treat.

Your goal with Sequence 1, the first of three Sequences, is to get your dog to roll over with a little help from you.

1. **Place your dog into the down position, either with a command or a treat.**

2. **Reduce your body posture by kneeling or squatting in front of your dog so that you're not leaning or hovering over him.**

3. **Hold the treat in such a way that your dog has to look over his shoulder while lying on the ground.**

4. **Say "roll over" and slowly make a small circle around his head, keeping the treat close to his nose.**

5. **With your other hand gently help your dog roll over in the direction you want him to go.**

   When the dog has completely rolled over, enthusiastically praise, reward, and release.

6. **Repeat until your dog is completely relaxed with you helping him roll over.**

Your goal for Sequence 2 is for your dog to roll over on his own.

1. **Place your dog into the down position, either with a command or a treat.**

2. **Reduce your body posture.**

3. **Say "roll over" and get him to follow the treat without any help from you.**

   When he does it, praise, reward, and release. If not, go back to Sequence 1.

4. **Repeat until your dog rolls over with a minimum of guidance on your part.**

Your goal in Sequence 3 is to get your dog to roll over on command.

1. **There is now no treat in your hand, but be prepared to reward immediately when you get the correct response.**

2. **Say "down" and then "roll over."**

   The first few times you do this, you may have to use the same hand motion as though you had a treat in it. Praise, reward, and release when your dog does it.

3. **Reduce the hand motion until he does it on command alone.**

   Praise, reward, and release.

Once your dog has learned the trick, he will offer this behavior anytime he wants a treat. Unfortunately, you can't reward him for that for the obvious reason that he is now training you to give him a treat on demand. Instead, go to random rewards when he does the trick on command.

Play Dead

This trick is an old favorite and a logical extension of roll over. It is easily taught to dogs high in flight behaviors. If your dog is high in fight behaviors, don't waste your time.

It consists of aiming your index finger and "firing" at your dog with a command such as "bang," and your dog falls on his side or back and plays dead.

The goal of Sequence 1 is to get your dog to lie down on his side or back.

1. **With a treat in your "gun" hand, down your dog.**

2. **Lean over your dog and in a deep tone of voice say "bang" as you point your index finger at him.**

   If he is high in flight behaviors, he will roll on his side or back.

3. **Praise and give him a treat while he is in that position and then release him with "OK."**

   If he does not roll on his side or back, use the treat as you did for the "roll over." Then praise, reward, and release.

Repeat this sequence until your dog responds to the "bang" command.

Your goal in Sequence 2 is for your dog to play dead from the sitting or standing position.

1. **Get your dog's attention by calling his name.**

2. **Lean over your dog and in a deep tone of voice say "bang" as you point your index finger at him.**

   If he lies down and plays dead, praise, reward, and release. If not, show him what you want by placing him in the "dead" position. Praise, reward, and release.

Practice this sequence until he responds to the "bang" command from the sitting or standing position.

The Sequence 3 is your dog plays dead at a distance.

1. **With your dog about two feet from you, get his attention by using his name and give the "bang" command as you point your finger at him.**

   If he responds, praise, go to him, and reward him, and then release. If not, show him what you want and start all over.

2. **Gradually increase the distance to about 6 feet.**

This last sequence will go quickly because your dog has learned to respond to the "bang" command and signal. You can then gradually increase the time between his response and the praise, reward, and release to 30 seconds. After that, start giving the reward on a random basis.

It is generally easier to teach tricks that use Buddy's natural tendencies. If your dog has a quirky habit, you may find that you can turn this into a fun trick. When you see a behavior you want to turn into a trick, tell your dog how clever he is and give him a treat. For example, when you see Buddy do a play bow (front legs down and stretched out in front of him, rear leg standing up), and you want to turn the behavior into a trick, praise him when you see him do it and give him a treat. Next, give the behavior a command, such as "Take a bow," and when you see him do it, give the command, praise, and reward. It will not take long before Buddy responds to the command. Another example is "Sit up and beg," which is a favorite of one of our Dachshunds who sits up and begs any time she wants a treat. She is now rewarded only rarely for the behavior, but that doesn't stop her from trying.

Find Mine

The find mine trick is one of the most impressive tricks you can teach Buddy. It combines the retrieve with the dog's use of his nose to discriminate between different articles. It's a terrific parlor trick that will astound and amaze your friends.

The goal of Sequence 1 is for your dog to retrieve something of yours, such as your keys.

1. **Get a leather or plastic key fob and put some keys on it.**

   Using something leather or plastic makes it easier for the dog to pick up and carry it.

2. **Get your dog excited about the keys and throw them a few feet in front of you with the command, "find mine."**

   When he brings them back, praise, reward, and release. If he doesn't, review the first few sequences of teaching the retrieve (see Chapter 12).

3. **Repeat until your dog readily brings back your keys.**

A dog's ability to differentiate between scents is far more acute than ours. Dogs can be taught to identify any number of objects by scent, including underground gas leaks.

Your goal in Sequence 2 is for your dog to find your keys.

1. **Tell your dog to "stay" and with him watching you, place the keys in the corner of an armchair or couch.**

2. **Go back to your dog and send him with the "find mine" command.**

   Praise, reward, and release.

3. **Repeat several times, each time changing the location slightly, so Buddy gets used to looking for the keys.**

Your goal in Sequence 3 is for Buddy to find your keys by using his nose. This sequence is the heart of the trick and the real fun part.

1. **Tell your dog to stay and without him watching, place the keys on the floor, just inside the doorframe of another room.**

2. **Go back to your dog and send him with the "find mine"command.**

   What you want him to do is to find your keys by retracing your steps and then using his nose to locate the keys.

Over the course of several sessions, make the find mine game increasingly difficult. For example, a fairly advanced search would involve you going into one room, coming out again, and going into another room and putting the keys behind a wastebasket. Anytime he gets stuck, help him by showing him where you placed the keys. Remember to praise and reward correct responses, although you no longer have to do it every time.

The goal in Sequence 4 is for your dog to discriminate between objects.

For many years, this has been our favorite trick. Like any good trick, it's baffling if you don't understand how it's done, yet childishly simple for the dog.

It starts with the knowledge that a dog's nose is far more powerful than a human's, and that he is able to discriminate between different scents. He can certainly tell the difference between you and anybody else. Armed with this knowledge, you are ready to fleece anyone gullible enough to take on Buddy.

1. **Crumple up a dollar bill, place it on the ground and have your dog retrieve it with "find mine."**

2. **Have a helper, and this can be a member of the family, also crumple up a dollar bill.**

3. **Place the bills on the floor about 6 inches apart and send your dog with "find mine."**

   At this point the odds are better than 50 percent that he will bring back your dollar bill. If he does, praise and reward. If he brings back the wrong one, ignore the response, that is, don't take it from him. Just send him again to get the correct one.

4. **Repeat until you are sure he is using his nose to identify your dollar bill.**

5. **Have your helper add another bill.**

   Each time your dog is successful, have your helper add another bill, until there are a total of 10 bills from which to choose. While Buddy is learning this trick, he will occasionally make a mistake and bring back a wrong bill. Without taking that bill from him, send him again with "find mine." Reward every correct response. You will need to replace the wrong bill that the dog brought back — it now has his saliva on it.

That is all there is to this trick. The fun part comes when you change the denomination and get other people involved. Say you have a half dozen visitors. During a lull in the conversation you say "did you know that our dog can tell a twenty dollar bill from a single?" Of course, nobody is going to believe you. So, you take out a twenty and say "anybody have any ones?" Crumple up your twenty and have the others crumple up their singles. Then have Buddy do his number.

A variation is to ask for someone else's twenty with the understanding that if your dog retrieves it, you get to keep it. Naturally, you can only handle that twenty and the person who gave it to you cannot contribute any singles. Good luck!

Jumping through Arms or Hoop

A hula-hoop makes a wonderful prop for this trick in which you first teach your dog to jump through the hoop and then your arms. Start by getting a hoop commensurate with your dog's size.

The goal of Sequence 1 is that your dog jumps through hoop on leash.

1. **Lay the hoop on the ground and take your dog over to examine it.**
2. **Put your dog on leash and walk him over the hoop.**
3. **Pick up the hoop and let the bottom edge rest on the ground.**
4. **Thread the leash through the hoop and encourage your dog to jump through with "jump."**

    You can use a treat to get him to walk through the hoop. Repeat until your dog readily goes through the hoop with the command "jump." Praise, reward, and release for successful tries.

5. **Thread the leash through the hoop and raise it a few inches off the floor.**

    If necessary, use a treat to get him through and then enthusiastically praise. As your dog gains confidence begin raising the hoop in two-inch increments until the bottom is eye level in front of him.

The goal of Sequence 2 is to get your dog to jump through hoop off leash.

1. **Take the leash off and present the hoop in front of your dog with the bottom no higher than the dog's knees.**
2. **Say "jump" and let the dog jump through.**

    Praise and reward with a treat. Repeat but change the position of the hoop so that the bottom is level with the dog's elbows, then shoulder. How high you can raise it depends on the athletic ability of your dog.

Keep in mind that as soon as you get to about shoulder level (the dog's, not yours), you need a surface with good traction on which the dog can take off and land. Wet grass and slippery floors are not good surfaces for this trick.

3. **Teach your dog to jump as you pivot in a circle with the hoop.**

   Pivot slowly at first and then increase speed, but never so fast that the dog loses interest or can't keep up.

Finally, Sequence 3's goal is achieved when your dog jumps through your arms.

1. **Review having your dog jump through the hoop at his shoulder level several times and then put the hoop away.**

2. **Squat down and let your dog see you put a treat at the spot where he is going to land.**

3. **Make a circle with your arms out to the side.**

   Keep the upper part of your body upright.

4. **Tell your dog to jump and when he does, tell him how clever he is.**

   Going around you to the treat is considered bad form, and you need to pick up the treat before he gets it. Then try again. It will not take him long to figure out the only way to the treat is through your arms. Stop after he has been successful.

Keep working on this trick until your dog jumps through your arms every time you make the circle.

Don't Cross This Line

This trick is an extension of door and stair manners (see Chapter 4). Its most useful application is to keep the dog out of one or several rooms in the house, either temporarily or permanently.

Because don't cross this line is a good review of door and stair manners, rember that you have to release your dog to go through doors or up and down stairs. If you get lax about it, your dog will start releasing himself, thereby defeating the object of the training.

The goal of Sequence 1 is to Review door manners on leash.

1. **Use the command "stay" or "wait until I tell you."**

   Put your dog on leash.

2. **Walk toward the front door, say "wait" and open it.**

   Make sure the leash is loose and that you are not holding Buddy back. If he starts to cross the threshold, check on the leash to bring him back in.

3. **Close the door and start all over.**

   Because you may have already taught him to sit at the door before you release him, this review on leash will go quickly.

4. **Repeat until he begins to hesitate crossing the threshold.**

The goal of Sequence 2 is that your dog learns to cross the threshold with your permission.

1. **Walk toward the front door, say "stay," and open the door.**

2. **Briefly hesitate and then say "OK" and cross over the threshold with your dog.**

With Sequence 3, your goal is for you to go through the doorway and your dog not.

1. **Approach the door and open it.**

2. **Say "stay" and go through the doorway.**

   If he tries to follow, pull him back by extending your arm through the door and then close the door on the leash.

3. **Open the door, but don't let him come out yet until you say "OK," and then praise.**

Your goal in Sequence 4 is to review Sequences 1–3 coming back into the house.

You have to release your dog to go through doors or up and down stairs. If you get lax about it, your dog will start releasing himself, thereby defeating the object of the training.

You can now apply the same principle to one or more rooms in the house. As a trick, you can teach this to your dog by drawing a line on the ground and using the line as a threshold. Once your dog understands the basic principle, he will catch on to anything you don't want him to cross.

You Have Food on Your Nose

This is a cute trick. It involves balancing a piece of food on Buddy's nose until you say "OK." Some dogs even toss it in the air and catch it on the way down.

Your goal in Sequence 1 is to be able to cup your hand over your dog's muzzle. If you have taught your dog to retrieve, he already knows this.

1. **Sit your dog and pet him for a few seconds.**

2. **Cup your hand over his muzzle from the top, just as you do for the retrieve (see Chapter 12).**

3. **Kneel or squat in front of your dog and keep your upper body straight.**

   With your other hand hold a treat near your dog's nose and get him to focus on the treat.

4. **Release with "OK" and give him the treat.**

   You need to be able to hold his muzzle so that you can put a piece of food on his nose.

5. **Repeat until you can cup his muzzle and he focuses on the treat.**

The goal in Sequence 2 is to put the treat on his nose.

1. **Gently hold his muzzle and put the treat on the dog's nose in front of your thumb.**

2. **Tell him to "stay" or "wait," and then release him.**

   The treat will either fall off or get bounced into the air.

Sequence 3's goal is to increase the time he balances treat.

1. **Start by holding his muzzle and placing the treat on his nose.**

2. **Say "stay" and have your dog balance the treat for ten seconds, then release him.**

3. **Repeat and increase the time to 20 seconds.**

With Sequence 4, your dog should balance the treat without help from you.

1. **Put the treat on his muzzle and then slowly let go of his muzzle, reminding him to "stay."**

2. **Get him to focus on your index finger by holding it front of his nose.**

3. **Wait a few seconds and release your dog.**

You should now be able to gradually increase the time he holds the treat before you release your dog, as well as gradually increase the distance of your finger from the dog's nose.

What if he drops or tosses the treat before you said "OK"? Well, if you can't get to the treat before he does (an unlikely outcome), reduce the time and distance until he is reliable again and you can increase them again.

Chapter 21

Seeking Expert Outside Help

● ●

In This Chapter

▶ Looking at outside training resources

▶ Knowing your options

▶ Choosing an obedience school

▶ Hiring a personal trainer

▶ Deciding on a dog camp

● ●

*Y*ou have a number of choices when it comes to Buddy's education. You can

✔ Train out of a book, such as this one.

✔ Participate in group classes.

✔ You can have someone else do the training.

Each one has its own pros and cons, and your own personality and life style will determine your choice.

The trouble with dog training is not that it is a completely unregulated activity and that anyone, regardless of experience, can set up shop as a dog trainer, but that so many actually do.

Moreover, there are enormous quality differences, not only in terms of effectiveness of the training, but also in how the dogs are treated. Dog training is a completely unregulated area, and anyone, yes, anyone, can proclaim himself a trainer.

When you attempt to make a rational choice, remember that there are many ways to skin a cat. Beware of anyone who says there is only one way to do the job. Successful dog training depends not so much on the "how," but on the "why." Dogs are not a homogeneous commodity, and the approach to training has to take into account the dog's personality profile, as well as your own personality.

Teaching skills are not the same as training skills. To teach people how to train their dogs, an instructor needs good communication and people skills, as well as a thorough knowledge of dog training.

Table 21-1 breaks down the three major categories of training resources available to you.

Table 21-1	Available Choices	
Choice	*Pros*	*Cons*
Training out of a book	Least expensive. You can train how you want, what you want, and when you want. You are not tied to a regular schedule. Location is not a problem.	You need to be highly self-motivated or training will fall by the wayside. You have no one to critique you. Possibly not enough exposure to other dogs.
Group classes	Very economical. There is someone who can tell you what you may be doing wrong. Opportunity to meet people of like mind. Keeps your training on track with weekly sessions. Continuous socialization with other dogs.	Schedule and location may be inconvenient. Instructor dictates how, what, and when. Training method may not be right for you or your dog.
Having someone else do the job	Little time commitment required from you.	Very expensive. Training method may not be how you would want your dog trained.

Within these three major categories, there are additional options. You can take private lessons from an instructor, either at your house or some other location. Under such an arrangement, the instructor teaches you what to do, and you are then expected to practice with your dog between sessions. In terms of cost, time, and effort, this is one of the most efficient arrangements.

Another option is a doggie day care center, many of which offer training for you, but again, you will have to learn how to get Buddy to respond to your commands.

Our own preference, and the one we recommend, is to take Buddy to an obedience class where you are instructed how to train him. Aside from the socialization with other dogs, the time you spend together will strengthen the bond between you and your dog.

Word of mouth is often the best way to find a trainer. Ask your veterinarian, friends, and acquaintances for recommendations.

Going to Class — Obedience and Training Schools

Having taught obedience classes for 30 years, we are naturally biased in favor of this choice. A basic class usually addresses your most immediate concerns, such as not pulling on the leash, the sit and down-stay, and coming when called.

The purpose of the class is to show you what to do, have you try it a few times to make sure you've got it right, and then send you home to practice. You should be prepared to practice at least five times a week. Most classes are sequential in nature. If you miss a class, you will fall behind and may have a hard time catching up. Falling behind is discouraging and may cause you to drop out. When you go to a class, do not expect the instructor to train your dog. That is not his or her job.

Obedience classes are conducted in almost every community and are an excellent way for you and Buddy to learn together.

We think taking Buddy to school is perhaps one of the best things you can do for both of you. It gets you out of the house into an atmosphere where you can spend quality time together. Both of you have fun while learning useful things that make living together that much easier.

Classes can be found in most communities. Until quite recently, the majority of classes were conducted by obedience or kennel clubs. Today, many classes are taught by schools or private individuals. The difference has nothing to do with the quality of the training, but relates solely to profit motive. Clubs are not-for-profit organizations and the instructors, usually members who have trained and shown their own dog, generally volunteer their services. Training schools and individuals who hang out their shingles are for-profit organizations.

To train for participating in performance events, you will be best served by joining an organization that offers training for that goal. You will be coached in the intricacies of the various requirements.

Choosing a good training class

To locate a class, look in the Yellow Pages under a heading such as "Pet & Dog Training" to find out what is offered in your community. Chances are you will have several choices.

Call one of the organizations listed to find out where and when the class meets. Ask whether you can observe a beginner class. If you are not allowed to observe a class, which would be highly unusual, forget that organization. When you find one where you can observe a class, do so, but leave Buddy at home so that he doesn't interfere with the class and you are not distracted.

Here are a few questions you should ask yourself about the class you're observing:

- ✔ What is your first impression of the class? You are looking for a friendly, pleasant, and positive atmosphere.

- ✔ Do the dogs seem to have a good time? You will be able to tell very quickly if the dogs are enjoying themselves or if they would rather be somewhere else.

- ✔ How does the instructor deal with the class participants? You want the instructor to be encouraging and helpful, especially to those who seem to be struggling.

- ✔ How does the instructor deal with the dogs? You want the instructor to be nice to the dogs, not yell at them or create anxiety or fear.

- ✔ Does the instructor appear knowledgeable? As a student, you are not likely to be able to tell whether or not the instructor actually is knowledgeable, but at least he or she should give the appearance of being so.

- ✔ What is the ratio of instructors to students? We always aim for a 1:5 ratio, with a limit of 15 students for one instructor with two assistants.

- ✔ Is the space adequate for the number of dogs? Insufficient space can be a cause for aggression in a class situation.

If you don't like what you see, find another organization. If you like what you see and hear, then this might be the class for you and Buddy. But while you are visiting, you need to find out a few more bits of information:

- ✔ The cost of the class and what is included. For example, our basic training course, or Level 1 as we call it, consists of eight 50-minute sessions and includes a training collar and leash, weekly homework sheets, and a copy of our book, *What All Good Dogs Should Know,* as part of the fee.

- ✔ The schedule of classes, the level of classes, and the length of the program.

  The length of the program, the fee and what you get for your money, varies. A beginner class can run anywhere from four to ten weeks, at a cost $50 to $200, depending on who teaches it and where you live. Price is not necessarily an indicator of quality, nor is the length necessarily an indication of how much you learn. The majority of beginner classes last from six to eight weeks and cost about $100.

> ✔ What is the goal of the program, that is, what can you expect from your dog upon completion of the class? This is pretty much under your control, because you are the one who is going to train Buddy. To be successful, you should be prepared to practice with him five times a week. Two short sessions a day are preferable to one longer session, but for most people that is not realistic. How long each session lasts depends entirely on your aptitude and Buddy's drives (see Chapter 2).

> ✔ Does the organization offer puppy classes? The ideal age to start training Buddy is around eight to ten weeks. His brain is fully developed, but he has not acquired any bad habits.

Puppy training classes

The joy of taking a puppy to class is that he can socialize with other young dogs, have fun, yet be taught manners and how to interact with his own kind. Buddy's brain at this point in his young life is just like a sponge, and everything you teach him now will be remembered for the rest of his life. He will learn all those lessons that will make him an ideal pet.

Taking Buddy to an obedience class as a puppy is the best investment in his future you can make.

Look for an organization that offers puppy classes, preferably one that teaches basic control to puppies, rather than just socialization and games. There is nothing wrong with socialization and games; both are necessary, but at the right time and in the right context.

You want Buddy to associate meeting other dogs as a pleasant but controlled experience, not one of playing and being rowdy. As he grows older, playing and being rowdy is no longer cute and will make him hard to manage around other dogs.

The ideal puppy class allows the puppies to interact with each other for up to three minutes before the class starts for the first two classes only. After that, the puppies are allowed to play for three minutes after class. This way Buddy learns that he must be obedient to you first, and the reward is playing after he has worked, a lifetime habit you wish to instill while he is young.

Look for a class where the people are having fun with their dogs, and where the instructor is pleasant and professional to the students. Above all, you want to see happy dogs.

Stay away from the classes where you are told that Buddy is too young to learn obedience exercises. This shows a lack of knowledge of dog behavior.

You can expect that your puppy will learn to sit, down, and stand on command, come when called, stay when told, and walk on a loose leash. An excellent program, with well-trained instructors, will also have Buddy doing the same exercises off leash, as well as on signal. For Buddy, this is easy stuff.

Advanced training classes

Many organizations also offer classes at higher levels, as well as for different activities, such as agility. You might get bitten by the training bug, and if you and Buddy enjoy what you are doing, go for it.

The majority of people who go on to advanced training, start training their dogs in a beginner class. They then discover that the organization offers more and perhaps even different activities. You may discover, for example, that in addition to obedience training, the organization also trains agility, perhaps even tracking, and that some of the members have therapy dogs, and so on.

To pursue your interests, you may to look for another organization or another instructor. In either case, you would apply the same criteria you used to choose your beginner class.

Finding a Private Tutor

You may have serious time constraints, and so you might want to consider a private trainer. Private trainers are not cheap, but it's better than not training at all, provided the trainer doesn't ruin your dog.

In selecting a private trainer, use the same criteria you would for selecting a nanny. Ask for references and call them. You also want to inquire into the trainer's experience.

Once you have found a trainer, he or she usually does the training at your residence. This is an advantage because the trainer gets to see where and how Buddy lives, and can tailor a program to meet your special needs. But before you sign on the dotted line, watch how he or she interacts with Buddy and especially how he or she works him.

At some point you will have to become involved and learn the various commands Buddy has learned and how to reinforce these commands. After all, the object is for Buddy to obey you, not just the trainer. You will be expected to work Buddy under the direction of the trainer so that you can learn what and how he was taught.

In selecting a private trainer, be choosy. This individual will have a great impact on shaping your dog's skills. Don't be afraid to ask for references and to grill the trainer on his experience. Remember, anyone can declare himself a dog trainer!

Off to Boarding School

When you outsource the job by sending your dog to a boarding school, Buddy will typically be boarded at the training facility for a specified period, such as three to six weeks.

This is our least preferred training option. We are not too thrilled about the idea of leaving one of our dogs somewhere to be trained. For us, at least, it seems to conflict with why we have a dog in the first place.

Sending Buddy to boarding school is not an option that we can strongly advocate. Why get a dog that you don't want to spend time with? We view this option as one of last resort, when you absolutely cannot make any other arrangements.

If boarding school is the only option for you, here are some things you should look for. Before you take this step, inspect the facility.

- ✔ How are the dogs housed?
- ✔ Is it clean?
- ✔ How do the other dogs look?
- ✔ Ask for a demonstration.
- ✔ Trust your instincts — Buddy is your dog!

After your dog has completed the program, the trainer will then work with you for several sessions to show you how to get Buddy to respond to you. It is then your responsibility to keep up the training.

As an alternative to sending Buddy off for three to six weeks, you may want to consider a doggie day care facility that also offers training. That way at least you can pick Buddy up in the evening and monitor his progress.

Don't overlook day care as another alternative. Many of these facilities also offer basic training while looking after Buddy.

The Great Dog Camp Adventure

Dog camps have been around ever since we can remember. When we became serious about training and competing with our dogs, dog camps are where we went. They were great fun and invaluable learning experiences. In 1977, we started our own camps, and since then have conducted almost 60, in the U.S., Canada, and England.

There are dog camps, just like tennis or computer camps, for you and Buddy. They can be great learning experiences and are a wonderful way of getting closer to your dog.

Most dog camps last from four to five days, and the number of participants can range from 20 to over 100. A few of the distinguishing features are

- Some are highly structured, with each hour of the day filled with specific activities, while others are more loosely organized.
- Some camps are program driven, where you learn a particular approach to training, and others are activity driven, where you are exposed to a variety of things you and Buddy can do together.
- Some are designed for a particular activity, such as agility or obedience competition, and others are more general.
- Some require prior training experience, and others do not.
- Some include room and board in the tuition, others only the camp itself.
- Some are held in full-fledged conference centers offering every conceivable amenity, others in more Spartan settings.

All camps combine a vacation element, where you and Buddy can enjoy each other. If you feel you would like to take a week's vacation with Buddy, where you can go have fun and learn more about dogs, training, or a particular activity, then dog camp is the place for you. A good starting point for more information about dog camps, including ours, is the Internet. The average cost of going to camp is about $100 a day, plus room and board.

The Volhard camps

Our own camps are held twice a year, in April and July, and require no prior training experience. They are five days long, tuition is all-inclusive, and they are held at a YMCA Conference Center. For maximum individual attention, participation is limited. Activities include

- Obedience training at all levels
- Problem solving
- Understanding and dealing with aggression
- Refinements of "drives"
- Understanding dog behavior
- Nutrition and health
- Complementary sources of health care
- Agility
- Tracking
- Water rescue work

Because few dogs can maintain an entire day's worth of activity, the training sessions alternate with lectures on a variety of subjects so the dogs can rest.

Current and past participants have given us a slogan for our camps: for the best time with your dog you have ever had!

Part VI
The Part of Tens

The 5th Wave   By Rich Tennant

"OK, I'LL LET HIM PLAY AS LONG AS YOU STOP SAYING, 'YOU CAN'T TAKE AN OLD DOG'S NEW TRICKS'."

In this part . . .

This part is packed with quick lists that you can read in a flash. Here you can find ten commands every dog should know, ten reasons why dogs do some of the things that they do, and ten sporting activities that you and Buddy can partake in together. Have fun!

Chapter 22

Ten Fun and Exciting Sporting Activities

In This Chapter

▶ Sharing sporting activities

▶ Activities for fun and games

▶ Activities that benefit others

*I*n addition to obedience competition, you and your dog can participate in numerous other competitions and events. Some are for specific breeds, such as herding trials, and others are for all dogs, such as agility. Many are conducted under the auspices of the American Kennel Club, and some are not, such as Schutzhund trials. Still others are for one breed, such as the Newfoundland Club of America's Water Rescue and Draft Dog competitions.

The American Kennel Club awards over 30 different performance titles in eight different categories. And other organizations have an almost equal number of titles.

The AKC alone has over 30 different performance titles that can be earned, albeit not all by the same dog, in the following categories:

- ✔ Obedience Titles — 6, plus 5 Versatility titles, each consisting of an agility, obedience, and tracking title
- ✔ Hunting Test Titles — 4
- ✔ Field Trial Titles — 2
- ✔ Herding Titles — 6
- ✔ Tracking Titles — 4
- ✔ Agility Titles — 9
- ✔ Earthdog Titles — 3
- ✔ Lure Coursing — 3

Obedience Competitions

Obedience competitions are one of the oldest performance events in which any breed registered with the American Kennel Club can participate. The AKC awards six obedience titles: Companion Dog (CD), Companion Dog Excellent (CDX), Utility Dog (UD), Utility Dog Excellent (UDX), Obedience Trial Champion (OTCh), and National Obedience Champion (NOC). (See Chapters 14–17 for requirements.)

In addition, the AKC has five Versatility titles. A versatility title requires that the dog has earned an agility, obedience, and tracking title.

Agility Events

Agility is one of the AKC's newest events. It has experienced phenomenal growth over the last ten years, and with good reason: Dogs love it, handlers love it, and it has enormous spectator appeal. Agility competitions began in England and were then introduced in the U.S. by Charles ("Bud") Kramer in the early 1980s. Bud was instrumental in its success as an activity in which all dogs could participate. After a slow start, the popularity of agility competitions exploded. For the past ten years, agility has been the fastest growing dog sport. It is an exciting and exhilarating sport for both handler and dog, and it has great spectator appeal. You may have already seen it on one of the cable television channels that specializes in televising dog events.

The AKC is not the only organization that sponsors agility trials, but it now has the largest number of trials. There are also international agility competitions.

The dogs, under the direction of their handlers, negotiate a complex obstacle course that includes walking over a 3- or 4-foot-high plank, weaving in and out of a series of poles, jumping over and through objects, and going through tunnels. To compensate for the size differences among dogs and make the competition fair, four height divisions exist. You and Buddy can earn nine AKC agility titles, as well as titles awarded by other organizations. The original four titles are

Title	Requirements
Novice Agility (NA)	Three legs under two different judges
Open Agility (OA)	Same
Agility Excellent (AX)	Same
Master Agility (MX)	Must have earned the AX title and then qualify ten more times

Other than the exercises themselves, there are some significant differences between agility trials and obedience trials.

Agility	*Obedience*
Your dog has to be able to work on both your right and your left side	Your dog always works on your left side
Minimum time limits during which you and your dog have to complete the course	No time limit (within reason)
The order in which the obstacles are to be negotiated varies, as do the obstacles	The exercises and the order of the exercises are always the same
Continuous communication with your dog is encouraged	During your dog's performance of an exercise you cannot talk to your dog and can give only one command

As with obedience, the level of difficulty increases with each higher class, as does the number of obstacles.

No doubt, part of the appeal of agility competition is its seeming simplicity. Almost any dog in reasonably good physical condition quickly learns the rudiments of the various obstacles. And, almost any handler who is also in reasonably good physical condition can compete in agility. But few things are ever as simple as they appear.

Beginning agility is deceptively simple, but it's not as easy as it looks. There is a premium on being able to communicate with your dog and the two of you really have to be in tune with each other.

Because the courses you and your dog have to negotiate are never quite the same, there is a premium on your ability to communicate with your dog. Any lapses in communication invariably result in Buddy's failure to complete the course correctly. You are also competing against the clock and have to make split-second decisions. In addition, you are required to memorize the course before you and your dog compete.

You can see what makes agility so exciting. The two of you really have to able to work as a team and keep your wits about you. We highly recommend that you try it. You will be amazed how your dog will take to it. We are not suggesting that you try to set up an agility course in your backyard — few of us have the wherewithal to do that. Find out from your local dog organizations where agility trials are being held and then take a look. In almost every community there will be a group or an individual who has classes that meet on a regular basis where you and Buddy can get started. Even if you are not interested in competing, it's good mental stimulation for Buddy, as well as good exercise for both of you.

Tracking Titles

The dog's fabled ability to use his nose and follow a scent is the basis for this activity. Any dog can participate, and if you enjoy tromping through the great outdoors in solitude with your dog, tracking is for you. Tracking is also the potentially most useful activity you can teach your dog. Many a tracking dog has been credited with finding a lost person, or lost article, not to mention the dogs that are used with much effectiveness in law enforcement.

Your dog's sense of smell is almost infallible, and dogs are used by various law enforcement agencies to sniff out bombs, drugs, and other contraband. They are even being used in cancer research to detect cancer in a person.

Buddy can earn three titles:

- Tracking Dog (TD)
- Tracking Dog Excellent (TDX)
- Variable Surface Tracking (VST)

The principal differences between the classes are the age of the track and the surface.

Title	Basic Requirements
TD	The track has to be at least 440 yards, but not more than 500 yards in length. The track is laid by a person 30 minutes to two hours before the event and it has to have three to five turns. There are no cross tracks and no obstacles.
TDX	The track has to be at least 800 yards, but not more than 1,000 yards in length. The track has to be not less than three hours and not more than five hours old. It has to have five to seven turns. It has two cross tracks and two obstacles, such as a different surface or a stream.
VST	The track has to be at least 600 yards, but not more than 800 yards in length. Age of track is the same as for the TDX. It has to have four to eight turns. It has to have a minimum of three different surfaces, such as, concrete, asphalt, gravel or sand, in addition to vegetation.

Your dog has to complete only one track successfully to earn its title, unlike obedience or agility titles, for which three qualifying performances are required. You can also continue to compete at any level, even if you have earned your VST.

The basic idea of successful tracking is the dog's ability to follow the track layer's footsteps from beginning to end. A dog that veers too far away from the track and has obviously lost the scent is whistled off and does not qualify on that particular occasion.

Field Trials and Hunting Tests

Field trials and hunting tests rival obedience and agility competitions in popularity. These events are for the pointing breeds, retrievers, spaniels, Beagles, Basset Hounds, and, you would never guess, Dachshunds. The tests are divided by type of dog and sometimes by specific breeds. Some of them, such as Beagles, work in groups of two, three, and seven or more.

Hunting tests and field trials are popular and test your dog's ability to demonstrate the function for which he was bred.

The performance requirements vary, depending on the specific breed and the particular event. If Buddy is a Labrador Retriever, you and he can participate in both field trials and hunting tests, and the sky is the limit.

Earthdog Trials

These tests are for dogs bred to retrieve critters that live in tunnels or dens. The Dachshund, which, translated, means "badger hound," and the smaller terriers are eligible to participate in these competitions.

The object is to locate the quarry in a tunnel or a den. In the tests, either rats, caged for their protection, or a mechanical, scented device, are used.

Tests are conducted at four different levels:

- An introductory test to see if the dog has any aptitude for this sort of thing. There is no title for this test, but it is a prerequisite for a title.
- After the dog has passed the introductory test, he is eligible to compete for the Junior Earthdog (JE) title.
- Next is the Senior Earthdog (SE) title.
- Last is the Master Earthdog (ME) title.

Naturally, the level of difficulty increases with each title. As the levels progress, the distance from which the dog has to locate the den is increased and the tunnels that the dog has to encounter become more complex.

The instinct of terriers is to discover and root out the critters that live underground. This can lead to monumental "landscaping." Our Dachshunds are forever digging for moles or anything else that might be under the ground. Of course, anything recently planted must be immediately dug up just to make sure nothing edible has been buried.

Earthdog trials are quite a specialized activity and explain the penchant these dogs have for redesigning the backyard.

Lure Coursing

An equally specialized activity is lure coursing, which is for the sight hounds. These dogs were bred to run down game over great distances. If you have ever seen a sight hound running flat out, you can appreciate how fast-paced and exciting lure coursing is.

In an AKC test an artificial lure is used, which the dogs follow around a course in an open field. Scoring is based on speed, which is blazing, enthusiasm and endurance. Of course, it helps if the dog is actually chasing the lure and is not off on a frolic of his own.

Again, the dog can earn three titles:

- Junior Courser (JC)
- Senior Courser (SC)
- Field Champion (FC)

Schutzhund Training

The word *Schutzhund* means "protection dog." After field trials, Schutzhund training is probably the oldest organized competition. It originated in Germany and is the progenitor of our obedience exercises, tracking, and, to some extent, agility. It is hugely popular in Europe, and worldwide competitions are held. Although Schutzhund is not an AKC performance event, it enjoys an avid following in this country.

Schutzhund training is the progenitor of many of our training activities today. It dates back to the early 20th century, and many of its exercises have been incorporated into today's performance events.

It all began when the German Shepherd came to be used as a police dog. Billed as the only true multipurpose dog, he was expected to guard and protect, herd, track, be a guide dog for the blind and, of course, be good with children. Rigorous breeding programs were designed to cement these traits into the breed. Behavior was bred to behavior, so that only those dogs with demonstrated abilities procreated. Looks were not considered as important as ability.

As a police dog, a dog's main responsibility is to protect his handler. He also has to be able to pursue and capture suspects, or track them down. Building searches required great agility, perhaps jumping into windows, negotiating stairs, even ladders. Naturally, he has to know all the obedience exercises.

It wasn't long before competitions began among and between police units to see who had the most talented and best-trained dog. Dog owners like you became interested and the sport of Schutzhund was born.

Schutzhund training consists of three parts:

- ✔ Protection
- ✔ Obedience
- ✔ Tracking

To qualify for a title, the dog must pass all three parts. When obedience and tracking were introduced in this country, they were patterned on the requirements for the Schutzhund dog. Agility competitions derived in part from the Schutzhund obedience exercises, which include walking over the A-frame as well as different jumps.

Schutzhund training is not limited to German Shepherds and can be done by any dog of the guarding breeds that has the aptitude. Even some of non-guarding breeds can do it, although you won't see them at the upper levels of competition.

It is a rigorous and highly athletic sport and the skills required are all-encompassing. It is also one of the most time-consuming of dog sports.

Flyball Competitions

Flyball is a relay race, with four dogs on a team, over four hurdles spaced 10 feet apart to a box that holds a tennis ball. The dogs, each in turn, jump the hurdles and step on a spring-loaded box that shoots out the tennis ball. The dog then catches the ball and runs back over the hurdles. When the dog crosses the finish line, the next dog starts. The team with the fastest time wins, provided there were no errors, such as a dog going around one or more of the hurdles, either coming or going.

Flyball was invented in the 1980s and is a popular, extremely fast-paced competition.

Freestyle Performances

Canine Freestyle is a choreographed musical program performed by a dog/handler team, sort of like figure skating for pairs. The object is to display the team in a creative, innovative, and original dance. In Freestyle, the performance of every team will be different, although the various performances often share basic obedience maneuvers.

Started in the early 1990s as a way to bring some levity to obedience training, Freestyle has caught on like a house afire. Chances are you have seen it on one of the cable shows featuring dog activities. Freestyle is fun to watch and fun to train.

Search and Rescue

Search-and-rescue groups all over the country train dogs to find people who are lost or injured in the woods or similar terrain. One of our Landseer Newfoundlands was a search-and-rescue dog. The dogs are trained to locate a victim by air scenting, which is different from tracking or trailing a scent. Once the dog has found a victim, he returns to the handler and leads him or her to the spot.

This training is quite rigorous. The dogs have to have great stamina and persistence, and may have to ride in a helicopter to get to the designated search area. You have to learn how to read a compass and other survival skills.

Therapy Dogs

Undoubtedly, the most rewarding dog activity is having a therapy dog. A dog's ability to cheer up and comfort a person in distress or need is legendary.

Therapy dogs visit nursing homes and hospitals, accompanied by their handlers. The dogs' power to cheer and comfort is legendary. This activity requires a special dog, a dog that is natural at dealing with people with special needs, such as those under medical care or people in wheelchairs, with walkers, and on crutches. This is perhaps one of the most rewarding activities for you and your dog.

Chapter 23

Ten Basic Commands Every Dog Should Know

··

··

*Y*our lifestyle will dictate the commands most important for you and your dog, and you may not need all of the ones we have listed. Nor does the order in which they are listed necessarily reflect their relative importance to you. Chapter 4 contains the information you need to train Buddy to respond to these commands.

Sit — The Safety Command

Permitting Buddy to barge uncontrollably through doorways is not a good idea — you may get mowed down in the process. Get into the habit of making Buddy sit before you open a door. After he sits, it doesn't matter whether you release him to go through first, or whether you go first and then release him, so long as he sits until you tell him it's okay to move.

Similarly, make him wait before you go up or down stairs, or get in and out of the car.

Sit — The Convenience Command

The sit command lets you control Buddy during periods of excitement, such as the happy greeting when you return home, when visitors arrive, and when you are about to take him for a walk and want to put his collar and leash on. "Sit" is also the easiest way to stop Buddy from jumping on people.

One question we frequently are asked is, "He doesn't jump on me anymore, but how do I get him to stop jumping up on visitors?" Our advice is to enlist the help of friends and neighbors to train Buddy. Show the visitor how to induce Buddy into a sit with a treat and the command, and then reward him with a treat. Ask as many people as you can to help you. It will not take Buddy long before he will sit on his own in front of a visitor in expectation of his treat. At that point, it is no longer necessary to give him a treat every time he responds correctly. A "good dog" with a friendly pat on the head will suffice.

Go Lie Down

"Go lie down" is another command of convenience. During meal times, you don't want Buddy hanging out by the table. The "go lie down" command tells him to chill out in his favorite spot until you are done. Or when you have guests and he insists on making a nuisance of himself.

Come

"Come" is as much a command of convenience as of safety. You need this command any time you want Buddy to come to you for whatever reason — after he has enjoyed a nice romp in the park or when he is chasing a cat. Unless he responds reliably to the "come" command, you should keep him on leash in situations where he might be a danger to others or himself.

Easy

We use the "Easy" command when we don't want Buddy to pull on the leash. "Easy" is a useful command for anyone who walks his or her dog as form of exercise, or jogs or bicycles with the dog. We also use it to teach our dogs to take treats from our hand without the alligator imitation.

Give

The "Give" command is useful for taking something out of Buddy's mouth that you don't want him to have and that he doesn't want to give up. The object can be anything, from one of your favorite possessions to the piece of meat he has just stolen off the counter.

Our favorite way of getting Buddy to give up whatever he has in his mouth is to trade — we offer him a treat in exchange for what he has in his mouth. If it is food, you may have to offer him something of equal value, such as a frozen chicken wing. We keep these in our freezer at all times since we use them as special treats. Of course, there are going to be times when you don't have a treat handy, in which case you just have to open his mouth and remove the object.

Off

"Off" is a commonly used command for getting the dog off the furniture. The command is also frequently used to stop dogs from jumping on people, although "sit" is a better choice because it is more specific.

Whether you allow your dog on the furniture is a matter of personal prefer- ence. You can certainly train him to stay on the floor, at least as long as you are in his presence. Chances are, however, that when you are gone, he will settle on his favorite couch only to quietly slide off when he hears you coming home.

For those individuals who are adamant about keeping the dog off the furni- ture, there are several options:

- Don't give him the run of the house.

- Place a broomstick on Buddy's favorite chair or couch while you are gone. The broomstick works well with most dogs, although we know of instances where the dog simply removed the stick.

- Invest in one or more *Scat Mats*. Scat Mats come in different sizes and are designed to keep dogs and cats off the furniture by giving the animal a slight electric shock when it steps on it. The intensity of the shock can be regulated.

   Scat Mats are also used to restrict access to a room or part of the house. Again, the device is not foolproof, as some dogs learn to jump over the mat.

Leave It

"Leave it" is another common command that tells the dog to ignore whatever interests him at the time. The object of his interest can be a cat, another dog, a person, or something on the ground.

No "No" Command

Our least favorite command is "No." We prefer to tell the dog exactly what it is we want him to do with an action command, such "Come," "Sit," or "Down." When the dog responds we can then praise him by telling him how good he is.

"No" is nebulous, negative, and overused, and most of the time does not give the dog any specific instruction or directive. Worse yet, "No" does not generally lend itself to being followed by praise. For example, Buddy wants to jump on you, you yell "No," and he stops. Can you now praise him? No, because he may still be thinking about jumping on you and praising him encourages him to try again, not the message you want to give.

All in all, it's better to eliminate the word from your communications with Buddy. Of course, in an emergency, you do what you have to.

Chapter 24

Ten Reasons Why Dogs Do What They Do

*W*ho knows why your dog does some of the things that he does? Or more importantly, who *wants* to know why your dog does some of the things that he does? Well, if you're curious, this chapter offers answers to a few of these critical questions.

Why Do Dogs Insist on Jumping on People?

The behavior goes back to the weaning process. As puppies grow, the mother dog begins to feed them standing up, so puppies have to stand on their hind legs to feed. Then, as her milk decreases, the puppies jump up to lick at the corner of her mouth, trying to get her to regurgitate her semi-digested meal. When she does, it is the puppies' first introduction to solid food.

As dogs grow, jumping becomes more of a greeting behavior, as in, "Hi, good to see you," much like we would shake hands when we are introduced to someone. Because the behavior is so instinctive, it is sometimes so difficult to modify. While you're probably pleased that your dog is happy to see you, you would also probably prefer a more sedate greeting, especially if Buddy is a large dog. And, because jumping up on people is a friendly gesture, we suggest modifying the behavior in a positive way (see Chapter 4).

Why Do Dogs Sniff Parts of Our Anatomy We Would Prefer They Didn't?

When two dogs meet each other for the first time, they often go through what looks like a choreographed ritual. After some preliminaries, they sniff each other's respective rear ends and genitals. Dogs "see" with their noses and gather important information in this way. They can identify the sex, age, and rank order of the other dog, information that will dictate how they interact with each other.

When meeting a new person, a dog wants to know that same information. Some are confirmed "crotch sniffers," while others are more subtle. Although embarrassing for the owner and the "sniffee," the behavior is harmless enough and easily remedied with the "sit" command.

Why Do Male Dogs Lift Their Leg So Often?

All dogs "mark" their territory by leaving small amounts of urine, the male more so than the female. You can liken it to putting up a fence; it lets other dogs in the neighborhood know he has been there. The scent enables dogs to identify the age, sex, and rank order of every dog that has marked that spot.

When you take Buddy for a walk, he intently investigates various spots and then lifts his leg to deposit a few drops of urine to cover the area, thereby reclaiming his territory. Male dogs also have a special fondness for vertical surfaces, such as a tree or the side of a building. Corners of buildings are a special treat. Height is important here because it establishes rank. Comical contortions can be the result, such as when a Yorkshire Terrier tries to cover the mark of a Great Dane. Females do not seem to have that need, which explains why they can do their business in a fraction of the time it takes a male.

Both males and females may scratch at the ground and kick the dirt after urinating to spread their scent, thereby claiming a larger amount of territory.

Why Do Dogs Mount Each Other?

Both female and male dogs can display mounting behavior. More normally associated with males trying to flirt or breed a female, this behavior can be seen male to male, female to female, and female to male. Most people think it has to do only with sex, but it can be a dominance display with dogs of the same gender — the one on top reminding the other who is in charge — or it can be a behavior that is displayed when dogs that know each other well have been separated for some time. The behavior is then a form of bonding, like a hug, meaning "I missed you." Rather than discouraging this behavior, we have found it better to leave the dogs alone; they work things out well between themselves. They have to, because they are pack animals and know exactly the message they are trying to convey, usually to bring harmony back into the household.

The only time this mounting behavior can be construed as abnormal would be if a female has some vaginal discharge indicating some sort of infection, which smells as if she is in season. In that case, other dogs will not leave her alone, and a visit to the veterinarian is the appropriate remedy.

Why Do Dogs Like to Chase Things?

Dogs chase things for a variety of different reasons:

- ✔ To chase intruders, be it people or other animals, off their property
- ✔ To chase a potential meal, such as a rabbit, squirrel, or chipmunk
- ✔ To chase just because the object is moving, such as cars, bicycles, or joggers
- ✔ To chase because it's fun

Whatever the reason, it's usually not a good idea because it can endanger the safety of people and the dog himself. Unless you are prepared to keep Buddy on leash under circumstances where he is likely to chase, you need to train him to come when called (see Chapter 4).

Why Do Dogs Roll in Disgusting Things?

Dogs delight in rolling in the most disgusting stuff, such as dead fish, deer droppings, and similar decaying debris. To make matters worse, the urge to roll seems strongest just after Buddy has had a bath. Do dogs like to smell putrid?

Behaviorists believe that because the dog is a pack animal, he is merely bringing back to the pack the scent of possible food sources. The pack can then track down a meal. The behavior is instinctive. Most dogs roll at one point or another, some to a greater extent than others. It's part of being a dog.

Why Do Dogs Eat Weeds or Grass?

Dogs come with many instinctive behaviors. One of those behaviors is the incredible knowledge of what weeds to eat and when. One reason a dog eats grass is to induce vomiting. He may have eaten something that disagrees with him, and the grass goes into the stomach and binds whatever it contains, which is then expelled. It's an adaptive behavior that protects the dog against indigestion and food poisoning. As a result, dogs that have access to the right kind of grasses, those with wide, serrated edges, rarely get food poisoning. Another reason dogs eat grass, wheat grass, for example, is as a digestive aid.

Dogs have an infallible knowledge of which weeds to eat. These weeds are often the very same that are found in capsules in the health food store to boost immune systems or any other system of the body. Should you stop your dog from eating weeds? Absolutely not! He knows much better what he needs than you do. The only thing you have to do is make sure you don't expose your dog to areas that have been sprayed with chemicals.

Dogs also seem to have a sense of the medicinal value of various plants. When one of our Newfoundlands became arthritic, he would seek out the large patch of poison ivy we have on our property. During our daily walks, he would make it a point to stand in that patch for a few minutes, eat the grass that grew there, and then move on. At first we could not understand his behavior. We subsequently learned that *Rhus Tox,* a homeopathic remedy for achy joints and rheumatism, is made from poison ivy.

Why Do Dogs Eat Disgusting Things?

Good question.

How Do You Explain a Dog's Grooming Behaviors?

Notwithstanding their occasional rolls in disgusting stuff, dogs do keep themselves clean. Most dogs will wash their genitals, their legs, and their feet. They may use their front paws to wipe their faces, their eyes and ears, then wash their paws clean. You may also see them nibbling parts of their body with their front teeth, which can be a sign of fleas. Dogs nibble each other, especially if they are closely bonded to one another. It's a sign of affection. Sometimes dogs will do this to their owners when they are feeling very cuddly. This should not be confused with biting behavior — quite the opposite.

Dogs also will also nibble themselves in areas that hurt or itch. They have an amazing sense of where to stimulate the best part of their bodies if they hurt. Once we learned acupuncture, we were amazed to see that a dog actually nibbles and licks on specific acupuncture points. So it seems that dogs also know how to treat themselves! If we watch them carefully, they teach us a great deal.

Why Do Some Dogs Scoot on Their Rear Ends?

Once in a while, your dog may appear to be sitting and then suddenly drag himself around on his front paws, with his rear end on the floor. It looks as if he is trying to clean his rear. This can mean that his anal glands — small scent sacks just inside the rectum — are full and need emptying. Get your vet to show you how to do this — takes but a minute and makes your dog much more comfortable. With some breeds, these small glands have to be emptied a couple of times a month. With other breeds, you never see this behavior.

Another reason for this behavior is tapeworms. The segments of worm are pushed out through the rectum and irritate the dog. To rid himself of the segment, he'll scrape his rectum on the carpet or on the grass outside. If you think your dog has worms, visit your vet and let him or her diagnose what is going on.

Why Do Dogs Show Nesting Behavior?

Around eight or nine weeks, after a female has come out of season, you may see her digging around her bed, turning in circles, collecting toys and putting them in her bed, and guarding the area from other animals and maybe even yourself. She is preparing a nest for her puppies. Sometimes even spayed females exhibit this behavior, and it is often accompanied by swelling of the mammary glands that may actually fill with milk.

In the wild, female dogs in a pack, even if they were not pregnant or did not have puppies, developed milk anyway. This phenomenon ensures the survival of the litter in case something happens to the mother dog.

Why Do Dogs Turn in Circles Before They Lie Down?

Why does the dog turn in circles, around and around, before finally lying down and going to sleep? Behaviorists speculate that the behavior was inherited from the wolf, who would circle in long grass to flatten it before the area was suitably comfortable.

Another theory is that the dog's spine has to be curled at a specific angle before he can lie comfortably on his side. So a young dog, one that is supple, turns just a few times before lying down. An older dog, whose spine is no longer as flexible, will circle a little longer to flex his spine to just the right angle.

Index

foods *(continued)*
beggars, 70–71
canned, 128–129
carbohydrates, 122–123
coprophagy (stool eating)
  issues, 114–115
crate-training uses, 174
Econo, 119
enzymes, 130
fats, 123–124
feeding strategies, 131–135
label information, 118–119
Light (Lite), 119
Low Protein, 119
meat requirements, 119–120
minerals, 125–126
Natural Diet Foundation
  (NDF) formula, 131–132
performance, 119
Premium, 119
preservatives, 124–125
protein requirements,
  120–121
puppy, 122
raw, 129–130
Regular, 119
selection guidelines, 118
semi-moist, 129
Super Premium 1, 119
vitamins, 125–126
water requirements, 127–128
Wendy Volhard's Natural Diet
  recipe, 132–135
freestyle performances,
  described, 354
freezing, inhibited flight
  behavior, 24
Front command, 251–252
frustration
  cause/treatment issues, 100
  digging reason, 107
fuzzy (soft) toys, ingestion
  cautions, 161

• *G* •

games
  Come command, 68–69
  Down/Stay command, 65
  sit-down-sit, 280
  trick training, 323–334
Gas Station Dog profile, 33
genetic testing, breeder
  criteria, 143
German collar, defined, 51

ginger cookies, car sickness
  treatment, 95–96, 114
Give command
  retrieve over high jump, 264
  retrieving training, 198–204
  when to use, 356–357
glove retrieve, teaching,
  288–290
Go Lie Down command
  basic training guidelines,
  64–66
  when to use, 356
Go to Bed command, crate-
  training, 173–174
Go-Out command, teaching,
  291–293
grass eaters, reasons for, 362
grinders, toenail trimming,
  81–82
grooming
  bathing guidelines, 79–80
  behaviors, 362–363
  breed selection issues, 139
  Canine Good Citizen (CGC)
  component, 210, 214–215
  ear cleaning, 82
  expressing anal glands, 82
  toenail trimming, 80–82
group exercises
  defined, 245
  increasing levels of difficulty,
  255
  out-of-sight stays, 271
  self-generated distractions,
  255
  yo-yo game, 256
groups, American Kennel Club
  (AKC), 84

• *H* •

hackles, defensive posture, 23
hair length, breed selection,
  139
hand signal to heel, 276
harness, reasons for use, 47
head halters, 52–53
health
  acupuncture benefits, 320
  bathing guidelines, 79–80
  behavior issues, 101
  Canine Good Citizen (CGC)
  requirements, 216
  car sickness, 95–96, 113–114
  cystitis, 112

ear cleaning, 82
expressing anal glands, 82
grass/weed eating, 362
holistic health, 321
homeopathic emergency kit,
  319–320
homeopathic product
  sources, 321
hypothyroidism, 317–318
musculoskeletal system
  issues, 318–319
nutritional needs, 83
nutritional product sources,
  321
over-vaccinating
  cautions/concerns,
  313–315
poison control information,
  321
protein deficiency results,
  121
rear end scooting, 363
shock treatment, 96
spay/neuter advantages,
  164–165
stress indicators, 90–91
thunderstorm stress, 95
titer test, 314
toenail trimming, 80–82
when to vaccinate, 315–317
health certifications, breeder
  criteria, 143
Healthy Dog Diet, coprophagy
  (stool eating) remedy, 115
heart rate, puppy test, 145
Heel command, 250
  action training, 10
  off leash training, 231–234
  training guidelines, 187
Heel Free exercise, 249–250,
  259
heel position, recall to, 290
heeling
  about-turns, 190
  automatic sit at heel, 187, 238
  changing pace, 238–241
  command reinforcement
  importance, 242–244
  defined, 10, 190
  direction changing, 189–190
  distraction training, 229–230
  down at heel, 191–193
  Figure 8, 240–242
  hand signal, 276
  left turns, 190

• U •

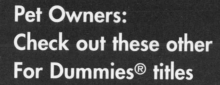

Pet Owners:
Check out these other
For Dummies® titles

Aquariums For Dummies®	ISBN 0-7645-5156-6	$19.99
Birds For Dummies®	ISBN 0-7645-5139-6	$19.99
Boxers For Dummies®	ISBN 0-7645-5285-6	$15.99
Cats For Dummies®, 2nd Edition	ISBN 0-7645-5275-9	$19.99
Chihuahuas For Dummies®	ISBN 0-7645-5284-8	$15.99
Dog Training For Dummies®	ISBN 0-7645-5286-4	$21.99
Dog Tricks For Dummies®	ISBN 0-7645-5287-2	$15.99
Dogs For Dummies®, 2nd Edition	ISBN 0-7645-5274-0	$21.99
Ferrets For Dummies®	ISBN 0-7645-5259-7	$19.99
German Shepherds For Dummies®	ISBN 0-7645-5280-5	$15.99
Golden Retrievers For Dummies®	ISBN 0-7645-5267-8	$15.99
Horses For Dummies®	ISBN 0-7645-5138-8	$19.99
Iguanas For Dummies®	ISBN 0-7645-5260-0	$19.99
Jack Russell Terriers For Dummies®	ISBN 0-7645-5268-6	$15.99
Labrador Retrievers For Dummies®	ISBN 0-7645-5281-3	$15.99
Puppies For Dummies®	ISBN 0-7645-5255-4	$19.99
Retired Racing Greyhounds For Dummies®	ISBN 0-7645-5276-7	$15.99
Rottweilers For Dummies®	ISBN 0-7645-5271-6	$15.99
Siberian Huskies For Dummies®	ISBN 0-7645-5279-1	$15.99

Look for these titles in early 2001:

Australian Shepherds For Dummies®	ISBN 0-7645-5301-X	$15.99
Dachshunds For Dummies®	ISBN 0-7645-5289-9	$15.99
Pit Bulls For Dummies®	ISBN 0-7645-5291-0	$15.99
Turtles and Tortoises For Dummies®	ISBN 0-7645-5313-5	$21.99

From the Pet Experts at Howell Book House, Titles of Interest to Dog Lovers

GENERAL

The Complete Dog Book, 19th Ed., Revised
By The American Kennel Club
ISBN 0-87605-047-X • $32.95

Dog Owner's Home Veterinary Handbook, 3rd Ed.
By James Giffin, M.D., and Liisa Carlson, D.V.M.
ISBN 0-876605-201-4 • $27.95

Holistic Guide for a Healthy Dog, 2nd Ed.
By Wendy Volhard and Kerry Brown, D.V.M.
ISBN 1-58245-153-2 • $16.95

DOGS TRAINING/BEHAVIOR GUIDES

*Dog Behavior: An Owner's Guide to a Happy
Healthy Pet*
By Dr. Ian Dunbar
ISBN 0-87605-236-7 • $12.95

Dog-Friendly Dog Training
By Andrea Arden
ISBN 1-58245-009-9 • $17.95

*DogPerfect: The User-Friendly Guide to a
Well-Behaved Dog*
By Sarah Hodgson
ISBN 0-87605-534-X • $12.95

Dog Training in 10 Minutes
By Carol Lea Benjamin
ISBN 0-87605-471-8 • $14.95

How Dogs Learn
By Mary Burch, Ph.D., and John Bailey, Ph.D.
ISBN 0-87605-371-1 • $19.95

ACTIVITIES

All About Agility
By Jacqueline O'Neil
ISBN 1-58245-123-0 • $22.95

Canine Good Citizen: Every Dog Can Be One
By Jack and Wendy Volhard
ISBN 0-87605-452-1 • $12.95

Flyball Racing: The Dog Sport for Everyone
By Lonnie Olson
ISBN 0-87605-630-3 • $14.95

Volunteering With Your Pet
By Mary Birch, Ph.D.
ISBN 0-87605-791-1 • $19.95

Books

Books by America's foremost teachers, written for pet owners and competitors alike and featuring Jack and Wendy's famous step-by-step teaching methods.

Videos

Jack and Wendy's training videos available through:

Dogwise
Post Office Box 2778
Wenatchee, WA 98807-2778
www.dogwise.com

Seminars and Camps

Want to take a vacation with Buddy? Take a week off and enjoy having fun with Buddy and training him at the same time. For more information, contact:

Top Dog Training School
30 Besaw Road
Phoenix, NY 13135
www.volhard.com

Feeding Buddy

Natural Dog Food, Vitamin and Mineral Supplements. Wendy's books, her Homemade Diet, Natural Nosh Dog Biscuits, and the Emergency Homeopathic Kit. For more information, contact:

PHD Products
404 Irvington Street
Pleasantville, NY 10570
www.phdproducts.com

FREE

RECIPE
"for the"
Perfect
DOG

Kong Dog Toys are used and recommended by veterinarians and dog trainers worldwide. To see how Kong can be utilized to achieve good behavior in your dog, send a self-addressed stamped envelope to Kong Company for a "Recipe for the Perfect Dog" brochure or simply log on to our website and click on **"How to Use Kong"**.

SAVE $1

Save $1 on **ANY SIZE KONG DOG TOY**. Limit one coupon per purchase. Not valid with any other offer for same item(s). Customer pays any sales tax in accordance with sales tax regulations for manufacturer coupons. Void if copied. Cash value 1/100¢. Void where phohibited. Good only in the United States. Expires 04/01/02. RETAILER: Redemption subject to Kong's published redemption policy. For complete details, call 303-216-2626.

16191-D Table Mountain Parkway, Golden, CO 80403-1641 • Phone: (303) 216-2626 • Fax: (303) 216-2627
E-mail: kong@kongcompany.com • Website: www.kongcompany.com   ©**KONG**CO, 2000

SPECIAL OFFER FOR IDG BOOKS READERS

Pet Music™

ASPCA RECOMMENDED

Over 3 Hours Of Music For Pets!

$5.00 OFF

Regular Price: $19.99
IDG Books Readers: $14.99
Shipping & Handing Charges Apply

Reduce Your Pet's Stress And Separation Anxiety

How to order your Pet Music™ 3 CD Set

✉ **Cut and mail the coupon today!**

☎ **Fax us at 1-215-628-2306.**

☞ **Order online at www.petmusic.com**
Use Discount Code: IDG or 789

ORDER TODAY!

Featured in Forbes, Fortune, Cat Fancy, The New York Times, Pet Age, and More!

Cut Coupon and Mail To: Music Offer, P.O. BOX 245, Ambler, PA 19002-0245 ✂

---

1. ORDER BY   PLEASE PRINT

Customer billing and shipping address must be the same.

Name _____

Address _____

City _____ State _____ Zip _____

Daytime Phone (_____) _____

Evening Phone (_____) _____

It may be important for us to contact you regarding your order.
Your phone number will not be released to anyone else for any purpose.

2. YOUR ORDER   PLEASE PRINT

ITEM	QTY.	UNIT PRICE	TOTAL COST
Pet Music™ 3 CD Set		$14.99	

3. METHOD OF PAYMENT

Sorry, no cash or CODS.

☐ MasterCard   MasterCard
☐ Visa   VISA
☐ American Express
☐ Check Enclosed Made Payable to **"Incentive Media"**

Card Number

☐☐☐☐ ☐☐☐☐ ☐☐☐☐ ☐☐☐☐

Credit card statement will read "Incentive Media, LLC."

Expiration Date _____ / _____

Signature _____

PLEASE ADD 6% SALES TAX FOR ORDERS SHIPPING TO PA	$
SHIPPING AND HANDLING TOTAL ORDER	$4.95
FOR SHIPMENTS TO CANADA ADD $2	$
YOUR ORDER TOTAL	$

MasterCard requires 16 digits.
American Express requires 15 digits.
Visa requires 13 or 16 digits.

incentive media

Fax Your Order 24 Hours A Day To:
1-215-628-2306

Offer valid in US and Canada. US funds ONLY. Allow 2-3 weeks for delivery. Pet Music™ is a trademark of Incentive Media, LLC. ASPCA® is a registered trademark of The American Society for the Prevention of Cruelty to Animals.

Discover Dummies Online!

The Dummies Web Site is your fun and friendly online resource for the latest information about *For Dummies*® books and your favorite topics. The Web site is the place to communicate with us, exchange ideas with other *For Dummies* readers, chat with authors, and have fun!

Ten Fun and Useful Things You Can Do at www.dummies.com

1. Win free *For Dummies* books and more!
2. Register your book and be entered in a prize drawing.
3. Meet your favorite authors through the IDG Books Worldwide Author Chat Series.
4. Exchange helpful information with other *For Dummies* readers.
5. Discover other great *For Dummies* books you must have!
6. Purchase Dummieswear® exclusively from our Web site.
7. Buy *For Dummies* books online.
8. Talk to us. Make comments, ask questions, get answers!
9. Download free software.
10. Find additional useful resources from authors.

Link directly to these ten fun and useful things at
http://www.dummies.com/10useful

For other technology titles from IDG Books Worldwide, go to
www.idgbooks.com

Not on the Web yet? It's easy to get started with *Dummies 101*®: *The Internet For Windows*® *98* or *The Internet For Dummies*® at local retailers everywhere.

Find other *For Dummies* books on these topics:
Business • Career • Databases • Food & Beverage • Games • Gardening • Graphics • Hardware
Health & Fitness • Internet and the World Wide Web • Networking • Office Suites
Operating Systems • Personal Finance • Pets • Programming • Recreation • Sports
Spreadsheets • Teacher Resources • Test Prep • Word Processing

The IDG Books Worldwide logo is a registered trademark under exclusive license to IDG Books Worldwide, Inc., from International Data Group, Inc. Dummies.com and the ...For Dummies logo are trademarks, and Dummies Man, For Dummies, Dummieswear, and Dummies 101 are registered trademarks of IDG Books Worldwide, Inc. All other trademarks are the property of their respective owners.

IDG BOOKS WORLDWIDE BOOK REGISTRATION

We want to hear from you!

Register This Book and Win!

Visit **http://my2cents.dummies.com** to register this book and tell us how you liked it!

- ✔ Get entered in our monthly prize giveaway.

- ✔ Give us feedback about this book — tell us what you like best, what you like least, or maybe what you'd like to ask the author and us to change!

- ✔ Let us know any other *For Dummies*® topics that interest you.

Your feedback helps us determine what books to publish, tells us what coverage to add as we revise our books, and lets us know whether we're meeting your needs as a *For Dummies* reader. You're our most valuable resource, and what you have to say is important to us!

Not on the Web yet? It's easy to get started with *Dummies 101*®: *The Internet For Windows*® *98* or *The Internet For Dummies*® at local retailers everywhere.

Or let us know what you think by sending us a letter at the following address:

For Dummies Book Registration
Dummies Press
10475 Crosspoint Blvd.
Indianapolis, IN 46256

BESTSELLING BOOK SERIES